Legend

Legend

THE BIOGRAPHY OF BRIAN O'DRISCOLL

MARCUS STEAD

JOHN BLAKE

Published by John Blake Publishing Ltd,
3 Bramber Court, 2 Bramber Road,
London W14 9PB, England

www.johnblakepublishing.co.uk

www.facebook.com/Johnblakepub facebook
twitter.com/johnblakepub twitter

First published in paperback in 2009 as *In BOD We Trust*
Revised edition published in paperback in 2011 as
Brian O'Driscoll: The Biography
This revised, updated edition published 2013

ISBN: 978-1-78219-729-4

British Library Cataloguing-in-Publication Data:

A catalogue record for this book is available from the British Library.

Design by www.envydesign.co.uk

Printed in Great Britain by CPI (UK) Ltd

3 5 7 9 10 8 6 4

Papers used by John Blake Publishing are natural, recyclable products
made from wood grown in sustainable forests. The manufacturing processes
conform to the environmental regulations of the country of origin.

Every attempt has been made to contact the relevant copyright-holders,
but some were unobtainable. We would be grateful if the
appropriate people could contact us.

CONTENTS

Chapter 1

RAPID RISE
TO THE TOP

Brian O'Driscoll was born on 21 January 1979 with rugby in his blood. He weighed in at 9lb 12oz and cried, it seemed, for months without stopping. It later transpired that this was due to hunger. Little did his parents know that he would actually turn out to be a shy and very quiet child.

His father, Frank, was a decent centre in his day, who has been described by his son as a mad kamikaze tackler with a good step and plenty of wheels. He had toured Argentina with Ireland in the 1970s and played in the 'Tests', but in those days caps weren't awarded for matches against the Pumas.

He was unlucky in some ways. With the great Mike Gibson around, he did not get to fulfil his ambition to play for his country more often; much later on he would get enormous pleasure from living his dreams through his son, who would become more of a friend than a son as the years progressed.

Brian's early years were spent in Clontarf, in north Dublin. Both of his parents were, and still are, GPs. His mother, Geraldine, keeps the whole family in order, and is very much the boss of the house. Brian was the youngest of three children, with two sisters – Jules, a nurse, and Sue, who is two years younger, and works in event management along with doing a bit of radio work.

The family are close-knit and to this day they spend Sundays together whenever possible. At the meal table nobody gets more than anybody else. The girls aren't slow to tell Brian if the dishwasher needs filling, and the closeness and security of his family unit has undoubtedly helped to keep his feet on the ground and stop him becoming too big for his boots.

Even from a young age, Brian was showing signs of having a strong work ethic. As a child he hung a golf ball from a tree in the garden and would spend hours thwacking the ball with one of his dad's clubs. Frank said he didn't think his son was showing signs of madness, but was learning to develop his hand–eye co-ordination.

In those days, Frank kept a greenhouse of which he was very proud. If anyone broke a window with a stone they would be in big trouble. Do it with a ball, though, and it was in a good cause!

The garden was full of balls in those days. Golf balls, tennis balls, Gaelic footballs, soccer balls. Brian's first hero was footballer Mark Hughes, who he admired for his attitude as much as his ability. Tap-ins were never his style. Brian was a big Manchester United fan from a young age, but he was never much of a one for posters. As a child, he was always someone who kept his feelings very close to his chest. He was never an exhibitionist, and everything was always under control, with all things in sensible proportions. So far as the nature of his personality went, little changed as he grew into an adult.

Yet there was another side to him, a side that was fiercely competitive even as a young child. At the age of around 13 or 14, he was playing a round of golf with his father at Royal Dublin. They were playing the 10th, a par four, where you have to hit the ball across a mound, but there's a hollow to the left, and if you get it in there you seldom make par. Brian hit his tee shot straight into the mound. His father told him that he would give him 20 pounds if he made a par from there. So Brian responded by hitting a three-iron, followed by a chip to 10 feet before sinking the put. It was clear that Brian had a massive in-built determination.

As he grew up, he had his share of difficulties. A severe astigmatism – when the shape of the eyeball is not truly spherical – meant he could not keep contact lenses in, and he was chronically short-sighted, meaning he has always needed glasses for reading.

3

He was painfully shy throughout his childhood, and his parents found it a real struggle to get him to come out of his shell. That was the main reason he was sent to Blackrock College in Dublin, a fee-paying Catholic secondary school, which provided an education to several rugby stars including Alain Rolland, as well as other famous people such as the comedian and actor Ardal O'Hanlon. There was something about that school that appealed to Brian's parents. Children walked out of there with their shoulders pinned back and their heads held high. This was exactly what their son needed.

It didn't take long for the school to make an impact on Brian. In his second year he was elected as a class rep, a first taste of leadership for a future Ireland captain. His passion for sport continued to grow during his time here. Someone had seen him playing football (soccer) in the Community Games and encouraged him to join Trinity Boys, but at Blackrock he found rugby.

The summer before he started at Blackrock, he watched the 1991 Rugby World Cup on television. When he saw Michael Jones, the All Black flanker, Mark Hughes was relegated from top spot in his list of heroes. Brian watched with awe at what Jones could do. He was a back and a forward rolled into one combining great skill and superb running skills. He could tackle and mix it when it came to the rough stuff as well. Brian had found his role model.

However, when it came to his own development, things were a bit slow to begin with. Alan MacGinty, his school principal, left him off the Junior Cup team, on the grounds that he was tiny. That decision has haunted Alan ever since.

The only rugby Brian played in 1994 was with the under-16s at Clontarf. They won their league and that summer came the trip to Wales. Hugh Fanning, the coach, made some throwaway remark to Brian along the lines of: 'Don't forget to send me a postcard when you play for the Lions'. Seven years later, the card was in the post.

From then on, his talent began to shine through and, in 1996, while still at Blackrock, he was capped by Ireland Schools three times.

Legend surrounds his performance against Clongowes, in what was his last schools match. The Blackrock senior team were trailing as the clock ran down. Four times in the last five minutes, Brian tried to rescue the match with drop-goal attempts. One soared right over the top of the posts. Another hit the woodwork and bounced back into play, and Blackrock lost the game. This was a bitter pill to swallow, but learning to accept defeat with dignity was, unfortunately, something he would have to get used to as a sportsman.

Even at this stage, people were describing Brian as the new Brendan Mullin, who was considered by many to be the greatest Irish centre of recent times. After being something of a slow developer, or, perhaps more specifically, a slow grower, his skilful hands and ability to change gear quickly made him a real one to watch for the future.

At under-19 level, Brian was selected for the Ireland squad to play in the 1998 IRB under-19s World Championship in France, under the stewardship of respected coach Mike Ruddock. This tournament would have a profound effect on his career. By Brian's own admission, there is no comparing the standard of the under-19s with senior rugby, which he says is 100 times better, but the opportunity to play in this tournament provided an important stepping stone and a chance for him to impress in front of some important people. And he was involved in some memorable matches in that tournament.

There was the quarter-final against South Africa, when Ireland were 17–0 down and battled back to make it 17–17. It eventually went to penalty kicks before Ireland won those on a technicality because South Africa had used a player that hadn't finished the game as one of their five kickers. Ireland had lost the shoot-out 4–3, and Brian had taken one of the penalties and missed. Brian initially thought he had cost his side dear; until the technicality with the South African kicker was noticed, Brian was experiencing his first major low as a rugby player.

In the final, Ireland beat France 18–0 in Toulouse. Certainly, it was a team effort and everyone deserved credit for their remarkable achievement that day, but little did Brian know that he had caught the eye of some highly influential people and he was just a year away from playing for the Ireland senior team. Other notable names playing that day included Donncha O'Callaghan and Paddy Wallace.

Despite making remarkably rapid progress as a rugby player, Brian's parents were keen for him to gain qualifications as a back-up should something go wrong. His father knew only too well that his gifted son was only one nasty injury or one piece of bad luck away from being unable to play rugby again, and he was keen for him to have something for him to fall back on should this happen.

For this reason, Brian attended University College, Dublin on a scholarship. While at the college, he gained a diploma in sports management, but it was for his progress as a rugby player that his time there will be best remembered. Under Director of Rugby John McLean, he first made the under-20 side, before being promoted to the senior squad at the end of his first year.

Meanwhile, the Ireland squad were undergoing something of a revolution under Kiwi coach Warren Gatland, who was professionalising the entire setup to bring it into step with the modern era, while building a team that would, in time, compete with the world's very best. This meant breaking in players now who would form part of the Ireland side for the next decade, giving them a chance to know each other as players and as people early in the day.

Brian made his under-21 debut in February 1999, and went on to gain four caps. However, Warren clearly knew he had something very special when, incredibly, he called Brian into his senior squad for the Six Nations match against Italy. This was before he had even made his club debut for Leinster, which would not come until the August of that year. Brian's job that day was just to keep the bench warm, but he retained his place in the squad for the summer tour of Australia, and, on 12 June 1999, at the age of just 20, he made his senior debut for Ireland against the Wallabies in the first Test in Brisbane.

This match certainly wasn't Irish rugby's finest hour, as they crashed to a record 46–10 defeat, with Tiaan Strauss scoring a hat-trick of tries, but Brian certainly made his presence felt on the field that day and helped Ireland claim a fine consolation try when he, along with Connor O'Shea, dragged deep into Australian territory before Kevin Maggs finished off an impressive move.

He was far from the finished article, and still had a lot of growing up to do both in terms of his physique and in the development of his rugby skills, but, by showing what he was made of that day, he sealed his place in the Ireland team for the foreseeable future at least.

On 7 August 1999, Brian finally made his debut for Leinster, playing in an Interprovincial game against arch rivals Munster. Once again, Brian was on the losing side as they fell to a 31–20 defeat at Temple Hill.

Brian's development as a player was rapid, and in the Six Nations Championship of 2000 he showed how good he was when he took to the field in what was to be a very special game of rugby in Paris. However, the game started disastrously for Ireland when David Bory scored France's first try in the left corner after just 47 seconds. Or so they thought. Touch judge Jim Fleming ruled the final pass to be forward, but the warning was clear. This was a French side that meant business and would be tough to break down. Gérald Merceron soon put France 6–0 ahead, after Ireland were caught offside twice in as many minutes.

The first quarter of the game was a disaster for Ireland, but the game was about to change dramatically thanks largely to Brian's breathtaking efforts. He firstly collected the ball well from a French drop-out and Peter Stringer and Peter Clohessy drove into the ensuing ruck. It sent the home side backwards and there was little to stop Brian when he appeared in the move for the second time to touch down underneath the posts.

The home side soon hit back when scrum-half Christophe Laussucq scored following a quick tap penalty. In a match of blistering pace, Kieron Dawson then came close to replying, but knocked on as he touched over for Ireland on the left.

Early in the second half, Merceron kicked over a long

penalty which saw the beginning of a period of play dominated by the home side, and it wasn't long before Merceron kicked over another penalty from right in front of the posts to stretch the French lead to 12 points.

Warren decided to bring on Paddy Johns to give experience to the flagging Irish pack, and his presence soon rubbed off on Brian. Some quality interplay between him and Rob Henderson saw him score his second of the game, silencing the French crowd. Ronan O'Gara converted to cut the lead to just six points. Although still relatively inexperienced at this level, Brian sensed this game was very winnable.

Disaster struck when Johns received a yellow card for blatantly lying on the ball. He left the field to French cheers as Merceron again increased the home lead. Warren then decided to replace Ronan with the experienced David Humphreys, who almost immediately scored a superb 40-metre penalty, but Ireland were caught offside far too often and Merceron soon put over another penalty of his own. The game looked to be heading firmly in the home side's direction, and it looked as though Ireland's appalling track record in France was going to remain. The last time they had won here was in 1972. Cue Brian O'Driscoll.

The French had been caught offside, after blatantly diving through a ruck. But an inspired piece of refereeing from Paul Honnis gave Stringer the opportunity to sidestep his way through a host of French tacklers, before offloading to Brian who went charging towards the try-line and secured his hat-trick. With just three minutes remaining, Humphreys converted to give Ireland a two-point lead. They managed to hang on, and won the game 27–25.

In the post-match interviews, Brian was typically shy and humble and heaped praise on David Humphreys's brave efforts. In Brian's eyes, David had been the hero of the day and he was keen to take the attention away from his own performance, which had just given Irish rugby one of the proudest days in its long history.

The Irish rugby fans had known that young Brian was good, but until that day they had not realised just how special he was. And they also had to remember that he was just 21 years of age, and there was plenty of room for improvement yet. Even people who didn't really follow rugby knew who Brian was after this. He was a true national hero and, even if he never played another game of rugby in his life, his would be a name they would never forget.

For Brian, life would never be the same again. From now on, media interest in every aspect of his life would be something he was just going to have to get used to. He was still very much a shy young man, and this was something he didn't always appreciate. But there would be an upside to it. All this attention would inevitably mean that there would be sponsorship opportunities and chances to make a great deal of money by having his name associated with big brands.

While Brian's progress remained rapid over the next few years, the same could not be said of the Ireland team. Warren was playing the long game, and his focus was more on the future than the present. The actions he was taking to professionalise Irish rugby would not bear fruit for several more years, and, on the pitch, his priority was to get his crop of talented youngsters used to playing together now, as they would form the nucleus of the team for the next decade. The price they would inevitably have to pay for this was that success would not be instant; on paper, the scorelines in big matches over the next few years were not pleasant reading and the prospect of picking up major trophies seemed a long way off.

Brian consolidated his excellent performance against France by playing consistently well for club and country over the next 12 months, and this led to him receiving a call-up to the Lions squad to tour Australia in the summer of 2001. Brian knew that there was still massive room for improvement in his game and there was still plenty of work to be done, but he knew this was an opportunity to impress on the world stage that he could not afford to miss.

The Lions were coached by Kiwi Graham Henry, who had experienced mixed fortunes as Wales coach over the previous few years. Brian and Graham did not enjoy an especially warm relationship during the tour; the main bone of contention being the importance of the preparation of the players for the midweek sides compared to those playing in the tests. The full extent of the disagreement that existed between Brian and Graham would not fully come to light for another four years.

However, Brian possessed undoubted talent and he was selected to play in all three Tests. It was in the first Test that he really made his presence felt, where he helped the Lions to a memorable win against the Wallabies.

The Lions looked firmly in control from the third minute when Jason Robinson scored in the corner. Brian's first major act as a Lions player came on 11 minutes, and it wasn't to be one of his finer moments. Rob Henderson tried passing to Brian, but it was intercepted by Joe Roff who almost broke free for the Wallabies.

He more than made up for any blame that could have been attributed to him in that move in the 32nd minute when he ripped the Australian defence to shreds in spectacular fashion before off-loading to Jason Robinson who drew Andrew Walker, waited, and sent Dafydd James in at the corner for a wonderful score.

However, it was in the second half when the Lions really turned on the class. With a slender 12–3 lead, the Lions could have been forgiven for going on the defensive. Instead, they ripped into the Wallaby rearguard like men possessed.

The forwards maintained a rock-solid base 30 yards out. Jonny Wilkinson fed the ball to Brian and he smashed through the Aussie back-line like a super-charged tank and crashed over the line to send the 12,000 Lions fans in the Gabba crowd into raptures. Brian had shown his class on the world stage with a memorable try.

From then on, the game looked in the bag in a display of free-flowing, open rugby at its best and a further try from Scott Quinnell helped seal a 29–13 win for the Lions. Brian was pivotal in this victory and was playing like a man with far more experience than his 22 years would suggest. Captain Martin Johnson was full of praise for Brian's efforts, and described the game as one of the best he had ever been involved with or seen.

However, this was to be his best rugby of the tour. In the remaining two Tests, the Lions lost momentum and some of Graham Henry's preparation methods came into question as the unhappy atmosphere in the camp spilled over into the media, particularly from the newspaper columns of Matt Dawson and Austin Healey. It was even suggested by the media that a number of players were preparing to leave the tour early. In the months that followed, it became clear that the tour was not a happy one, with Henry saying in his own tour diary that he felt 'betrayed' by several players, namely those who gave accounts of the inner workings of the camp in their lucrative newspaper columns.

In the second Test at the Telstra Dome, Brian managed to break through the Australian line on a number of occasions but didn't receive the backup needed to capitalise upon his efforts, and the Lions suffered a humiliating 29–14 defeat.

In the final Test, Brian's only major contribution to the game was when he was on the receiving end of a high tackle from Herbert, which sent him crashing to the ground. The game was competitive and there was rarely more than a score in it, but ultimately the Lions were the poorer side and fell to a 29–23 defeat, handing Australia the series in the process.

The series was among the most competitive in history, and Brian had been one of the shining lights of the Lions team. He was only 22 years old and there was still a lot of room for improvement, but already he had established himself as one of the best centres in the world and had shown he was unfazed by the big occasion.

Yet in the months that followed the tour, his career saw something of a blip and he was far from at his best for the remainder of the year. Maybe something had to give. His life had changed beyond all recognition in a relatively short space of time. He had gone from being a shy, unassuming schoolboy to rugby superstar and national hero. All of this was going on while he was still in the process of becoming an adult, and it's arguable that people were expecting too much of him and the pressure was beginning to tell.

That said, in mid-December, he won his first silverware as a professional when Leinster won the inaugural Celtic League. The competition was experiencing all sorts of teething problems and followed a very different format to the one it would eventually settle on. The league, which ended before Christmas, climaxed with a final between Leinster and arch rivals Munster in front of 30,000 fans at Lansdowne Road.

Leinster coach Matt Williams had some notable names in his ranks, including Gordon D'Arcy, Shane Horgan, Malcolm O'Kelly, Denis Hickie and captain Reggie Corrigan. However, it was Munster who made the early running, and went into the break with a 12–6 lead and a man advantage after Eric Miller's sending off. Ronan O'Gara added another splendid kick after 51 minutes to extend his side's lead. But if anything, the Munster score seemed to spur Leinster on.

Shane Horgan, later named man of the match, immediately produced another burst deep into Munster territory and Brian maintained the pressure with a break which earned a penalty, and Nathan Spooner's successful kick left six points between the teams again.

Another Spooner penalty reduced Munster's lead to three points in the 64th minute after Hickie's break had earned the chance. Hickie's involvement was central to the 66th minute try which put Leinster ahead for the first time. His counter-attack saw the ball being fed to Horgan on the burst and the centre off-loaded possession to the overlapping D'Arcy who scored in the corner.

Spooner, who had recovered his composure after a nervous first half, brilliantly added the conversion to extend Leinster's lead to 19–15. Leinster were now firmly in the ascendency and Brian's superb chip and chase yielded his side's second try in five minutes. Oozing a confidence that had been lacking in recent months, he seemed certain to score the try himself but after he was hauled down illegally, Horgan continued to win the race for the try line.

Munster produced a typically battling response as they attempted to fight back, and Anthony Horgan did grab an injury-time try for Munster, but after Ronan O'Gara missed the conversion, referee Nigel Whitehouse blew his whistle. Leinster had done enough to beat their old rivals for the first time in six matches to claim the very first Celtic League title, giving Brian his first silverware in professional rugby.

When the Six Nations came around the following spring, Brian returned to form in spectacular fashion, with Ireland's third match against Scotland proving to be one of the highlights of his career. The Ireland team took to the field at Lansdowne Road, eager to make amends for the catastrophic defeat to England they had suffered in the last round of matches.

Ireland kept Scotland pinned in their own half for the first 10 minutes, but their only reward came in the first minute through a Humphreys penalty. Gregor Townsend eventually relieved the pressure with a bombshell clearance and, when Mick Galwey fell over at a ruck, Brendan Laney levelled from 35 metres out. Laney kicked another one over just four minutes later to put Scotland in front.

Scotland, playing with the strong breeze, were putting together some excellent passages of keep-ball which had the Irish defence scrambling. The pressure paid off for the visitors when Laney put his third penalty over in the 22nd minute. Ireland were looking down-and-out, but Brian was about to return to form in spectacular fashion and turn the game in his country's favour.

Just three minutes after Laney's penalty, Stringer whipped the ball away left to Humphreys who put Brian through a yawning gap as the Scottish defence was caught by the decoy run of Kevin Maggs. At last, Brian's poor run of form seemed to be over, and this special try seemed to help him put the demons that had haunted him since the previous summer to bed.

Brian seemed psyched up and ready to take on the world, back to his most bold, confident and deadly, and just seven minutes later he was at the centre of the action once more. He started the move with a powerful kick upfield, and then helped finish things off when his long pass drifted wide to left-wing Shane Horgan, who ran in unaccompanied.

More was to follow before half-time when the Scotland midfield dropped the ball in the home 22. Up stepped Brian who moved in swiftly to scoop it up and sprint all the way in. Humphreys added the conversion. Suddenly, all Brian's problems with confidence seemed like ancient history. This was more like the Drico who scored a hat-trick against France.

Laney reduced the Scots' deficit with a penalty either side of half-time, before Humphreys relieved some of the pressure now being put on Ireland with two rifled penalties, passing Michael Kiernan's record of 308 points for his country in the process.

With 15 minutes remaining, Ireland added another try when the Scottish midfield clumsily dropped the ball for the umpteenth time in the match, allowing Horgan to feed Humphreys who in turn switched direction for Simon Easterby to glide in.

Scotland scored a consolation try but it was Brian who was to have the final word on the game, when a quick ball from an Irish scrum allowed him to dart between Andrew Henderson and James McLaren, to score his second Six Nations hat-trick and seal Ireland's only second victory over Scotland in 15 matches, by a comfortable 43–22 margin. Brian O'Driscoll was back in business.

As for the Ireland team itself, it soon became clear that this was still very much a side in transition. Frustration at the lack of consistency had seen Warren sacked as coach and he had been replaced by his assistant, Eddie O'Sullivan. Consistency was still very much a problem. On the one hand, they had beaten Wales and Scotland, yet on other days they had suffered humiliating defeats at the hands of England and France.

Longstanding Ireland captain Keith Wood announced his retirement after the autumn internationals of 2002.

In Eddie's mind, Brian was the natural and most obvious successor to Keith, and the announcement that Brian would be captaining Ireland in the 2003 Six Nations surprised few. It is true that, at just 24 years of age, he lacked the kind of experience most previous captains had seen, but there were clearly many good reasons why Brian was ready for the job.

Mainly, Eddie's eye was very much on the future. Yes, there was no reason why Ireland shouldn't be serious contenders for the upcoming Six Nations, but there were a crop of truly outstanding players on the horizon who would not reach their peak for another few years. Like his predecessor, Eddie believed in getting them used to playing together early on, so that, when they were all at the top of their games in a few years' time, they would know one another's games inside out.

Brian was still very much an improving player. Incredibly, he still had his critics. There were, for instance, still those who believed his kicking game was not up to scratch, yet this previous weakness had come on in leaps and bounds over the previous 12 months. In reality, Eddie knew that Brian had what it took to make an outstanding captain, despite his relatively young age. He had shown battling qualities in so many Ireland performances to date and, despite his reserved and humble personality, was proving to be a ruthless warrior on the pitch.

Every serious rugby fan in the world now acknowledged that he was one of the world's greatest players, and was still getting better all the time. The Ireland fans had taken him to their hearts, so much so that T-shirts bearing the slogans 'In BOD We Trust' were soon printed following his appointment as captain and have remained popular at Ireland matches ever since.

In his first Six Nations as captain, Brian led Ireland to four wins out of the first four matches, which included an impressive try of his own against Italy. The scene was set for a Grand Slam decider at Lansdowne Road against a powerful England side. On the day, Ireland struggled to get going and were simply outclassed by the more mature England side, and, despite Brian and Geordan Murphy testing the resolve of the England defence early on, the result never looked in any doubt and England secured a walloping 42–6 victory. After the game, Brian told the press that slowly, but surely, they were getting there and it was only going to be a matter of time before Ireland ranked among the world's greatest sides. For him, it was disappointing to lose the game but he was still hugely optimistic for the future, as he knew the sheer quality of the young players coming through.

This defeat set alarm bells ringing in certain quarters and not everybody at the IRFU was willing to play the 'long game' that Eddie and Brian were committed to. Keith Wood, who had barely even featured for his club Harlequins during the season, was coaxed out of international retirement. It was decided that he, rather

21

than Brian, should lead Ireland in the upcoming World Cup, which was to be his third as a player.

Brian could easily have felt cheated of the opportunity to captain his country in the World Cup, but instead he stuck his head down and quietly got on with the job, knowing that, once the tournament was over, Keith would be off the scene for good and the role of captain would be his once more. This decision was certainly a controversial one, as it went against the youth-based ethos that Eddie had subscribed to throughout his tenure so far. Yet it was the long, patient game that had cost Warren his job and the powers that be weren't willing to wait much longer for Ireland to become serious contenders. This meant that it was Keith's job to add some much-needed experience to this very young squad.

The first three matches of the tournament saw Ireland notch up convincing victories against Romania and Namibia in the Pool stages, before defeating a resilient Argentina by a single point thanks to a try from Alan Quinlan. Brian made his presence felt in Ireland's final group game against Australia. In the second half, with his side 14–6 down, he scored one of the most memorable tries of his career to date. The video referee was brought in to judge whether the Irish ace had touched the ball down in the left corner before his feet went into touch, but the Irish faithful inside the stadium were never in any doubt.

Ronan added the conversion, to put Ireland within a

point of the world champions. Elton Flatley kicked another penalty to make the gap four points, but a drop goal from Brian with 13 minutes to play kept Ireland in the hunt. Unfortunately, Australia were just that little bit too strong for them and the more experienced side managed to hang on for victory.

Despite the defeat, Ireland had done enough in their earlier matches and set up a mouth-watering quarter-final clash against France. Although Ireland were the underdogs, Brian had remembered how his side had beaten France 15–12 in a closely fought match in Dublin during the Six Nations and knew this game was very winnable.

However, come the day, the French stormed to a 27–0 lead at half-time and amassed four tries in the process. Even so, Brian was at the top of his game and things could have been so much worse for the Irish had he not been playing. Early on, he made a crucial last-gasp tackle on a flying Tony Marsh to deny him an almost certain try.

Crenca scored France's fourth try inside the first 10 minutes of the second period, effectively ending the game as a contest, but Ireland soon got on the scoreboard with a try from Kevin Maggs. This was now an exercise in damage limitation, and Brian was clearly keen to give the thousands of Irish fans at least some momentum they could be proud of from this game.

Sure enough, Brian delivered Ireland's second

consolation try when he got a touch on Humphreys's grubber kick, and on the final whistle he added a second to bring respectability to the scoreline, which read France 43 Ireland 21. Things would have been a lot worse without Brian.

Ireland's World Cup had been typical of the sort of form they had been showing over the past year. On occasions, they looked like they could beat any team in the world yet they were a young squad and on the really big occasions their lack of experience and squad depth really did show, but at the same time it was clear that this side was going to be one to watch for the future.

As expected, Keith Wood announced his retirement from rugby immediately after Ireland's defeat to France, and Brian was immediately reinstated as captain for the Six Nations campaign in the spring.

Ironically, Ireland had to face France in Paris in the first round of fixtures, and unfortunately for Brian the game turned out to be a recurring nightmare of the World Cup quarter-final as Ireland crashed to a 35–17 defeat in similar style to their World Cup exit. The Grand Slam chance may have been lost, but this was an Ireland side that needed to show the world that they were maturing fast and that the day when they would be winning major trophies was near.

At home to a lacklustre Wales side, Brian turned on the class, scoring two of Ireland's six tries as they stormed to a commanding 36–15 victory. Next up came an away match against the newly crowned world champions, England, who had crushed Italy and Scotland in their opening two fixtures, despite having to do without an injured Jonny Wilkinson and a number of retirements following the World Cup triumph.

England scored the only try of the first half through Matt Dawson but some superb kicking from Ronan saw the visitors take a 12–10 lead at the break. However, England came out firing in the second half and Ben Cohen went over only for the video referee to rule out the try for a double movement. This seemed to inspire Brian and within minutes he made a superb break, the ball was spread wide and Leinster full-back Girvan Dempsey crossed over in the corner. Ronan converted, and England could only offer a Paul Grayson penalty in response, giving Ireland an incredible 19–12 victory against the world champions, thanks largely to some stubborn and determined defending.

After the game, Brian could not hide his delight and the normally reserved and quiet Ireland captain could not wait to tell the world that this side had arrived on the world rugby scene and meant business. At long last, the young team that had shown so much promise had finally delivered the goods.

A fortnight later, Ireland consolidated their excellent performance against England when Brian guided his side to a 19–3 home win against Italy, which included a try of his own. Going into the final round of fixtures, the Triple

Crown was still on, but, realistically, the Championship was out of the question unless England managed to thrash France by an enormous margin. Instead, Brian had to focus all his attentions on beating Scotland at Lansdowne Road. The game also saw Brian notch up his 50th cap for Ireland at the age of just 25. He was keen to make this a day for all Irish rugby fans to remember, a day when they finally had a trophy to parade around their historic home ground, which was the oldest in the world.

The home side had a nervy first period against a fired-up Scotland team but Geordan Murphy's try just before the break gave Ireland a 16–9 lead; however, the visitors did level the scores with an Ali Hogg try on 48 minutes. This Scotland side was clearly keen on causing an upset after a dreadful tournament to date. However, three tries in the final 24 minutes, including a second for Gordon D'Arcy, sealed the win for Ireland. The final quarter of the game was hardly vintage rugby from either side, but Ireland had done enough.

Finally, Ireland had something to show for their efforts: the Triple Crown. After years of showing promise but failing on the big occasion, this was a massive sign that things were finally starting to come together for this promising young squad. The final game was a quiet one by Brian's standards, but his impact in earlier matches had been enormous and his efforts as both player and captain had been pivotal in contributing to Ireland's historic achievement.

Brian celebrated with a night at Kehoe's Bar in Dublin. This was a day to remember. But Brian was also aware that, from now on, this was the minimum requirement, and that next year, and thereafter, the fans expected even better from the team.

That autumn, Brian led his team out at Lansdowne Road to face a South Africa side that had been rejuvenated under the stewardship of coach Jake White. Ronan scored all Ireland's points as they beat the Southern Hemisphere giants 17–12, but the win was in no small part down to Brian's no-nonsense approach from start to finish. Ireland had defended and tackled superbly and richly deserved this victory. They consolidated this with an expected thrashing of the USA, before ending the autumn series by beating a rapidly improving Argentina side 21–19, with Ronan providing all the points once again.

Brian might not have managed to get his name on the scoresheet against South Africa and Argentina, but he had steered Ireland to two memorable victories, and had led by example by giving his best from start to finish. After a shaky start, 2004 had ended on a high, and it seemed that, after over five years of preparation, this Ireland side had finally come of age. Things were not perfect, and a number of players were far from the finished article, but it was clear that Ireland were to be a major force in world rugby in the years ahead. The years of patient preparation had finally paid off, and the reality was that Brian was now the captain of one of the world's best rugby teams.

Brian's status as one of the world's greatest centres was secure, but he was quickly developing a reputation as a strong leader and great motivator of those around him. With such status comes increased responsibility and raised expectations, and Brian knew that the year ahead would be one of the most important of his life.

Chapter 2

COMING OF AGE

The following year, 2005, was always going to be pivotal in Brian's career. He was now 25 years old, and the previous few years had seen him mature rapidly as a person; the stature and esteem in which he was held by both his team-mates and rugby fans in Ireland and beyond had risen sharply.

On paper, it looked like being a gruelling 12 months, and expectations were high. Leinster were in with a very real chance of winning the Heineken Cup. The Ireland team looked stronger than ever, and fans were expecting nothing less than their country capturing their first Grand Slam in 57 years.

There was to be no summer break. Brian would undoubtedly be selected for the Lions tour to New

Zealand, where they would be looking to win a Test Series against the All Blacks for only the second time.

The year got off to a bad start, when on the evening of New Year's Day Brian lined up for Leinster to take on old rivals Munster at Musgrave Park. Brian had never found it difficult to psych himself up for matches against Munster, and was fully prepared for the challenging 80 minutes that lay ahead. This was his chance to get an important year off to the best possible start, and he didn't want to let the opportunity slip through his hands without a fight.

With both sides at full strength and Munster in superb form, it proved to be a typically physical encounter between the traditional rivals, which saw Irish fly-half Ronan O'Gara breaking a bone in his right hand, leaving a serious question mark over whether he would be available for the early Six Nations fixtures which were now only a month away.

Leinster lost the game 19–13, and Brian's year had got off to the worst possible start as far as he was concerned. Losing is never pleasant, but, with rivalry between the two provinces so intense, the defeat was especially painful to take.

However, Brian had no time to dwell on this defeat as the following week he had to travel to Bath as Leinster's quest for Heineken Cup glory continued. Things didn't look good and with four minutes to go Leinster were trailing 23–13. But there was still time to turn it around, and a late surge saw tries from David Holwell and Malcolm O'Kelly to make it 27–23 at the end.

Bath coach John Connolly knew his team had thrown the game away, and was quick to praise Brian's contribution. In a post-match interview with the BBC, he said, 'The guys were focused, the effort was phenomenal but the odd mistake cost us the game and the players are incredibly disappointed. Any team that has Brian O'Driscoll and up to six potential Lions in their line-up always has a chance.'

But Brian was far from happy with his performance in the game, and cursed himself for a sloppy pass he made to Girvan Dempsey early on that probably cost his team a try. That said, a win is a win and Brian's efforts that day played no small part in Leinster's stunning turn-around in the final few minutes.

In the professional era, matches come thick and fast and there is little time to dwell on defeats or revel in victories. Within a week, Brian would be meeting up with the Ireland squad as they prepared for their Six Nations campaign. On 21 January, just two days before the squad was due to meet, Brian should have been celebrating his 26th birthday. Instead, he opted for a quiet day, knowing that this really wasn't the time for a night's boozing with mates. If he and Ireland were serious about completing the Grand Slam, they had to be in the peak of physical fitness, and this meant making sacrifices early on.

Brian enjoyed playing with an iPod given to him by O_2, one of Ireland's sponsors, before heading to the barber's to cut off the blond locks he had been sporting in favour of a short-back-and-sides look. A serious haircut for a serious man. There was no clowning around now, and Brian used this small gesture as a statement of intent for the challenges that lay ahead.

Two days later, and Brian joined the Ireland squad at the City West hotel in Dublin. This would be his base until the end of the Six Nations.

From now on, each day's activities would run to a strict schedule. Essentially this meant a daily ritual of eating, training and sleeping. As usual, Brian did not enjoy the prospect of having to be away from home for such a long period of time. The novelty of having everything laid on for him never took long to wear off. He felt the daily training ritual was not especially different to that he underwent at home and he much preferred to be around those closest to him, especially with such a long build-up to the first game of the Six Nations.

Brian has gone on record as saying that he doesn't necessarily believe that spending long periods together as a squad is the best way to prepare for a game. He points out that in the 1970s international sides put together breathtaking performances on the back of a maximum of just two days together.

It's easy to see where he's coming from, but in the professional era few would argue that the highest levels of fitness and the correct diet are essential in preparing for big games and that joining together as a squad early on plays an important part in getting this right. They might not enjoy being away from those closest to them for so long, but it is a fact of life for the modern international rugby player.

Brian's left-shoulder injury, sustained early in his career, soon came back to haunt him in the days that followed and he wasn't able to train as rigorously as he would have liked. After each training session, he would apply an electro-magnetic TENS pain-relief gadget to his shoulder to alleviate the persistent problem. This was far from ideal preparation for the tournament.

Brian was the first to put his problems into perspective. Irritating though this was, it was nothing compared to those suffering the effects of the Tsunami disaster just a few weeks earlier, and watching the terrible pictures of the aftermath from his hotel room helped him realise this.

Being captain, and being the biggest 'celebrity' in the squad, meant Brian had to do more than his fair share of media work in the lead-up to the tournament. He has never been a natural extrovert and shyness was a problem early on in his career, with his personality never coming across on television. Things had improved as he grew into the captaincy, and by now Brian's approach to interviews was every bit as professional as his approach to other aspects of being a rugby player.

On the day of the Six Nations press launch, Brian had to make himself available for a number of interviews with journalists from various organisations from around the world. This in itself proved something of a challenge. He was expected to treat each interview with the seriousness of the last one. In all likelihood, this meant being asked exactly the same questions as before, which meant having to give exactly the same answers.

Brian always stuck to the official party line, never speaking out of turn. He knew full well that making one light-hearted comment or poking a bit of fun at the opposition could easily be taken out of context and backfire on him spectacularly, which was exactly what had happened to him the previous year.

In an interview before the Ireland–England game, Brian had made a comment along the lines that an Ireland win would give the prawn-sandwich brigade at Twickenham something to choke on.

Of course, the Celtic nations love nothing more than winding up the 'posh boys' of England and his remarks went down well back home. Brian was simply parodying comments made by Roy Keane about Manchester United's corporate 'supporters' some years previously. But his rather lame attempt at humour certainly seemed to psych up his opponents. Lawrence Dallaglio seemed to take it very personally and appeared more angry than usual as he took to the field that day. The remark was blown out of all proportion but it certainly seemed to stick and speculation was rife that it had done serious damage to Brian's relationship with Sir Clive Woodward.

In the context of those remarks, it came as a huge surprise to Brian when, in the middle of his preparations for the Six Nations, he received a phone call from Clive inviting him to his home in Henley for a chat about the upcoming Lions tour. Brian had no idea what this could mean. Yes, the press had grossly exaggerated the extent of his rift with Clive but he could hardly be described as one of his closest confidants.

Not knowing what to expect, Brian took a flight to Heathrow where Clive picked him up at Arrivals and drove him to his sublime home. The whole evening turned out to be a very relaxed and friendly occasion. The two men just talked frankly about the upcoming Lions tour, with Clive appearing to take a keen interest in which players Brian rated. The alleged falling out of 12 months previously suddenly felt like a million years ago. Then the true purpose of the meeting was revealed.

Clive asked Brian how he felt about captaining the Lions. It was phrased as a hypothetical question rather than an offer, but Brian knew exactly what this meant. The hairs stood up on the back of his neck, and, as he put it, his whole rugby career flashed before him. To captain the Lions is almost certainly the greatest honour any rugby player from Britain or Ireland could ever receive, and now it was practically being offered on a plate to Brian. He answered the question with an enthusiastic 'Yes' before going on to say that he was a big believer in the Martin Johnson style of captaincy, but he wasn't looking to be a clone of him.

The rest of the evening was spent discussing a strategy for the tour. Both men agreed that the tour of New Zealand should be fun. They both knew full well that many players didn't enjoy the 2001 Lions tour of Australia. This was partly due to a large number of players being marginalised in the midweek side early on. Both men agreed that back then the Lions simply needed more back-room staff to do the job properly. Clive agreed to set up two different teams of coaches and medics. There was obviously no way every member of the squad could play in the Test team, but making every player feel valued and properly supported was vital in making for a happy, coherent squad.

With more emphasis on fun, Clive made sure the tour allowed time to absorb the country and the culture, as well as allowing for a few decent nights out. This didn't have to mean heavy drinking sessions, but it did mean avoiding a siege mentality within the camp. They were away from home for a long time, and making the tour an enjoyable experience was now considered an important aspect of making it a success on the field. After all, if they were playing a series of matches at home with that length of gap in between, there would certainly be space made for some 'down time'.

At the end of their meeting, Clive made it clear that

he would not be making any final decision on the captaincy until after the Six Nations. But Brian was aware that it was now his to lose, and that, if he remained professional in his leadership of Ireland, the job would be his.

The following day saw the official media launch of the Six Nations in London. Brian was growing sick and tired of constant interviews, press gatherings and posing for pictures by now. The build-up seemed never ending but this was just something he had to learn to put up with. It came as part of the job and that was that.

Brian nevertheless coped well with the many interviews he had to do, until about halfway through the day when he got bored with repeating the same old lines to one journalist after another and decided to say something that would stir up a degree of controversy.

He commented that world champions England had lost their aura of invincibility. This was by no means an outrageous remark, since several former England captains had publicly said exactly the same thing in recent weeks. After all, the England team that would be taking to the field in the Six Nations was missing the likes of Martin Johnson, Jonny Wilkinson and Richard Hill, to name just three of the stars of their World Cup campaign.

Inevitably, the English press spun his words into a severe dig at the current England squad. The reality was that the squad were rebuilding in between World

Cups and few could seriously deny that this was an England team in transition, but these remarks were pinned very firmly on Brian and he had to live with the fall-out that followed.

He knew that this would wind up several members of the England squad and that the best way to cope with this would be to fight fire with fire. Ireland had been made pre-tournament favourites and Brian employed the mentality of the All Blacks, who are favourites before just about every match they play. They then embrace this thought and build it into their preparation.

Ireland were pre-tournament favourites and had an experienced, yet developing squad, and, as captain, Brian saw no reason why they couldn't go on and take the Six Nations by storm.

The campaign was due to start with a trip to Italy. Brian decided to sit out Leinster's game against Gwent the week before so as not to aggravate his shoulder. This meant he hadn't had much match practice in the run-up to the Italy game, but he went for the lower-risk strategy of doing a full week's training instead.

The away trip to Italy was never going to be a walkover. They had come on in leaps and bounds since John Kirwan took over as coach and their days of being the whipping boys of the Six Nations were well and truly over. Worryingly for Brian, they tended to put in their best performance of the Championship in their first match. Italy were fresh, had prepared well and, as it was the first game, were generally free from any significant injury worries within the camp.

This was always likely to be a baptism of fire for Brian. A week before the match, a journalist who had known Brian for many years put it to him that he had matured as a person and would now handle comfortably the sort of situations that would have fazed the Brian O'Driscoll of five years previously. It was more a statement than a question. Brian had been captain for two years by now, but never before had he captained a team as well prepared and well balanced as this. It was up to him to lead by example. The time had come to deliver.

As expected, Italy didn't roll over easily on home soil. They took an early lead through a Luciano Orquera penalty after seven minutes. Italy had the better of the first quarter before a Ronan O'Gara penalty drew the scores level. With Ireland struggling to maintain possession, it looked like being a long, hard slog to get anything out of the game. Cue Brian O'Driscoll.

Just before the half-hour mark, he ran a dummy scissors and made a breathtaking outside break before passing to Geordan Murphy who scored in the corner. However, an Italian penalty followed, leaving Ireland trailing 9–8 at half-time.

In the second half, Brian really turned up the heat and led by example, and it was his break that set up Peter Stringer's try. For most of the second half, though, it looked as though Italy could quite easily have snatched the game as they tested the Irish defence time and time again. A Denis Hickie try made sure Ireland didn't lose the game, but it could hardly be described as a convincing victory. It was a sluggish performance by Ireland and the 28–17 scoreline was flattering to say the least.

Brian's predecessor as Ireland captain, Keith Wood, was working as a pundit for the BBC and said that if Brian hadn't been playing it could easily have been a different result. Worryingly, Brian picked up a hamstring injury in the last minute. There was no way Ireland could have lost the match that late on, but Brian took his dedication a tad too far by getting involved scrambling around with the pack in the final seconds. Judging by his team's performance on the day, he should have thought of the greater good and not taken any unnecessary risks.

Yet this was typical of Brian's character. He only knows how to play rugby one way, to get stuck in and stay involved for the whole 80 minutes. That night, and during the following morning, he nursed his injury with ice back at the hotel. All he could do was be as still as possible and get bored out of his mind sipping tea.

The flight home was delayed so Brian was left sitting around for even longer than he would have liked. Clive Woodward put in a call asking how bad the injury was. By now it seemed Brian would be laid off for weeks rather than months, and fingers crossed he would be ready to captain the Lions. But for now, there was no hiding the disappointment that he was unlikely to feature much more in Ireland's Six Nations campaign.

With the rest of the Ireland squad preparing for the next game against Scotland, Brian would spend the week working around the clock with the medics on his hamstring. It soon became clear to all in the Ireland camp that neither Brian nor Gordon D'Arcy was going to feature in the Scotland game, but this was to remain a closely guarded secret all week. After all, why put the Scotland squad at ease by giving them this crucial information sooner than they had to? It seemed far better to let them sweat a little. It was only when the Ireland squad left for Edinburgh on the Thursday that their secret was out.

Instead, Brian and Gordon were off on a little trip of their own, to somewhere very different. On the Sunday, they were to fly out to the Cryotherapy Chambers in Spala, Poland, for five days' intensive treatment to try to get them fit for the England game.

During Warren Gatland's reign as Ireland coach, the whole squad had been to the complex for intensive training sessions. It is a gruelling, unforgiving place but the facilities there are state-of-the-art and leave nothing to chance.

It has a well-equipped fitness centre with some added bonuses, such as the ice chambers for cryotherapy, where they can set the temperature to minus 120 degrees, enabling you to triple your workload on any given day. The theory is that the extreme cold boosts your circulation and thereby flushes out the toxins that release chemicals into the system, such as lactic acid. Brian and Gordon hoped the experience would speed up their recovery by up to two weeks, allowing them both to take to the field against England.

Brian checked out of the City West hotel just as the rest of the of the squad headed for Edinburgh, and decided to spend a few days at home before flying off to Poland. He watched the Scotland game there with his sister Jules. Brian has never enjoyed watching matches he should be involved in and this was no exception.

As had been the case all too often in the recent past, Ireland got off to a sloppy start and Scotland took the lead through a Hugo Southwell try. However, the Ireland team recovered as the boys led by stand-in captain Paul O'Connell turned on the style. Ronan O'Gara was back on superb kicking form, and five superb tries saw Ireland come out 40–13 winners. In truth, the scoreline flattered the Scotland performance as Shane Horgan spilled the ball over the line in what was otherwise a great effort by him, and the Irish defence were superb throughout.

Brian flew out to Warsaw early on the Sunday morning, but getting there proved to be an adventure in itself. The IRFU had booked Brian and Gordon under different names to avoid drawing unwanted attention to their trip. Brian became Brendan O'Donovan and Gordon was Graham Delaney.

When Brian went to check in, he didn't know whether he should keep up the pretence or whether the ground crew were in on the scheme. When asked his name, Brian froze, as though it was a tricky question or he had something dodgy to hide, so he just gave a daft grin.

It didn't get any easier in the departure lounge. A middle-aged lady came up to him and asked him if he was the young actor in the O_2 advert on television. Brian couldn't wait to get on board, put his earphones in and get back to sleep.

Upon landing in Warsaw, Brian and Gordon faced a two-hour drive to the complex. The journey wasn't particularly welcoming. The temperature was well below freezing and dirty snow was piled high on the sides of the road amid grim, barren scenery.

For the next four days, the two would undertake a punishing daily routine that usually included no fewer than three cryotherapy sessions per day, combined with fitness work and sessions in the pool, complete with bungee straps and cords. The cryotherapy sessions weren't a miracle cure by any means, but they did do a great deal to speed up the recovery process.

The challenge was to stay in the chamber for as long as you were able to. Medics were on hand to ensure the players did not stay in for longer than was safe, monitoring their blood pressure closely. At a stretch, Brian could manage eight minutes in the chamber.

At the end of each session, Brian would feel freezing

cold and would hop straight on the exercise bike, working frantically to warm himself up. In the evenings, the two would go to a nearby restaurant with their translator. On the way back, it would be pitch black and there was sheet ice everywhere. Brian became very aware of the strange noises coming from the woodlands and felt that slipping on the ice and breaking a leg or being savaged by a pack of Polish wolves would be a strange way to bow out of the Six Nations. Brian hated being in Spala and found it a grim, miserable place, and wasn't sorry when his four-day stay was over. That said, the trip could be deemed successful. Brian was now well on the road to recovery and had lost half a stone in weight during the week.

The journey back to Warsaw airport proved even more miserable than the journey to Spala. A twin-carriaged bus slid out of control on a roundabout and Brian's taxi driver slammed into the side of the bus with an almighty thud. Luckily, nobody was seriously hurt but it was a frightening experience for Brian and Gordon to endure.

When he got back to Dublin, Brian received a number of text messages from his team-mates asking him how the trip had gone. He sent them sarcastic replies telling them Spala was gorgeous and that he was planning a holiday there in August. Most of the squad should probably have known better since so many of them had been there at some point over the previous few years.

A few days later, *The Times* reported that Paul

O'Connell was about to be named as captain for the summer's Lions tour. Of course, those close to Brian knew different but it was still a closely guarded secret. Paul's captaincy of Ireland in Brian's absence had been well received and comparisons were regularly being made between him and Martin Johnson, as both players and personalities. Over breakfast that morning, the rest of the squad wound Paul up about the rumours, and told him to put in a good word to Sir Clive. Brian didn't take the reports too seriously, and knew he was still on course to captain the Lions.

That same day, Brian was declared fit to start against England the following weekend, but Gordon wasn't quite ready.

Brian didn't take any unnecessary risks in the days leading up to the game. Come the day, he remained cautious and was still quite worried that his hamstring could give at any time. Lansdowne Road is a notoriously cold place, and Brian knew that standing around for such a long time before the whistle blew was not going to be good for him.

Preliminaries there tended to take longer than at other grounds. The players were first presented to Ireland's President, Mary MacAleese, after which came the away team's anthem, followed by Ireland's two anthems. On a cold February day, this allowed more than enough time for Brian's hamstring to play up.

The game that followed will be talked about for

decades. England had lost their two previous games and Ireland were on a high. The whole squad, Brian more than most, really believed they had what it took to crush England.

An early drop goal from Ronan gave Ireland a slender advantage but England took the lead with a try by Martin Corry. This only stirred Brian up even more. He was now more determined than ever to break England down and Ireland were on the charge for much of the rest of the first half, with Brian leading by example by trying to break through the English back row time and again.

However, it was referee Jonathan Kaplan who became the centre of attention as half-time approached. Mark Cueto thought he had scored after a Charlie Hodgson cross-field kick but Kaplan ruled that he had started in front of the kicker.

England were the stronger team at the start of the second half, and a rare Irish break-out gave Ronan a chance to kick at goal, which he missed. A Charlie Hodgson drop goal extended England's lead still further, but the tide of the game was about to change dramatically.

Ireland took control of possession and passed the ball around well. Geordan Murphy played a clever dummy on Hodgson, before passing over to Brian who touched down between the posts. Brian's hard work had paid off and his try was well deserved.

From then on, it was Ireland all the way. Some clumsy kicking from Ronan wasn't enough to dampen the spirits. Ireland had beaten England and had deserved to win. Several members of the English squad were less than gracious in defeat, and did their best to deflect attention away from their own shortcomings by blaming the referee for the result. Kaplan had disallowed 'tries' from Cueto and Josh Lewsey during the game, which, upon closer inspection, pretty much showed he had got the decision correct. If anything, Ireland were hard done by when Kaplan missed Danny Grewcock blocking Ronan on the edge of a ruck.

England coach Andy Robinson led the complaining in the post-match press conference. His team had now lost nine of their last fourteen matches under him and he knew he was under a lot of pressure.

It took several days before any member of the England squad owned up to the painful truth. Martin Corry admitted in an interview that England had 'stuffed up' and that the team, not the referee, were responsible for the defeat.

Brian's heavy involvement in this physical encounter left him feeling very sore the following day, but his hamstring had survived the ordeal and after a session in the pool that afternoon he realised he was in one piece and ready to prepare for the next challenge.

Next up were France at Lansdowne Road, who had just suffered a narrow defeat to Wales, despite playing some of the most exciting attacking rugby the Championship had seen in years.

Brian managed to squeeze in a trip to Twickenham for a North v South Tsunami benefit game. Although he was nominated captain, it would have been foolish to play in the game but his presence there certainly gave the event some welcome publicity. Clive Woodward was coaching the North side and had organised a team dinner, which gave Brian a chance to get to know some of his future Lions team-mates in relaxed circumstances. Brian also had to shoot an advert for Adidas for the Lions tour. He had his reservations about doing the advert when the make-up of the final squad was far from certain, but by now a large part of him was growing to enjoy all the posing and hype these shoots provided. It certainly came as a welcome break from the City West hotel.

In the week that followed, the Grand Slam hype in the media just grew and grew. The squad, and Brian in particular, knew all along it wasn't out of the question, but the wider public were only just starting to cotton on to how good this Ireland side really was. However, this French side were good, and Ireland were going to have to overcome them without the likes of Horgan, D'Arcy and Maggs. This was always going to be a tough game.

It wasn't long before Brian was called upon to make his presence felt when after just two minutes he made a try-saving interception after Julien Laharrague went on the charge. A penalty kick from Ronan saw Ireland take an early lead, but France equalised with a drop goal just three minutes later.

Brian was on the receiving end of a high tackle from Yann Delaigue that gave Ronan the opportunity to restore Ireland's lead after 18 minutes. Yet again, France levelled the scores almost immediately after Simon Easterby was caught offside. French indiscipline allowed Ronan to put his country 9–6 up after 25 minutes, but things were to go rapidly downhill from then on.

Just three minutes later, France put together a brilliant move that ended with a Christophe Dominici try, which was followed by another French try just a few minutes later after some shambolic Irish defending allowed Benoit Baby through to score, putting France 18–9 up at half-time.

Ireland restored some form of respectability early in the second half, courtesy of Ronan's reliable kicking; however, this was cancelled out by a French penalty after 61 minutes. Ireland were down and out, but Brian wasn't going to quit until the final whistle had been blown. With just eight minutes to play, and his side out of the game, he broke through three French tackles to score under the posts. Ronan duly converted, putting just two points between the teams, providing a nail-biting final few minutes of the game. Once again, the Irish defence leaked, allowing Dominici to score for France, sealing a 26–19 victory.

The Grand Slam dream was in tatters, leaving Brian at

the lowest ebb he had ever felt in his professional career. He had done well enough in the game, and he knew his team had what it took to defeat the French. He also knew that a chance like this only came once in a generation for sides like his. He also had to accept his share of responsibility for the second French try, which was partly due to a sloppy error on his part.

Despite his disappointment, Brian knew he had a professional duty to remain positive for the post-match interviews. The Irish public saw the upcoming game against Wales as a Championship decider and they wanted to hear from Brian that there was still all to play for.

Coach Eddie O'Sullivan was as disappointed as any of his players, but he knew that there simply wasn't time to dwell on this defeat. He decided that the whole squad needed a two-day mini-break to take things easy and lighten the mood in the camp.

They stayed in the grounds of the City West for the duration of the break. There was golf for those who wanted it, as well as time for massage and sauna sessions. Brian decided to take the opportunity to enjoy a few lie-ins and lounge around for a while.

On the Thursday, the squad flew to Cardiff for the crunch-match against Wales. The sheer number of cameras flashing when they arrived at the airport reminded Brian that this was no ordinary game, and fans from both nations expected big things from their players in two days' time.

Wales had been breathtaking in the Championship thus far. Brian knew Wales coach Mike Ruddock well from his days at Leinster. In fact, it was Mike who had offered Brian his first-ever professional contract. Mike had got Wales playing attacking, running rugby, making Wales a team that could give every nation on the planet a run for their money for the first time in two decades. Brian knew his side would have their work cut out in this massive game.

The day before the match, the squad tested out the Millennium Stadium pitch. Brian was taken aback by his impressive surroundings, and he said at the time that it put the state of Lansdowne Road to shame. He liked the atmosphere the ground could generate, but this was the professional era and Ireland was now a prosperous country that deserved a national rugby stadium far better than this.

Redevelopment was on the cards within the next few years, but there was talk that Ireland would have to play their games at Twickenham or Cardiff while the work was being carried out. This frustrated Brian, who thought the matches could be played at Croke Park, the home of Gaelic football, just a few miles down the road. At the time, it looked as though this was not going to happen for political reasons stated in Rule 42 of the GAA Constitution. In the end, the GAA voted to allow Croke Park to be used temporarily until 2008 for non-Gaelic sports such as rugby and soccer, while Lansdowne

Road was redeveloped, and Ireland would play their home games in the 2007 Six Nations at the stadium, which ranks among the world's best.

Although Brian greatly admired the surroundings of the Millennium Stadium, he knew that the Welsh crowd would give the home team a massive boost and this would be an intimidating place to play.

On the day, the squad made the short coach journey from the Hilton Hotel to the Millennium Stadium and Brian was struck by the sheer number of people out on the streets of Cardiff wearing red. Welsh rugby had never known a day quite like this, certainly not since Wales's heyday in the 1970s. This was going to be a massive test for his team.

The atmosphere inside the Millennium Stadium was no less intense. Brian felt the full force of a boisterous Welsh crowd as he led his men on to the pitch. The match that followed certainly lived up to its billing.

Ronan's early penalty kick gave Ireland the lead and Stephen Jones missed the chance to level the scores with a kick of his own a few minutes later. A drop goal from Gavin Henson brought the scores level.

Ireland had the better of the opening exchanges until the 16th minute when Wales scored a try in bizarre circumstances. Brian impressively turned over the Welsh ball and passed out to Ronan, who took rather too long to put the ball into touch, allowing Gethin Jenkins to charge it down, after which he kicked the ball ahead, patiently allowing it to fall over the line before placing himself on top of it. Hardly the sort of try people had got used to seeing in games of this standard, but the fact was it put Wales in front, leaving Ireland with it all to do. Stephen Jones duly converted, before Gavin Henson put another three points on the board with a mammoth kick from inside his own half.

Brian didn't disappoint with his level of commitment in trying to get Ireland back into the game when he sent Denis Hickie on the charge with the ball, but Girvan Dempsey was held up on the line by a superb Stephen Jones tackle. However, a while later, Brian let his enthusiasm get the better of him when he came in at the side of a ruck, which resulted in Jones adding three more points to the Wales tally.

Ronan's kicking was as reliable as it had been for most of the tournament and his penalty narrowed the lead shortly before the break, but there was no hiding the enormous fight back Brian and the team had to mount in the second half.

Things went from bad to worse in the opening exchanges of the second half as two penalties from Jones extended the Wales lead to 26–6, and Ronan didn't make the task any easier by pushing one wide when they most needed him to be on form.

Anthony Foley had a decent chance to score but was forced into touch by Shane Williams. It was clear by the hour mark this wasn't going to be Ireland's day. A Kevin

Morgan try sealed Ireland's fate and by now the scoreline was impossible to turn around with just 20 minutes left to play.

Wales became complacent allowing a close-range try by replacement Marcus Horan to bring the score to a respectable 32–20 with seven minutes left, making it a nervous finale for the Welsh fans. However, Wales held their nerve and the Grand Slam was in the bag, in what was one of the most memorable days in Welsh rugby history.

Brian was not as distraught as one might expect following the defeat. He was stoical and gracious, accepting that his team had been beaten by the better side on the day, and there were no excuses and certainly no English-style whingeing from him or any of the Irish camp. Brian said a sincere well done to his old friend Mike Ruddock at the captain's reception that night.

The following day, he and the rest of the squad headed for Kehoe's bar in Dublin for the traditional end-of-tournament wind-down. The purpose of this had become a sort of unofficial debrief and to make sure the players felt good about themselves and the state of Irish rugby for the rest of the season. If any of the players had been feeling downbeat following the Wales defeat, they had certainly snapped out of it by the Sunday night and this was to be an old-fashioned rugby gathering, the sort that had largely disappeared in the professional era, and it was time to have some fun and let themselves go at the end of a long, hard campaign.

Brian and some of the others headed out into Dublin for a proper night out that lasted well into the early hours. Needless to say, Brian took the rest of the day off before returning to training with Leinster on the Tuesday. That night was to be the last time the Ireland squad would see each other and be on the same side for a number of months. The end of the Six Nations also marked the end of another era. The Ireland team manager Brian O'Brien was retiring after five years in the post. A quiet, unflappable yet canny operator, he was somebody who Brian O'Driscoll held in high regard and he was sorry to see him leave the setup.

The Six Nations campaign that promised so much yet ultimately led to disappointment was at an end. The first phase of the most important year of Brian's career was over. It was time to look to the challenges that he was going to face in the months ahead.

Chapter 3

THE GREATEST HONOUR, THE GREATEST CHALLENGE

In the following Wednesday morning, Brian was listening to the radio while having his breakfast when he heard an interview with Clive Woodward, who gave details of what he was looking for in a Lions captain. He used the exact same words he'd used to Brian at his home in Henley. Not a Martin Johnson clone, but somebody with his single-minded approach.

Brian knew that the interview was probably pre-recorded as Clive was away on holiday that week, but what could this mean? Was the captaincy in the bag? Or was Clive taking some time away to ponder his decision? Brian's heart began to race as his thoughts turned to the future and what this could all mean.

Within a day, he had snapped out of it and reassessed

his priorities. He reminded himself that first and foremost it was a privilege to even be selected for a Lions squad and if picked to play he owed it to himself and the team to try to produce the best rugby of his life.

In the meantime, he had to focus on his responsibilities with Leinster but this was easier said than done. The Six Nations had completely dominated his life since Christmas and he had thought about little else day and night over the past three months. Now it was over and he felt a real sense of anti-climax. The adrenaline had gone from his body and all of a sudden every bump and knock he had experienced during the tournament had come back to haunt him. His body felt battered, bruised and exhausted, but he knew he couldn't sit back and relax for too long as Leinster's vital Heineken Cup match against Leicester was just around the corner and he had to be back in shape for that.

Most importantly, his hamstring wasn't quite right and he knew that it was important to give it time to heal if he was to be fully fit for the Leicester game, so he decided to sit out Leinster's Celtic League fixture the weekend before.

His relationship with model Glenda Gilson – of which there had been much gossip in the Irish press in the preceding months – was back on, but Brian was keen to keep things as low profile as possible. Comparisons had been made in the Irish press to Posh and Becks, but in reality nothing could have been further from the truth. Their relationship had been on and off a few times before and they certainly did not do much to court press attention, especially outside Ireland, where hardly anybody had heard of her. But the fact he was seeing such a glamorous woman inevitably meant their relationship would attract the attention of the press.

Yet there was an upside to the high profile Brian now enjoyed in Ireland. He had become something of a marketing dream in his home country, and now, more than ever, advertisers were keen to have him associated with their products. Second only to Roy Keane, he was Ireland's most marketable sportsman.

The Irish rugby press had noted that Brian would regularly be seen drinking from a bottle of Powerade, and argued that it was happening too often to be a coincidence. Then there was the golf club on the Wicklow–Wexford border that Brian had described as 'an amazing place'. He had just signed an exclusive sponsorship deal with the club. He said of it, 'When I visited [the club], I knew right away I had found what I was looking for; I can finish training and be on the first tee here in just over an hour.'

Observers depict Brian, who holds qualifications in sports management, as level-headed and financially savvy. In 2001, he set up a company to handle many of his commercial deals. His father, Frank, is a director of the company and advises his son on which offers to take. ODM Promotions made a profit of around €125,000 for the year ending 31 August 2003 and had retained profits of €188,000. But, by now, things had moved on considerably.

One Irish sports agent said that, if Brian was offered the Lions captaincy, he could charge whatever he liked. He said, 'For example, he's in such high demand to make personal appearances he can probably ask for around ?5,000 a day. He's in a take-it-or-leave-it position.'

Fintan Drury, chief executive of Drury Sports Management, tried to put Brian's earning power into perspective. He explained, 'Other than being a fantastic player, he's bright, articulate, young and has a good image. However, there's a very simple equation at work here – rugby players don't earn as much as footballers, there is a massive gap.'

Drury was blunt in comparing Brian's earning power with that of Roy Keane. He said, 'If Brian were to have as long a career as Roy Keane has had, regardless of what he is getting paid by his employers at the IRFU, he still wouldn't be in the same league. It doesn't matter how successful he proves to be with the Lions – Adidas is always going to be able to sell more pairs of boots with a football player.'

Another agent, who has experience in handling several Irish rugby players, backed up this view, saying, 'It's a Mickey Mouse sport compared to soccer. Roy Keane makes more in one month than Brian O'Driscoll could possibly make in a year. Keane can get away with asking for £10,000 a day for personal appearances. In rugby that's just not on. You can't even really compare it to the likes of tennis or golf. Padraig Harrington probably makes several million a year in prize money alone.'

Times have certainly changed since rugby turned professional, but these accounts go a long way towards showing that the earning power of even the most glamorous and high profile of rugby players does not even come close to matching that of other sports. As the press attention surrounding his private life proves, Brian was, by now, much more than just a rugby player in his homeland – he was a celebrity in his own right. So, the fact that he does not have the financial clout of other sports stars from Ireland may come as something of a surprise, yet it is clear that Brian has benefited considerably from the professionalisation of rugby and his earning power is considerably higher than it would have been had he come along a decade earlier.

One down side the professional era had brought was the criticism he had to face for not turning out for Leinster in Celtic League matches as often as many traditionalists would have liked. On this occasion, he really did need to rest his hamstring and save himself for the Heineken Cup.

To this point in the season, he had played four Celtic League games, six in the Heineken Cup, which require a similar standard of preparation to internationals, and eight Ireland matches, giving a total of 18 full-on games by the middle of March. In the old days, there would have been one international in the autumn and four games in the Five Nations, plus some far less demanding club games, and that would be about it. There is no comparison between the intensity of the two eras, and the physical demands placed on the modern players is undoubtedly more intense. On this basis, few would argue that leading players such as Brian should be preserved for the key games.

Since he was 'resting' that weekend, Brian decided to head on a night out with his mates in Dublin on Friday night. On the Saturday morning, he headed for brunch at a local café. While he was there, he received a voice message on his mobile from Clive Woodward, who was still on holiday somewhere in the Caribbean. Clive asked him to call back as soon as possible, but Brian had difficulty getting through to him. He tried again 15 minutes later. Still no luck.

Brian knew full well that this phone call would either make or break his hopes of being Lions captain. All this waiting to get through to Clive was torture.

It seemed like many hours, but in truth only about 20 minutes had passed when Clive's phone finally rang. They exchanged pleasantries for a few moments – it turned out Clive was in Barbados in the baking heat and had just come back from a morning swim. Then came the big news. Brian was formally offered captaincy of the Lions. Brian immediately accepted, and clenched his fist and punched the air for joy.

It took a minute or two to sink in. He recalled the

meeting in Henley a few months earlier, but then in the past few weeks the press had bandied about other names and Clive was playing his cards very close to his chest. Brian needn't have worried. Clive had pretty much decided on the night of the Henley meeting that Brian had matured enough as a person and was now absolutely the right man to captain the Lions.

There was no time for wild celebrations as Clive immediately began talking about the hectic schedule that stood in front of him in the months ahead. First up was the big lunch on Monday, 11 April at the Hilton Hotel, Heathrow, for the management and captain. Brian would be expected to arrive on the Sunday night and the big announcement would be made live on Sky on the Monday afternoon.

Brian's attempt at humour fell flat: 'I'm not sure I will be able to fit that in,' he said.

There was a long pause at the other end. Clive seemed irritated.

Brian came back with: 'Well, of course I suppose I could try to clear the diary,' to try to show he was joking.

There was another long pause. Clive clearly didn't see the funny side and said, 'Well, it would be nice if you could find time to pop in, Brian.'

Hardly the best start to his tenure, but it was all soon forgotten. Brian was sworn to secrecy for the next two weeks until the official announcement was made. He was allowed to tell his parents, but that was about it.

During the course of the following week, Clive phoned Brian a number of times to discuss the tour. Brian was pleasantly surprised by the amount of input Clive was giving him regarding squad selection. Clive made it clear to him that he was the man leading the team and ultimately he had to be happy with the men he was leading out.

Brian had some very clear thoughts on the players he wanted to be included. The exception to this was the front row, about which he admits he knew very little, but there were a number of people on hand whose views he respects to make recommendations for him.

By the end of the week, he had put together a list of 53 players that had to be reduced to 44 by the following weekend. Thirty-five of these were definite, but there were still a few either/ors and there was plenty to play for in the week ahead for a number of players.

That Saturday was the day of Leinster's vital Heineken Cup game against Leicester Tigers at Lansdowne Road. Brian knew he could not underestimate the sheer power of the opposition who were going for their third Heineken Cup. In truth, Leinster took an almighty hammering that day as the Tigers became the first English side to win a Heineken Cup quarter-final away from home.

The Leinster defence did remarkably well to keep the score down to a respectable 29–13 but in truth they were never in the game, and had to settle for a late consolation try from Shane Horgan.

Chapter 4

LEADING BY EXAMPLE

As captain, he was eager to set an example to the rest of the squad so he threw out all the junk food he had in his kitchen and stocked up on fresh fruit and veg, as well as chicken and fish cutlets. He knew that it would be boring rabbit food all the way for the next few months, with very few beers and heavy nights out with the lads. He owed it to himself and the team to be in the peak of physical fitness and to prepare properly for the tour.

Brian began the week well and stuck rigidly to his new regime. But his plans were interrupted on the Wednesday when it was announced that Declan Kidney had resigned as Leinster coach and was taking over at arch rivals Munster. Declan cited family reasons for the move, but his side's thrashing the previous weekend made his position at Leinster less secure. Brian had heard a rumour the previous week that Declan had applied for the vacancy at Munster and was sure he'd take it if offered.

It's fair to say that Brian's relationship with Declan had never been particularly close or easy. They first worked together when Brian played in the side that won the under-19 World Cup in France in 1998. At the time, they worked well together, with Declan teaching Brian never to go out on to the pitch feeling inferior to his opponent – a lesson he has never forgotten. That was probably the high point in their relationship, and at Leinster things had never been as good between them.

The previous week, Declan had wanted to talk to Brian about the way ahead for the rest of the season. Knowing something was up, Brian cut him short, telling him it was a pointless exercise because he knew full well he wasn't going to be there. Mentally, Declan had not made the break from Leinster and even offered to stay there for the remainder of the season, but that was never going to be an option.

Some of the other members of the squad were certainly not sorry to see him go. He had just finished a round of contract negotiations and told several prominent members of the team their contracts were not being renewed, and Brian tended to side with the players over Declan over this.

Brian could not hide his frustration with the way

things had developed at Leinster under Declan's tenure – he did not believe his overall game had progressed as he would have liked.

He knew what he would like to see in Declan's successor at Leinster – a technically brilliant coach who had new ideas and innovations he wanted to put in place. He also knew that such coaches wouldn't come cheap and that he had to detach himself from the mess at Leinster because of his commitments with the Lions.

It was now less than a week until Brian would be unveiled as Lions captain at the big press conference in London. Brian spent the weekend doing some quiet sightseeing with Glenda in London. Clive phoned Brian and told him the make-up of the final squad. Brian was delighted with Clive's choice; every 50-50 decision had gone the way he'd hoped and he was comforted to know that he and Clive thought alike on matters of team selection.

They both knew the importance of persevering with Jonny Wilkinson, allowing him extra time to recover from his injury. The Kiwis would have loved them to announce this early on that Jonny was injured and wouldn't be on the plane, so they agreed it would be better to do exactly what the Kiwis didn't want them to do. The same went for Mike Tindall and Phil Vickery, both of whom were extremely doubtful but would keep the opposition guessing until the very last minute.

Brian checked into the Hilton Hotel in Heathrow

under the name Marcus Jansa, who was presumably friends with Brendan O'Donovan and Graham Delaney. He spent the night before the big day watching Tiger Woods winning the US Masters golf after a nail-biting play-off.

On the day itself, he was not allowed out of his room until midday to keep the growing press entourage guessing for as long as possible. He was then smuggled via the service lift to the press-conference room where he was kept waiting behind the curtain before being unveiled.

Clive had not really prepared Brian for the occasion. There was to be no autocue or script. He wanted it to come from the heart. Brian had to overcome his shyness because the truth was that once in New Zealand there would be press conferences most days and he simply had to get used to this intense level of media interest.

Brian played it safe at the press conference. He knew that every word he said was being taken down by a large number of journalists and that there were many thousands of people listening live on television. This was not a time for any of his lame attempts at humour.

Instead, he just went through the motions, saying what an honour it was, how moved and emotional it was to be selected as captain, and how hard it had been not telling anyone other than his parents about it those past few weeks.

Inevitably, the journalists were more interested in the

apparent absence of Jonny than in Brian being named captain, and this press conference proved relatively easy for him. The only question that really came his way was when he was asked about his memories of previous Lions tours. Aside from the tour of four years previously, his memories were virtually nil and, when asked what he remembered from the previous Lions tour to New Zealand in 1993, all he could say was, 'I was much more interested in Mark Hughes and Manchester United in those days'.

After the press conference was over, they split up for one-on-one interviews that gave Brian the chance to say all the things that had been playing on his mind over the last few weeks.

At mid-afternoon, Brian took a flight back to Dublin and organised what he intended to be a small gathering for close family and friends. This soon erupted into a wild party with at least 40 people turning up at his house, which included no fewer than six members of the Leinster squad who had been selected for the tour.

Denis Hickie, Shane Horgan and Gordon D'Arcy had been on edge for at least a week. They knew they were borderline selections and the build-up to this day had been a nervous one for them. Brian had known for several days that their seat on the plane was secure but he was sworn to secrecy and had to watch them suffer, unable to say a word.

Shane Byrne and Malcolm O'Kelly would be joining

them, as would Ronan O'Gara, a controversial selection but one Brian was very keen on, believing him to be the best fly-half available. Yes, there had been the occasional very bad performance with the boot, but he had generally been in good form over the previous four years, though he would face stiff competition from Stephen Jones to make the first XV.

The night started with some serious talk about how Brian saw the tour progressing, but before long they had all had plenty to drink and the lads, continuing the celebrations, headed to Flannery's pub – a haunt often frequented by nurses who had just come off shift. After that, they went on to a club and let themselves go before a daily disciplined routine had to set in.

The following weekend, Brian was spurred on by the news that Jonny had played a successful 50 minutes for Newcastle on the Friday night and was looking good for the tour. Brian played in Leinster's Celtic League win over Glasgow, although he was disappointed with the way his team fell away in the second half and blamed himself for not fully concentrating. However, considering all the upheaval at Leinster, it wasn't a bad performance by the boys.

On the Sunday, Brian travelled to the Vale of Glamorgan hotel near Cardiff for a two-day Lions get-together, exactly a month before they were due to fly to New Zealand. Waiting for Brian at the hotel was a large brown parcel. He opened it to find a Blackburn Rovers shirt signed by Mark Hughes, who had heard Brian's reference to him at the press conference and took the opportunity to write Brian a personal note wishing him all the best for the tour. 'Sparky' was Brian's all-time sporting hero and he felt greatly touched by this gesture; the shirt now takes pride of place on Brian's wall at home.

The purpose of this exercise was just to spend a bit of time together as a squad. They had been used to knocking lumps out of each other for the past four years, now they were on the same side and had to get to know each other as rugby players and as people.

In the evening, Brian and a few others had a great laugh filming the tour trailer for Sky. Brian spent half an hour roaring like a lion in front of the cameras, but couldn't help falling about laughing every time he tried to look remotely menacing. The finished article saw their heads turned into those of lions, thanks to some help from computer animation, and certainly made for an impressive advert.

Training wasn't a massive priority during this gathering, though Brian did put in several weight sessions, but gave his legs a well-earned rest. The most important aspect of this gathering was the briefing given by Clive and tour manager Bill Beaumont, which included a lot of emotive language about the Lions.

Representatives from each of the four nations, Martin Corry, Gordon Bulloch, Gareth Thomas and Paul

O'Connell, were asked to explain what the Lions tour meant to them. Then it was Brian's turn to give his speech. For once, he knew exactly what he wanted to say and there was a very important message he wanted to convey to his players.

He pointed out that the only previous Lions tours people really remembered were the tours of 1971, 1974 and 1997, which were all winning tours for the Lions. Hardly anyone mentioned the 2001 tour, and that was only four years ago. Other tours such as those in 1993, 1983 and 1977 are almost entirely forgotten, because the Lions were defeated. Brian made it clear to the squad that it was up to them to make this tour one people would be taking about in fifty and hundred years' time.

Brian also made it clear that, after a night's celebrating on the day of the squad selection, he had knuckled down to training like never before in his life. He was leading by example, and expected every single member of the squad to follow suit.

Brian then talked about what he and Clive had discussed in Henley at the start of the year. This tour had to be fun. They would be together as a squad for seven weeks. This would be the only time in their lives they would play together as a squad, and it was important they had fun and enjoyed each other's company.

He told them to enjoy New Zealand, a country like Ireland in many respects with its relaxed pace of life, village feel and warm welcome. He pointed out that the

New Zealand players were far more humble and friendly than their Southern Hemisphere counterparts. Warriors on the pitch, but gentlemen off it. The New Zealand public were rugby-mad and would give the players a warm welcome if they walked into a hotel or a bar, and the players should enjoy mixing with the ordinary people. There were also to be some old-fashioned school and hospital visits, something that hadn't happened too often in recent years.

Brian got his message across well. It would be a tough tour rugby-wise, but ultimately playing for the Lions is the pinnacle of any player's career and it was an experience to cherish and enjoy, especially in such a beautiful country as New Zealand.

There were a number of other 'getting to know you' exercises during the get-together, which included one member of the squad interviewing another in depth. Brian got paired off with Welshman Shane Williams, who he didn't know all that well, and it proved to be an interesting exercise. Brian learned that Shane wasn't some wonder-kid and had been something of a late developer. This meant he had to work hard for everything he had earned in the game.

This was music to Brian's ears. He knew instantly that Shane was a grafter and was exactly what was needed for the battle that lay ahead. Brian knew from the interview that if Shane was feeling a bit down on tour he responded better to the carrot than the stick. He also discovered that Shane was mad on motorbikes and that was his main interest outside rugby.

Then the roles were reversed and it was Shane's turn to interview Brian. Shane asked whether Brian had any embarrassing moments and if he had any regrets. Brian had one good story that answered both of those questions.

A few years earlier, Brian had done some advertisements for men's pants that resulted in some horrendous posters of him posing in his underwear. They were unflattering to say the least and Brian had kept a low profile for some months afterwards.

Later on, Clive and the rest of the management team quit the room and left the players on their own to come up with their own Code of Conduct and outline their tour objectives. Brian allowed Lawrence Dallaglio, a veteran of the successful '97 tour, to head the discussion. Obviously, there would be disappointed individuals who would not be selected for the Test side and they had to agree now the best way to deal with this. They also discussed the best way to support players who were having a bad day at the office.

At the end of the meeting, Lawrence came over to Brian and gave his take on the matter. As a veteran of two Lions tours, and the holder of a World Cup winners' medal, Brian took what he said very seriously.

Lawrence made it clear to Brian that there could be no bad days at the office on this tour. These matches were among the most important any of them would ever play and they had to give 100 per cent all the time. This was the philosophy they had to live by and this was the message they had to get across to the rest of the squad. It was as simple as that.

Clive returned to the room after an hour and the squad presented their findings to him. He agreed to give them every important thing they wanted. The tour charter was agreed and it would be printed into a booklet and given to each player the following month.

There were some amusing team-building exercises during the get-together that, on the surface, look silly but which Brian actually found a very effective way of getting to know members of the squad better and understand how they work as a team. Firstly, there was a mosaic exercise with a Lions theme which saw all the national flags and emblems split into 100 squares. Each team had to paint a few of those squares, which meant co-ordinating with the teams in charge of the squares bordering yours. It was a good laugh and they looked like primary-school children at the end, covered from head to toe in paint, but it achieved an important objective.

There was more fun after the team dinner when the squad was split into nine teams and each team was expected to perform cabaret. This kind of extrovert behaviour really didn't come easily to Brian and he just had to make the best of it. Ben Kay's celebrity impersonations were undoubtedly the highlight of the cabaret exercise, with a small number of others just about managing not to make complete idiots of themselves.

But again, there was a far more serious wider purpose to the task. A squad of players, who didn't really know each other that well beforehand, had come together and learned a bit about each other and learned to work together as a team. Of course, there is no substitute for training and playing together, so Brian was delighted when a pre-tour game against Argentina was set up, but this gathering had done a great deal to boost team spirit and morale.

Brian returned to Dublin at the end of the get-together, and it was only a matter of days before he discovered there was a nasty flipside to his elevated level of fame.

He had been living very happily at 'number 35' and had found he could go about his business quite easily without too much hassle. He lived surprisingly modestly for a man of his stature and was happy just being an ordinary bloke when he was among his local community. However, his profile had undoubtedly rocketed in the last few months, especially in the few weeks since he was named Lions captain. Things were about to change, and Brian was about to get a very rude awakening and see the other side of life as a famous sports star.

Brian returned from the get-together in Wales to find youngsters literally camped out in his garden waiting for him. Across the road, he could see several photographers hiding. He had no front gate and no privacy. This was becoming a problem and potential threat to his safety. He knew the time was right to move.

He had his eye on a property in Dublin's Herbert Road, but he couldn't afford it just yet. Brian had become something of a property bore just recently, and would flick to the property pages in the local paper even before checking the rugby results.

Brian was also still slightly distracted by the Leinster situation. They had finished a disappointing third in the Celtic League, way behind the Ospreys and Munster, and Brian met with some senior members of the squad to discuss the best way forward. Brian held the view that Leinster urgently needed a specialist coach who could take their individual games forward as well as put an overall game plan into practice.

In the days and weeks that followed, Brian found himself obliged to do more interviews than he had ever done before. As Ireland captain, he was now well used to having to do a number of interviews per day. Now he was captain of the Lions, and this meant the intensity and quantity of the interviews would only increase. But Brian stuck to his well-rehearsed routine. He remained firmly on message and made sure he said the same thing in every interview. He knew from past experience that an attempt at trying to be humorous could easily be taken out of context and this was certainly not the time to be starting a war of words with anyone.

The key point Brian tried to get across in every interview was that all 44 players getting on the plane on 25 May stood a realistic chance of getting in the Test side. The same could not be said of the 2001 tour. There was competition for places. Even a fit Jonny Wilkinson could not take his place in the team for granted with Stephen Jones in such superb form.

Brian made it clear in these interviews that he did not even dare take his own place in the team for granted. Yes, he was captain, and, by right, that should mean that he was an automatic choice. Yet he knew that he had to prove every day that he was worthy of his place as there were players who would more than hold their own at centre. He knew he had to lead by example, to play the best rugby of his life and encourage those around him to do the same.

Brian stated that, for him, a Lions tour to New Zealand held as much gravitas as playing in a World Cup final. He also repeatedly praised Sir Clive Woodward and the coaching setup, and said the preparation to date could not have been better.

At the end of April, Brian took a break from the Lions build-up by playing for Leinster in their Celtic Cup quarter-final clash against Glasgow. The tournament might not have been at the top of Brian's priority list at the beginning of the season, but Leinster had crashed and burned in all other competitions and capturing this piece of silverware would give a much-needed morale boost to the squad following Declan Kidney's departure.

Leinster won the game but the performance was hardly convincing. They had moments of skilful brilliance but these were more than outweighed by shoddy defending that almost allowed Glasgow to steal the game.

Unsurprisingly, it was the in-form Brian who was at the heart of Leinster's most impressive move of the match when he charged into the defence and threw a back-flip pass into space, knowing full well Gordon D'Arcy was running into it. Gordon then passed out to Girvan Dempsey to score a well-rehearsed, perfectly executed try.

The following week Brian declared that enough was enough and there would be no more press interviews for the time being. He decided that there was enough physical and psychological preparation to be done in the short time that remained before the plane left and he felt he had been more than generous with the time he had given the press and had easily fulfilled his obligations as captain.

In one of his last interviews, Paul Ackford in the *Sunday Telegraph* drew attention to the size of Brian's arse. Paul was taken aback by how stocky Brian was when he saw him in the flesh. The truth was that the game had changed a great deal in the last few years and Brian was a good example of how world-class centres in the future would be built.

Brian received some encouraging news from Clive when he was told that Jonny had come through a full 80 minutes for Newcastle, scoring six goals and setting up a try against London Irish. It's hard to see how the news could have been more encouraging, but Clive wanted to see him play another 80 minutes before making his final decision.

Brian began to focus purely on the rugby, and there was nothing quite like a match against Munster for focusing Brian's attentions. This was the Celtic Cup semi-final, and Brian did not underestimate the importance of this game.

Yes, it was undoubtedly important for Leinster to receive a lift after the season they'd had. Yet it was also important that Brian and all of the other Lions tour players who took to the pitch had some competitive match practice with the days ticking by until the plane left.

The match was a typical niggly encounter between the two sides. Kiwi Dave Holwell was sent off for Leinster over a petty incident with just five minutes to play. The game was tight and this left Leinster feeling unbalanced and allowed an Anthony Foley try to steal the game for Munster in the final minute.

It was a disappointing and frustrating end to a pretty miserable season for Leinster. The season promised so much yet everything fell away, although there was no denying the part off-the-field problems at the club contributed towards the disappointment.

Brian knew there wasn't time to dwell on it and he simply had to focus on the Lions from now on. That same evening Clive phoned Brian to tell him that Jonny had come through another 80 minutes and was fit to go on tour. This gave Brian's mood a massive lift. He firmly believed that Jonny was the best fly-half in the world and his inclusion in the squad would rumble the All Blacks. He also knew that Stephen Jones was in the form of his life and Jonny would have to stay on his toes to keep his place in the team. Inevitably, there were a few injury worries in the squad but this news gave a massive boost to Brian and lifted the morale of the whole squad.

Clive was less happy with his former employers at the RFU over their attitude towards England coaches and staff involved with the Lions tour. They had each received a letter asking them to log any time over 15 minutes they spent on Lions business before their contracts officially began on 17 May. Clive was understandably outraged at the pettiness of it but soon decided not to waste his time fighting a battle when the squad needed to be focused on other things. Brian saw this for the comical squabble it was, and decided not to waste his time elbowing in on something so silly.

The following day, Brian's problems were put firmly into perspective when he discovered that the Leinster team doctor had suffered an unbearable tragedy on the

Saturday. Jim McShane's three-year-old son Teddy had been killed in a drowning accident. Brian was very fond of Jim and his wife Dolores and was greatly saddened by the tragedy. At the funeral just two days later at Dun Laoghaire, Brian was moved to tears by the sight of the little white coffin being carried down the aisle at the beginning of the service.

The whole Leinster squad attended the service and it reminded every one of them that there were far worse things in life than losing a game of rugby.

They had been planning a squad night out to say farewell to a number of players who were moving on. Victor Costello was retiring, while David Holwell was returning to New Zealand. Meanwhile, Shane Jennings and Leo Cullen were moving to Leicester. The original plan was to meet in Kiely's in Donnybrook, but following the tragedy nobody was in the mood for celebrating. Instead, they had a few quiet pints before agreeing to meet up again under happier circumstances.

The rest of the week was a rare lull in Brian's hectic schedule. It was very much the case of being the calm before the storm. He kept his body in shape but didn't over-train; instead, he used the week to tie up some loose ends.

He took some time out to read the sack loads of good-luck cards and letters he had received, which included a letter wishing him well from Taoiseach Bertie Ahern. Other notable well-wishers included former Lions captain Ronnie Dawson, which Brian greatly appreciated.

The squad were going to get together at the familiar surroundings of the Vale of Glamorgan hotel in the days before the flight to New Zealand, and the time had come for Brian to say goodbye to friends and family. It wasn't so much a case of saying 'goodbye' to those closest to him – most of them would be taking a trip out to New Zealand to watch him play at some point – but it certainly was a case of saying goodbye to his home, to his familiar surroundings and to Dublin, a place he would not see again for another two months. From now on, he would be living out of a suitcase.

Brian checked into the hotel early on the Monday morning, before making the two-hour trip to London for a TAG photoshoot, then back to Cardiff for another shoot with Gillette and then back to the Vale for some more snaps for Adidas. The hectic schedule of that first day away from home helped Brian forget the nervous feelings he had been experiencing for the last few days. That evening, he bumped into Jonny – who was looking in trim shape and ready for battle to commence – in the hotel lobby.

The following day was far more boring, with most of it spent on administrative matters such as filling in insurance forms and autographing piles of memorabilia. During the course of the day, most of the rest of the squad arrived at the hotel and checked in. The one notable exception was Iain Balshaw who was forced to withdraw from the tour with a quadricep injury.

Brian felt a great deal of sympathy for Iain's predicament and it served as a firm reminder to him and the rest of the squad that they were all just one bad tackle away from being out of the tour themselves. An in-form Mark Cueto took Iain's place in the squad, which came as some consolation to Brian who had seen the rich try-scoring form he had been in for Sale during the season.

It so happened that the Manchester United team were staying in the same hotel that week as they were playing in the FA Cup final at the Millennium Stadium that weekend. This allowed Brian an opportunity to talk properly to one of his all-time heroes, their captain Roy Keane.

Known for his no-nonsense captaincy and blunt way of getting his point across, Roy had some firm advice for Brian. He told him to be his own man, to look after himself and make sure he was on top of his game. Brian was already doing exactly this, but hearing it from someone who had been there, done that and got the T-shirt, as well as being a fellow Irishman, certainly meant a lot. The principles of captaincy in both sports are much the same and this chat went a long way towards boosting Brian's confidence in his own ability.

On the Saturday, the whole Lions squad headed to the Millennium Stadium to watch Manchester United play Arsenal. As a massive United fan, this was a dream come true for Brian who had not had the time to watch his beloved team play for 18 months. He had also never been to an FA Cup final before, so this was a big day for him, and a chance to take his mind off the upcoming tour for a while.

The whole squad had VIP tickets but Brian insisted on turning up in United colours and certainly wore his heart on his sleeve during the game.

The match went to penalties following a goalless, but entertaining 90 minutes. Arsenal ultimately won the shoot-out, which left Brian in a grumpy mood as he had to endure a great deal of taunting from Llanelli coach Gareth Jenkins, a fanatical Gooner. Nevertheless, Brian enjoyed the opportunity to switch off and let others do the hard work for a change.

After dinner that evening, Brian and the others not taking part in the warm-up game against Argentina on the Monday were given permission by Clive to go into Cardiff for a night out. It would be their last opportunity to have a proper drink for at least the next two weeks.

They headed off into town in their Range Rover, complete with minders who had previously served in the SAS. They had got a few miles down the road when their vehicle suddenly ground to a halt. The minders leaped out instantly to protect the players from any kind of sabotage, though there was nothing to worry about.

After using their military experience to identify the problem, the SAS veterans discovered that the problem was, rather embarrassingly, that they had run out of petrol! Another standby vehicle was provided and they were soon on their way again.

Cardiff was still buzzing from Wales's spectacular Grand Slam victory and Brian and the lads enjoyed mixing with the Welsh public in the clubs and bars that evening. Inevitably, as the evening wore on and the drink began to set in, a small number of people approached Brian and the others looking for a fight. Fortunately, the minders were never too far away and there were times during the evening when their presence was greatly appreciated.

Chapter 5

DOWN TO BUSINESS

The following day, Brian had a bit of time to himself as the emphasis switched to those playing against Argentina. At a bit of a loose end, he decided to have a listen to the iPod every member of the squad had been given. On it was a favourite tune selected by every member of the touring party. Many of the Irish players chose U2. Will Greenwood was a big Neil Diamond fan. Alastair Campbell, the former New Labour spin-doctor and press secretary to Tony Blair, was part of the tour party to work on the PR side of things. His selection for the iPod was Abba's 'The Winner Takes It All'. He had told Brian it was the first song he'd heard on the radio when he woke up the morning after the 1997 general election.

The team selection for the warm-up match against

Argentina was always going to pose difficulties. Clive had decided some weeks before that it would not be a good idea to let Brian play in the game as to lose your squad captain to injury under those circumstances would obviously be considered a disaster.

Gareth Thomas was an absentee as he was playing in the Heineken Cup final, and fellow Welshman Stephen Jones had club commitments in France. The five Sale players were needed for the Challenge Cup final, and Neil Back was serving a two-week suspension for punching Joe Worsley. Others would also be sitting out as they were recovering from knocks, but the big news was that Jonny would be taking part. It was felt he could do with playing a competitive 80 minutes against a world-class side given the length of his latest injury lay-off.

The instructions to the team for this game were simple – it was not to be treated as some kind of meaningless warm-up game. The priority was to win the game, and put in a good performance, in that order. Sections of the press were ridiculing the fixture as pointless, and a bit of a joke. Others said the fixture was reckless risk-taking, which could lead to key players picking up injuries with just a matter of days to go until the plane left.

Brian and Clive didn't see it like that. Only a fool would fail to acknowledge that Argentina were now a force to be reckoned with in world rugby and they would offer the Lions a highly competitive match.

A number of automatic picks were being rested, which allowed a degree of experimentation. This meant those lucky enough had to put in a good performance. Those who could expect to play in the Test side had to confirm to Clive and Brian that they were in top form, and those players considered fringe members of the squad had to make the most of this opportunity to state their case for Test selection.

So Brian took his place in the stand to watch the match. The performance was somewhat disjointed and a number of basic errors allowed the Pumas to dictate the game. A try from Ollie Smith kept the Lions in the match but the star of the game was Jonny who kicked an injury-time penalty to secure a 25–25 draw. This game was certainly no warm-up for Jonny – it was a statement of intent on his part. He proved to the world that he was back and that he meant business in the tour ahead. Brian didn't become too distracted with the fact the Lions didn't manage to win and instead expressed delight at Jonny's return to his very best.

Shortly after the match, Clive revealed some disappointing news to the rest of the squad. Jason Robinson would not be flying out with them later in the week as he felt he needed to spend some time with his wife, who was pregnant and the situation was causing him some anxiety. Gareth Thomas and Stephen Jones would also be joining up late, as they couldn't be released from club commitments in France. Michael

Owen would be flying out but would be returning home just a week later to attend the birth of his child. Clive's decision to take a huge squad was now beginning to look like a very smart move.

On the day the squad flew out to New Zealand, Brian received some welcome news from Leinster. Michael Cheika had been appointed Director of Rugby while David Knox would be joining as backs coach. This news was exactly what Brian wanted to hear. Knox becoming backs coach especially pleased him, as he was a man Brian knew a fair bit about and greatly respected. He was confident that the new Australian coaches at Leinster would help take his game forward.

And so Brian took to the skies in a flight lasting more than 24 hours. He boarded wearing his Lions blazer and full suit, though soon changed into a T-shirt and tracksuit bottoms once on board. The whole tour party was large enough to require two planes since there weren't enough business-class seats on board for everybody. Brian stopped over briefly in Singapore prior to flying on to Sydney to meet up with the rest of the squad before they embarked on the final leg to Auckland together.

Upon arriving in Auckland, he was greeted by around 150 hardcore Lions supporters who had already made the long trip, along with one New Zealand supporter who challenged him with his unique version of the haka.

Brian and the rest of the squad decided it would be

best to try to stay awake for as long as possible to adjust to the New Zealand time and so headed for a few beers and a stroll along the harbour front after they'd checked into the hotel.

The following day, Brian met up with some members of the New Zealand squad who were involved with promotional work with Adidas. Brian especially enjoyed the chance to spend some time with his friend (at the time) Tana Umaga, who is regarded by those who know him as a complete gentleman off the pitch, softly spoken and very charming, despite his fierce, warrior-like persona during battle.

Brian knew that, away from the field, relations between the two squads were going to be very good. The New Zealand players were exactly as he expected them to be – warriors on the pitch but humble and unassuming off it. He knew from then on that the tour was going to be good-natured and there was going to be no unpleasant war of words between the two groups of players.

Later that same day, Brian spent some social time with Jonny. The conversation that followed was to have a profound effect on him. Jonny began to tell him how his life had changed since England's World Cup win two years earlier. Jonny was very much the star of the team and had become rugby's answer to David Beckham.

Like Brian, Jonny had never been an extrovert off the pitch and was not comfortable with some of the aspects fame had brought him. He now needed full-time security guards and was mobbed everywhere he went. He was forced to spend most of his spare time indoors and simple things like walking down the streets near his home had become extremely difficult. The long injury lay-off had given him time to think and he had decided that once this Lions tour was over he was going to take measures to try to lead a more normal lifestyle.

This chat made Brian consider just how lucky he really was. Yes, there had been problems recently with his own security, hence his need to move home, but generally he was allowed to go about his business without massive difficulty and the way ordinary people were with him rarely gave cause for concern. Yet he knew that now he was Lions captain this could all change. Until now, his fame was largely confined to Ireland. Now, he would be as well known in Great Britain and this could have consequences when he made his regular journeys there. Would it be practical for him to go for nights out in British cities from now on? Would he be able to go shopping in London with his girlfriend without being mobbed? He needn't have worried, but at the time these were very real concerns for him.

The next day, the whole squad attended the official Maori welcoming ceremony, which was a plane ride away at Rotorua. They were greeted at the airport by thousands of rugby fans, before being taken by coach to the venue, which, due to the heavy rain, had to be moved indoors.

They were told on the way that they would have to respond to the Maori warriors' song with one of their own. Brian knew that Matt Stevens had a great voice and asked him if he fancied the challenge. To his credit, Matt knew all the words to 'Bread of Heaven' and responded in style.

Once inside the hall, Brian was greeted by a Maori elder who gave him a warm welcome. Brian went on to make a polite speech in which he said that, while his team were there to win, they were also in New Zealand to make friends and to enjoy everything the country had to offer. The tour manager, Bill Beaumont, then accepted the challenge laid down to him from the spectacularly dressed Maori warrior, complete with spear. Brian thoroughly enjoyed this ceremony, which was the first of many experiences the squad would have of New Zealand's rich culture.

One aspect of the preparation Brian did not enjoy was being coached for the many press conferences and interviews he would have to undertake as Lions captain. He believed he was already doing well in interviews, generally playing it safe, remembering to repeat the same party line in all interviews, no matter how repetitive it had become. As Ireland captain, he thought he had gained enough experience to be considered pretty good at this.

Alastair Campbell had been brought on the tour party to deal with PR issues and to make sure everybody was singing from the same hymn sheet. While Brian liked Alastair as a person and enjoyed his humour and passion for sport, he did not like some of the advice he was given.

Alastair had come from the world of politics where he had gained a controversial reputation in his role as Tony Blair's press secretary. In Brian's mind, politics and rugby were worlds apart. He understood that politics was essentially a murky and cynical world where a few words taken out of context could be twisted to mean something very different, whereas rugby was an entirely different matter. The game was generally played in a gentlemanly manner and there was a strong moral code among players that was generally adhered to. Compare the response a rugby referee gets from the players to that received by a Premier League football referee. The game is played in a gentlemanly spirit and differences can usually be resolved over a pint.

Brian felt he already knew how to behave in interviews and didn't always feel Alistair's attempts to manage them were necessary. From time to time, he had strong views and said things that needed to be said, and felt it important that he would continue to be allowed to express himself honestly and frankly during the tour.

The first training session brought home to Brian the extent to which the squad's every move would be followed by the public and media. The training session was watched by around 2,000 supporters. It was intended as an Open Day so there was no great disruption caused by the crowd, although it did provide a fair few laughs.

Sky commentator Miles Harrison was providing commentary for the crowd and the players had to do an official run-on. Being the captain, Brian led the party and sprinted on to the field, only for the rest of the party to stitch him up by staying put in the tunnel, much to the amusement of the crowd. However, a few moments later Brian got revenge thanks to the wonders of modern technology.

A promotional video was being played on the big screen, which, it turned out, wasn't quite big enough, as it cut off the first two letters of everybody's names. For Brian, this was no big deal, as he simply became 'ian O'Driscoll'. Things weren't quite so straightforward for Steve Thompson and Gethin Jenkins, who picked up rather unfortunate nicknames for the rest of the tour.

The one serious issue that arose as a result of this session was that Clive and the coaches decided that the group training sessions were too shambolic and that there would be no more such sessions for the rest of the tour. It was a decision Brian didn't completely agree with as he felt there were benefits to be had from everybody training together, but on this occasion he had to bow to Clive's decision.

Attention soon turned to the first match of the tour where the opponents would be Bay of Plenty, who had finished third in the National Provincial Championship (NPC) the previous year. Club rugby in New Zealand is intensely competitive, and Brian knew there would be no easy games against club sides. Every match would be a battle. And so it proved.

At half-time, the scores were level at 17–17 as the opposition gave everything they had. The Lions managed to run in three tries in the second half, although there could have been a fourth courtesy of Brian but he messed things up. Mark Cueto was unmarked on the outside and was calling for the ball, but Brian chose to pass to Josh Lewsey on the inside who couldn't do much with it. Mark was furious and started shouting at Brian, before realising it was the captain he was speaking to and apologised profusely. He needn't have worried. Brian knew he had messed up and deserved everything Mark was throwing at him. The Lions eventually won the game 34–20.

Brian's main concern following the game was Lawrence, who had been taken to hospital with a broken ankle. The injury was severe and threatened to end his career. Lawrence was a larger-than-life character, and an experienced old head who Brian greatly appreciated having around. His loss was a huge one for the team, but also a major psychological blow to Brian, and certainly took the gloss off an impressive second-half performance.

After the game, the players headed off for a few quiet drinks. There was little point in trying to sleep as the adrenaline was still pumping. It wasn't a heavy night out, but it was a good chance to unwind after the baptism of fire they had just experienced.

Brian used the following day to relax – there was no way a heavy training session would benefit him at all. He watched the New Zealand version of *Strictly Come Dancing* in his hotel room. Former All Black hooker Norman Hewitt was the star of the show, getting perfect marks from the judges for his *paso doble*, which included a haka in the middle. Later that day came the more sombre task of welcoming Lawrence back following his operation. His tour was over, but he wouldn't be able to fly home for another 10 days and offered to help Brian out with the preparations, which he greatly appreciated.

Simon Easterby was being flown out as replacement for Lawrence, and within a matter of days the squad would be at full strength. Stephen Jones and Simon Shaw had just arrived and had joined up, too. Gareth Thomas would be joining up shortly as Toulouse had just been knocked out of the French Championship, and Jason Robinson would be arriving at around the same time.

Halfway through the following week, Brian was hit by a nasty dose of food poisoning after he had made the mistake of eating scallops, his favourite seafood, the previous evening. He tried going to training but soon had to throw in the towel and was violently sick. Within

24 hours, he had lost four kilos but he was soon over the worst.

Later that week, he flew up to New Plymouth for the first of the community days. Brian spent an hour watching a group of 16-year-old boys taking part in a full-on contact session. Brian told them that what they were doing was deeply impressive, but it was equally as important to brush up on basic ball skills, which they didn't seem to put as much emphasis on.

Brian was asked to do some babysitting for one of the mums who was more interested in watching the training session. Ever the gentleman, Brian held the newborn girl on his lap. In New Zealand, they get the children keen on rugby from a very young age, and the baby, who can't have been more than a few months old, was already kitted out in All Blacks gear as she slept in Brian's arms.

He returned to the hotel to prepare the squad for that evening's game against Taranaki. Brian was going to sit out the game because a huge test against New Zealand Maori was only a few days away, and he needed to rest his shoulder, because the old injury had come back to haunt him once more.

Brian watched the game from the stand with his cousin Jenny. The Lions were captained by Martin Corry who led the side to a 36–14 victory against strong opposition, which included two superb tries from Geordan Murphy. A number of fringe players had certainly staked their claim for a place in the Test team.

Brian flew straight back to Auckland after the game to prepare for the match against Maori.

Brian chose to take things easy the following day, aware that any heavy training sessions could aggravate his shoulder problem and could force him to miss the game. Instead, he spent part of the day in the casino, where he made a small profit, before going with Shane Horgan for a haircut. The woman cutting Brian's hair claimed she used to work in Dublin and knew his favourite bars.

The day was very much the calm before the storm. The match ahead had been billed as the 'Fourth Test' and there was undoubtedly going to be a Test match atmosphere inside the ground come the day. Thirty-five per cent of all rugby players in New Zealand were eligible to represent Maori, and Brian was well aware that they were a proud race and would be taking this game very seriously.

Those players that might or might not be eligible to play for the Maori have their credentials examined by the Maori kaumatua, who traces the players' genealogy. The process is famously complicated, one notorious example being that of Christian Cullen, who it was discovered was 1/64th Maori and therefore eligible to play.

Later that evening, Brian watched a rugby programme on TV1, which had no fewer than six studio guests. Former All Black wing Stu Wilson was one of them, and he refused to join in with some of the harsh criticism the

Lions had faced in the press the past few days from the likes of Jon Mitchell. Instead, Stu said that he had been impressed with what he had seen so far and expected some fiercely competitive games ahead.

Following the rugby came the weather forecast, presented by the gaffe-prone Brendan Horan, who described the weather as: 'Bloody ugly, just like the Lions front row.' This sort of thing only spurred Brian on even more.

The day before the match Brian did some light training, though he remained cautious because of the shoulder problem. In the evening, he watched the highlights of New Zealand's warm-up game against Fiji on television. The All Blacks thrashed Fiji 91–0, but Brian still picked up on weaknesses, particularly with regards to their tackling. This was, nevertheless, the first time the All Blacks had played together since the previous November and Brian knew that the team that had thrashed France the previous year would soon get it together again and the challenge that lay ahead would still be incredibly tough.

The match against Maori was watched by a sell-out crowd of 30,000 at the Waikato Stadium. The atmosphere was exactly as Brian had anticipated, and it was clear to everyone involved this was a full Test in all but name.

The opening exchanges were physical with neither side giving an inch. Stephen Jones opened the scoring with a penalty but Maori soon brought the scores level. The pressure on the Lions was relentless until eventually Martyn Williams handed the Maori the lead when he deliberately slowed the ball down, giving Hill a kickable penalty.

Stephen Jones brought the scores level but soon sustained a nasty injury after colliding with a Maori shoulder. He left the field with blood pouring from his face and was replaced by Ronan, but he was soon patched up and was able to come back on for the remainder of the game. Andrew Sheridan was then given 10 minutes in the bin for a punch on Luke McAllister but the resulting penalty was not converted, making the scores six a piece at half-time.

The second half saw Maori turn on the class and kick three penalties early on. This was followed by a try from Leon MacDonald which was converted. Several Maori penalties were added soon after and the Lions became increasingly frustrated and sloppy.

With the game lost, Brian restored some credibility by scoring a try following a rolling maul, which was converted by an in-form Jones. The captain had led by example, but it was only ever going to make the score look more respectable. Brian had captained the first Lions side ever to lose to Maori.

Once back in the dressing room, Ian McGeechan tried to lift the team's spirits following the historic defeat. He compared that night to the first game of the 1997 tour when the 'Test' team were defeated by a very average Northern Transvaal side. Apart from a few moments of brilliance from Jeremy Guscott, the Lions played incredibly poorly. Ian told the players that for about half an hour after the game they were feeling down, but then the true spirit of the Lions came through and they decided that from then on they would destroy every South African team that came their way. Just four days later John Bentley scored a breathtaking try and the tour was back on course.

Clive reinforced this point by telling his players that this defeat would make them, not break them, and that, between now and the next game, they would concentrate on the good, and work on the bad. Brian simply told his men to ignore whatever criticism the papers threw at them over the coming days. It was what went on within the squad that mattered. Everything else was irrelevant.

Despite scoring a try that night, Brian felt he had put in a poor performance and asked Clive if he could play in the Wednesday game against Wellington to make up for it. Clive agreed, and named a strong team for that game, which included the likes of Jason Robinson and Gareth Thomas, who were making their tour debuts. Clive also decided that this would be a good time to unleash Jonny, who would be making his Lions debut in New Zealand on the day.

The squad flew on to Christchurch in preparation for the Wellington match. They trained on the grounds of

Christchurch School, one of the best rugby schools in the country. Brian had seen many hakas by now and felt he had become immune to its effect, but nothing could have prepared him for what he saw at the end of that training session.

It was a longstanding tradition for the school to issue the haka when Lions tour parties used the ground. Brian stood in awe as around 600 boys, some as old as 18, lined the quadrangle to perform the haka. He had never seen anything like it in his life. It was a truly breathtaking experience for him, and one that would stay with him.

Brian hadn't spent much time reading the papers over the previous few days. It was inevitable that his team were being criticised left, right and centre by the press following the defeat. However, he had found out about one story that annoyed him more than any other.

Several papers had reported that there had been a training-ground bust-up between Gordon Bulloch and John Hayes that had left Gordon needing a few stitches. Brian firmly denied there had been any such bust-up, and that Gordon's injury had been caused by a boot when they were practising their rucking. For him, this was a story out of nothing, a bit like the day before the squad was announced when one national paper declared that Matt Dawson had been excluded, when in fact he knew full well there was a plane ticket with his name on it.

The Wellington match took place before a crowd of 34,000 at a ground affectionately known as the Cake Tin. The opposition was strong – they were missing their All Blacks stars but they would still provide formidable opposition. This time the Lions performance was far more impressive as tries from Welsh duo Gethin Jenkins and Gareth Thomas helped secure victory. It wasn't perfect and there were still plenty of things to iron out in training, but it gave a much-needed morale boost to Brian and the rest of the squad.

The following day, the papers were not talking about the result; instead, they focused on Jonny's tour debut and what this would mean for the team selection for the upcoming Test. He was brought on after an hour as replacement for Gavin Henson, switching Jonny to inside centre alongside Brian and bringing Stephen Jones on as fly-half. Clive had considered moving Jonny as far back as the initial meet-up in Cardiff, and he was using this opportunity to experiment and see how it worked out.

However, this got the papers and, more importantly, the All Blacks guessing as to what they were really up to. Were they trying out variations just to give Stephen Jones more time? Nobody except the Lions themselves knew for sure.

In the end, the decision was taken to play Jonny at 12, thereby allowing the Welsh Grand Slam half-backs to remain together. The only person who would be disappointed by this arrangement would be Gavin Henson.

Gavin's tour was far from over but he made little attempt to hide his disappointment at being omitted from the Test team. Shortly after the tour, he published a diary in which he slated several members of the Lions squad and questioned some of the tactics employed and preparation for matches. There had been some bad blood between Gavin and Brian that had spilled over into the public arena around this time.

The fall-out began during the Wales–Ireland Grand Slam decider earlier that year. Gavin had claimed that Brian swore at him and called him 'cocky' during the game. He also claimed that Brian had tried to 'jackal' him, a term players use to mean stealing the ball from your opponent on the ground.

Gavin's criticisms didn't end there. He claimed that Brian had pulled his perfectly styled hair during the game and also tried to gouge his eye for good measure, before saying, 'How do you like that?'

Once Gavin's book was published shortly after the tour, he gave his reasons for not liking Brian, in as strong terms as he would be allowed to use. Essentially, it seemed that there was a simple clash of personalities between them. Gavin objected to Brian's in-your-face, confrontational manner on the pitch, whereas he preferred to keep quiet and let his play do the talking.

They were also poles apart away from the pitch. Gavin

and his girlfriend, the singer Charlotte Church, had become a celebrity couple in their own right, especially in Wales. They liked to be seen together in public, courted media attention and enjoyed living the celebrity lifestyle. Gavin was also gaining something of a reputation for his appearance. His hair always looked as though he had styled it with meticulous attention to detail, and he was often ridiculed for shaving his legs.

In sharp contrast, Brian's approach was more that of the traditional rugby player. Yes, he kept himself in the peak of physical fitness and was a role model for the professional era, but it would be unthinkable for Brian to lead a 'showbiz' lifestyle. He preferred a few beers in the company of close friends to attending film premieres, and, although he and Glenda could easily have become a showbiz couple if they'd wanted to, Brian preferred things to be low key and to keep his private life private.

Once the tour was over and Gavin's book was published, Brian said in an interview that Gavin had criticised certain players in the book but had never criticised them to their faces. The book caused much controversy and also saw Gavin say negative things about members of the Welsh Grand Slam squad, which led to a souring of relations between himself, his team-mates and the Welsh Rugby Union. Since then, Gavin's game has been in decline and he has never fully recovered from this episode.

Preparation for the first Test began in earnest and

Clive decided that work had to be done to improve line-outs. The problem seemed to be that the codes were too easy for the opposition to crack so they were deliberately made more complicated in the days leading up to the match.

Clive gave the players the impression that the All Blacks were spying on them and using underhand techniques to find out their game plan. It was equally as plausible that he was doing it to strengthen squad unity and make them think and act more cohesively, but either way, security had been stepped up significantly.

Brian found out the sheer professionalism and scale of the security operation while chatting to one of the regular security men who had been around him since the start of the tour. He told him that since the start of the week there had been three or four extra security men put in place. There was no point in Brian trying to find them, because they were so professional and so well hidden.

There were obvious security implications in having such a large number of world-class rugby players in one place. They were a high-profile target for terrorists so nothing could be left to chance. But, with Clive telling his men that the All Blacks were trying to spy on them, the role of the security men took on a whole new purpose.

From now on, nothing was left to chance. There would no longer be opportunities for waiters and other hotel staff to listen in on their conversations. Scribbled notes would no longer be thrown away in wastepaper baskets, as it would be all too easy for someone to pick them out of the bin and pass on vital information to the All Blacks. Every time the squad moved to a new hotel, every room would be swept for bugs and other listening devices.

If he was being serious, it wouldn't be the first time something like this had happened on a Lions tour. There had been speculation four years previously that South Africa had learned their line-out calls and the Lions had paid a heavy price for this in the third Test. Martin Johnson, one of the best in the world in a line-out, lost several balls he would normally be expected to grab with ease. There could be no repeat of that this time around.

All meetings would now take place in the 'War Room' as opposed to the Team Room. That would be the place where game plans, line-out calls and all notes would be kept. It was to be guarded 24 hours a day and no paperwork was to be taken from there under any circumstances.

For Brian, the consequence of this was that he became more withdrawn and less willing to interact with the public than usual. He was still willing to sign autographs when out and about in the streets, but he became a very private person in his hotel and didn't appreciate strangers coming up to his door for trivial reasons. This atmosphere of suspicion, combined with the fact that the first Test was now only a week away, resulted in considerable changes in Brian's personality. He became very focused, his whole life was consumed by the Lions. Other things did not matter and he did not allow himself to get distracted by them.

Even on his days off, he was thinking about nothing other than the Lions. If he went for a walk, it would be by himself. He got some bad publicity in the local press after withdrawing from some community events, but deep down he knew this was the lesser of two evils.

Those who have met Brian in passing or at a function nearly always agree that he is quiet and affable, and pretty generous with his time. At this moment in time, that was not the case, and it was better to just allow him to shut himself away from outside distractions. The usual Brian O'Driscoll simply did not exist until after the first Test.

This change in mood had consequences for his relationship with Glenda. Things seemed to be going well between them, and Glenda had planned to come out to see Brian during the fortnight, but he was now dead set against the idea. The last thing he wanted to do now was go for quiet meals in restaurants or take walks with her around some of the spectacular scenery that surrounded the hotel.

Sleeping next to her at night would also pose problems. He was prone to waking up, full of adrenaline and needing to go for short walks to clear his head.

Other members of the squad, especially those who were married, seemed to love having their partners around during this crucial time. Perhaps for those who were married things were different. They would know one another's faults far better and knew when to give each other space. Brian's relationship with Glenda was still in its early days and there was no way he was going to jeopardise things by revealing this darker side to his personality at this stage.

His parents were due to fly out shortly to watch him play, although he preferred not to meet up with them either just then. His relationship with them had always been fairly close and he knew that allowing them to see him when he was like this could not be a good thing.

Brian was by no means the first rugby player to behave like this when away on tour. He had found out that former All Black Colin Meads would never even phone his then fiancée Verna when away on tour, following an incident when Colin, who was clearly in a similar frame of mind to Brian, had a blazing row with her while away in Australia. This brought out an uncharacteristic side to him she had not seen before, and from that point onwards they agreed to communicate twice a week, by letter. He had obviously done something right because they have now been married for more than 40 years.

It was clear that Brian would have some making

up to do once the tour was over, but that was something to think about later. For the time being, only one thing mattered.

Chapter 6

THE CHANCE OF A LIFETIME

Brian travelled down to Dunedin to watch the second string take on Otago. The side, captained by Gordon Bulloch, put in an impressive display as they secured a 30–19 victory. There were two major talking points that came from the game.

The first was when Otago captain Craig Newby accused the Lions of 'cheating like buggery' at the breakdown. Coach Ian McGeechan shrugged off Newby's comments in the post-match press conference, telling journalists that they must have been doing something right to get him to make such an outburst.

Secondly, there was Ryan Jones's breathtaking debut at number eight, earning him the man of the match award. He had only been a part of the squad for a few days, having just flown in from Wales's tour of Canada where he was taking the place of the injured Simon Taylor. He scored one try after Shane Williams did the groundwork, then later on he returned the favour by setting up Shane following an almighty charge at Otago.

The following day's papers highlighted Ryan's performance as well as that of Simon Easterby, and several journalists pondered why it was that in such a close-knit squad the star performers were those who joined the party late. This was a fair question, but Clive put it down to them being extremely determined to impress when their chance came. The truth was that these two were now not far off being selected for the Test team.

The day had arrived when Clive would announce which players would make up the Test side, and which would be left out. To put it politely, those who were left out would make up the squad to play Southland. The whole squad were gathered for the big announcement. Aside from Gavin's absence, which Brian had known about for several days, there were a number of other very able players who had done little wrong, but were nevertheless destined to take on Southland rather than the All Blacks – Geordan Murphy and Charlie Hodgson to name but two.

Clive told the disappointed men that their contribution in training in the run-up to the big day was vital. They were well-intentioned words, but they came as little consolation to the men who had come so near, and yet so far, to making the Test team.

The Southland squad were then asked to leave the room, leaving just the 23 members of the Test squad and the coaches. The make-up of the squad provided no real surprises. Shane Horgan was chosen over Shane Williams for a place on the bench, which was a very tight call, but beyond that the press chose to focus on Gavin's omission and Jonny's switch to number 12.

Clive then went on to talk through the game plan, aided by diagrams he had drawn on the board. The chosen few looked on in a dazed silence, many of them still coming to terms with their inclusion in the side, while eager to absorb what Clive was saying at the same time.

At the end of the talk, Brian retired to his room and watched the final of the New Zealand version of *Strictly Come Dancing* on television. Brian watched as Norm Hewitt proved once again that there was far more to him than just his skills as a rugby player. Norm put in a brilliant performance on the dance floor, and Brian sent in a few text votes to prop up his chances. Sure enough, the New Zealand public agreed with Brian and Norm was crowned champion.

At midweek, Brian watched from the stands as the second string just about managed to scrape a win against Southland. It was by far the Lions' worst performance all tour, and was not the kind of preparation the squad needed for the first Test, which was now only a matter of days away.

There were some highly talented players in the Lions team that took to the field that night, and Brian expected far more from them. Many critics believed that the players who took to the field were playing as individuals, rather than as a team unit. They were inevitably extremely disappointed at not being part of the Test squad, and felt they had a point to prove to earn their place for the second Test. As a result, team play went out of the window and they all suffered because of it.

Clive had told Brian that Wales's Australian backs coach, Scott Johnson, was flying out to act as an observer for the Lions. Scott had caused massive controversy the previous autumn when, during the build-up to Wales's game against the All Blacks in the Millennium Stadium, he referred to New Zealand as 'just a poxy little island in the Pacific'. The proud nation of New Zealand was about to take its revenge on Scott.

Upon arriving at the airport, Scott showed his passport to the girl at the desk and, after she typed his number into the computer, she looked a little concerned and went to fetch her supervisor. Scott stood around for a long time, and got increasingly worried about what might be happening. Then, a huge man wandered over with his passport in his hand, before making a show of inspecting it in minute detail.

After a lengthy delay, he said, 'Ah, Mr Johnson, we have been looking forward to your arrival for some time. A thousand welcomes to our poxy little island in the Pacific. I do hope your stay with us isn't too awful.'

Scott was for once lost for words.

The build-up to the big day was gathering pace, and Brian joined the squad for the big team announcement opposite the hotel that evening, which was broadcast live on New Zealand television. It was a glitzy occasion, complete with a big screen and musical fanfare as they entered. However, what was meant to be a well-rehearsed formal occasion soon turned into a bit of a farce.

Enough seats had been set out for the squad, but one of the journalists decided it would be funny to take a few of them away to try to encourage a scrap between players for the seats that remained. To make sure all formality went out of the event, Paul O'Connell couldn't resist the opportunity to pull Alastair Campbell's tracksuit bottoms down, turning a revered and feared spin-doctor into a figure of fun.

The day before the big game, Brian tested out the pitch at the Jade Stadium, aware that wet weather, possibly even snow, would be on the way the following day. Later that evening, he spent time in the company of his sisters. Still very much in his withdrawn, focused mindset, these were the only people in the world he could bear to spend time with at the moment. They knew all about his mood

116

swings and were willing to make allowances for them, considering the highly pressured circumstances.

Brian went to bed that night knowing he could not be more ready. His preparation had been perfect. He was in the peak of physical fitness, and had never felt as sharp as this. His mental preparation had been spot on and he knew what he wanted and what he expected from his team-mates. His recurring shoulder injury was holding up well, and there was no way that was going to stop him from taking to the field. Even the dreaded hamstring that messed up his Six Nations campaign was holding up well now. He would be able to run at full speed, confident that it would not let him down. He was in the form of his life, and the tour couldn't have come at a better time. There were no excuses, Brian was ready for battle and he slept well that night, confident he could handle whatever the All Blacks threw at him.

The day Brian had waited six months for had arrived, and Brian led his Lions team out on to the field in the intimidating, yet electric atmosphere of the Jade Stadium. After the anthems had been played, it was time to face the haka. Brian and Clive had discussed at length the most appropriate way to accept the challenge. They agreed that the last thing they should try to do was upset their opponents. This was, after all, a longstanding tradition and they were ultimately guests in their country. Of course, there was also a chance that if they upset the All Blacks at this stage it might spur them on

117

even more and increase their determination to beat the Lions, which is the last thing they wanted to do.

Brian recalled a conversation he'd had with a Maori elder at their official welcoming a few weeks before, who outlined the most appropriate and respectful way to accept the challenge, and decided to follow his advice on the night.

Brian, as warrior chief, stepped forward to directly oppose their chief, Tana Umaga, accompanied by the youngest member of the team, Dwayne Peel. The rest of the team spread across the pitch, completely motionless. It was one of those moments that everyone involved would never forget. Tana led the haka with extra enthusiasm and it was very clear that Tana the gentleman was left behind in the dressing room and Tana the ruthless warrior had taken to the field. He put everything into it and tried to look as intimidating as possible as Brian stared straight into his eyes. Yes, it was steeped in ancient tradition, but it was also the perfect curtain-raiser for the battle that would follow. When the haka was finished, Brian remembered what the Maori elder had said and leaned forward while still maintaining eye contact, clutched a piece of grass and threw it to the wind. In the days that followed, the New Zealand media claimed that the Lions had insulted their hosts with the manner in which they had accepted the haka. Clearly, Brian and Clive knew more about the history of the haka than most of their critics did. They had done their homework perfectly. Brian had chatted to a Maori elder, and he and Clive had kept in contact with him via email to make sure they got it exactly right. Brian couldn't win. They could not have done more to get it right and it was clear that he was right and they were wrong.

With the formalities over, it was time for the rugby to begin. Within a matter of seconds, Brian tackled Leon McDonald, but Leon laid the ball back well, and Jerry Collins formed a protective bridge. Brian got back on his feet and started leaning on Jerry to try to get him to crash into Justin Marshall and spoil their possession.

Brian became aware of their hooker Keven Mealamu trying to pick him up by the left leg, which was completely illegal, but he might still have considered the ruck to be live. Brian was considerably stronger than Keven and managed to get the better of him. Tana had driven through the ruck, and moved left as Marshall cleared the ball. With the ball now well away from them, Tana turned back to Brian, grabbed his right leg and lifted him up. Keven helped Tana lift Brian, before turning him upside down.

Brian was about to crash to the ground, and his priority was to break his fall. He knew if he landed on his head he would break his neck and face a life in a wheelchair. He stretched out his right arm just in time and hit the ground hard. He was in agonising pain, and quickly realised he had a dislocated shoulder. He tried shouting out to touch judge Andrew Cole, who was still standing by the ruck, but he had no voice at all. Maybe he had been winded, maybe the shock had made it impossible for him to speak. Meanwhile, play had moved to the far side of the pitch and Brian was left the forgotten man.

The incident occurred close to the Lions fans and they knew exactly what had happened. Eventually, play was stopped on the other side of the field when the Lions halted the All Blacks close to the line. Brian's pain was only increasing and it wasn't long before physio Phil Pask called for the cart and diagnosed a dislocated shoulder.

Many rugby watchers described Tana's spear tackle as the worst they had ever seen. It was illegal, reckless and the ball was well away from them by the time Tana dropped Brian to the ground, so there can be no possible excuse for it. Yet it was four months before the authorities decided to punish him.

At first, they accepted his explanation that it was 'accidental' but all those months later some amateur footage shot by a well-placed spectator showed the sheer dangerousness of the tackle. The fall-out from the incident was enormous.

It's clear that Tana didn't acknowledge Brian as he was being taken off the pitch that night, in fact, the only All Black to enquire after him was Justin Marshall.

Some time afterwards, Tana phoned Brian, and a hostile exchange took place.

The details of what was said remained a secret until late 2007. Brian left the details out in his official Tour Diary book and his ghost writer was forced to tone down some of the more severe criticisms aimed at Tana, at the insistence of a sportswear company who sponsor both men. In his book, Brian says that the two had agreed not to divulge the details of their conversation.

Tana however claims that Brian was angry that he had not called him sooner to discuss the matter. He also says that Brian was furious that he hadn't gone over to see how he was, and accused him of being involved in a lot of off-the-ball incidents.

In his own book, Tana accuses Brian of being a 'sook', a New Zealand slang word meaning 'cry baby'. He says that he never went out to injure Brian and that, in the heat of battle, rugby players do occasionally sustain serious injuries. It appears likely that Brian was absolutely furious with every aspect of the tackle, and wasn't willing to dismiss it as just one of those things.

Few would disagree that the tackle was extremely dangerous, reckless and completely unnecessary, but the incident also ended what had until then been a good friendship between Brian and Tana. The incident certainly left a sour taste in the mouth and the remainder of the tour would not be played in the spirit of goodwill and friendship that had existed until that point.

Phil and Brian's cousin, Gary, tried to push the shoulder back into place but they couldn't. The cart that took Brian off the pitch was also completely inappropriate, as Brian felt every bump on the grass. An old-fashioned stretcher would have been better. It didn't help that Brian was paraded the long way around the ground before reaching the medical room. Brian has since said that the journey around the ground as he lay there, in agony and sweating profusely despite it being freezing cold, was the most embarrassing experience of his life.

When they finally arrived in the medical room, they were greeted by a scene of chaos. A spectator in the stand had been taken ill and the supply of morphine had been taken to help him. Sadly, the spectator subsequently died, which helped Brian put his own set of circumstances into perspective when he found out about it later on.

With no morphine available, Brian was lifted on to the table and the stadium nurse started to cut his Lions shirt off. Brian was now in excruciating pain, by far the worst of his life. A medic started using laughing gas on him to ease the pain, but Brian didn't take kindly to them forcing it down his throat. He pushed it away and asked them to just hold it above his mouth, which made things slightly better.

Incredibly, the nurse had the nerve to ask Brian if she could have his Lions shirt. Brian couldn't believe what he was hearing. He tried to use some very bad language but couldn't get the words out. The nurse persisted, saying she had two children and they would love to have it. She had no chance. The shirt was Brian's only artefact from the tour and he wouldn't part with it for the world. What else did he have left?

His father had fought his way through security and reached his son, who understood what Brian was fretting about. To Brian's eternal relief, the shirt was now in safe hands. After what seemed like an eternity, but what was probably no more than a few minutes, the medic found some more morphine and injected it into Brian's arm. Instead of giving it a few minutes to kick in, the medic immediately started trying to push the shoulder back into place. Brian was screaming in agony, he had never known pain like this before and just wanted it all to end.

From the corner of his eye, Brian could see Richard Hill coming into the room. His knee trouble had come back and he was out of the game, too, but was immediately taken to another room as Brian's screaming would have been hugely unpleasant to have to listen to. Eventually, his shoulder clicked back in. It was very painful, but Brian was relieved that it was firmly back in its socket.

Brian was then taken to the hospital, where the X-ray revealed no break, which came as a huge relief. The morphine was starting to kick in by now, so Brian can recall very little of his time in hospital. After a few hours, he returned to the hotel to meet up with his team-mates.

The match itself had been a disaster for the Lions, and the whole game had been played in a bad spirit following the tackle that was to end Brian's participation in the match and, inevitably, the tour. The All Blacks took the lead through a Daniel Carter penalty, which was followed by another soon after.

The first try came courtesy of Ali Williams after some clumsy work in the line-out from the Lions. Things went from bad to worse after the break when a stunning try from Sitiveni Sivivatu added to the misery. The only consolation came in the form of a Jonny Wilkinson penalty, but the final score was 21–3, which, if anything, flattered the Lions.

Back at the hotel, the atmosphere was as grim as Brian had ever known after a big game. The players were obviously down after the defeat, but they were outraged at what had happened to Brian. Every member of the team shared his view that he had been the victim of a malicious and dangerous tackle, and this was not just one of those hard but fair tackles that sometimes happen in a competitive game of rugby.

Later on, Brian met up with his family. Twenty-four hours previously, he didn't want them anywhere near him as he remained totally focused on the task that lay ahead. Now, though, he was only too pleased to see them. His family had always been a massive source of comfort and support for him, and now he needed them more than ever.

They sat in the corner of the hotel restaurant, saying very little. Brian's sister, Jules, was especially upset and had clearly been crying, although she made a good effort not to appear upset in front of him. At one point, the girls left the table, leaving Brian and his father alone together. Brian had never seen him as angry as this. His normally quiet and composed father was outraged at the tackle that had ruined his son's tour, shattering months of hard work and sacrifice in the process. It wasn't long before the girls returned, and he immediately calmed down to his usual self once again.

Brian knew full well that he wouldn't be able to sleep that night, so there was no rush to leave the table. At about 2am, he received news that the South African citing commissioner, Willem Venter, had refused to cite the two All Blacks involved in the tackle. This would have meant taking a proper look at the incident and interviewing all those closest to it. Incredibly, Mr Venter was intending to fly home in just a matter of hours. Brian was stunned by the extraordinary attitude the official was showing.

That said, Brian needn't have been so surprised. The precedents for bringing New Zealand players to justice on home soil weren't favourable. Two years previously, Ali Williams had been cited but cleared of stamping on the head of Josh Lewsey, an incident which left the England player with stitches and a badly bruised face.

Despite it being the middle of the night, Brian was inundated with requests for media interviews. He decided that he would release a statement. As Alastair Campbell had long since gone to bed, he did it on his own, and gave a full and frank account of what had happened from his point of view. The statement was completely blunt and spin-free. He was angry, and he didn't care who knew it. He had suffered a grave injustice at the hands of two of the world's toughest and most feared rugby players, and in the hours that followed the authorities didn't do anything to bring the men to justice.

He finally went to bed at around 4am, but he couldn't sleep. The whole episode just kept going round and round in his head. On the Sunday morning, Clive gave a press conference, as he had done on every other Sunday morning, for the benefit of Sunday-newspaper journalists in the UK. Even now, Brian wasn't going to let Alastair in on the act and reinforced everything he had said the night before.

Later that day, Brian was outraged by an interview he saw with All Blacks coach Graham Henry. He had played under Henry on the previous Lions tour when he was their coach and was hurt by his comments. In a nutshell, Henry brushed off the incident, but said that Brian was a good bloke and it was disappointing if his tour was over.

In the days that followed, Brian was outraged by the attitude taken by almost every New Zealand paper, with the exception of the *Herald*, which gave a fairer assessment. All other papers unquestioningly swallowed the line of the New Zealand camp, and didn't even entertain the possibility that Tana and Keven had been massively in the wrong. On television, the incident dominated every news bulletin. One of the channels managed to interview Andrew Cole, who had already flown back to Australia. He said that he didn't remember coming on to the pitch or ordering the players to put Brian down. After that, Cole clammed up in front of the camera when challenged and told the interviewer that he shouldn't really say anything. Incidentally, this was the same Andrew Cole who would be refereeing the second Test the coming Saturday.

Within a few days, Brian received the news that he would need a pinning operation to make sure the ligaments tightened properly so that the injury would not recur. It was already becoming clear that he was likely to miss the autumn internationals, which did little to lift his still very black mood.

As the week progressed, events did little to dissipate Brian's anger. Graham Henry stuck to his guns and said that Tana had apologised after the game, whereas in reality he had done no such thing. Someone from the New Zealand Rugby Union had been in touch asking for Brian's mobile number, which didn't impress him much. The hotel where the All Blacks were staying was only down the road, and it really wouldn't have taken much trouble for Tana, or even Keven, to pop over for a few minutes.

The All Blacks' spin machine proved more than a match for Alastair Campbell as they started briefing journalists that Henry had apologised on Tana's behalf, although anyone who had heard him speak during the press conferences knew his words fell well short of a proper apology. Their camp also accused the Lions of spinning the incident to make it appear more serious than it really was.

Brian was furious with Henry by this stage. He had worked with him four years previously but had never really warmed to him as a person. Yet he was still upset that Henry didn't have the grace to be more open about what had happened and accept that two of his players had been in the wrong.

On the Tuesday, the midweek team took on second-division side Palmerston North and won by a record margin of 109–6, with several players earning a place in the Test squad, including Shane Williams who scored five tries in the game. Brian watched from the stand and greatly appreciated the support being shown to him from the Lions crowd, who sported T-shirts bearing slogans such as: 'Keven Mealamu, Tana Umaga… all innocent. Yeah, right.'

This was the day that saw Brian's spirits begin to lift. He had a long chat with his father, who said that it was time to reflect on the fact that he was in one piece and to be thankful that he did not break his neck. In the evening, Brian received a text from his old friend Donal O'Flynn.

Donal had been a fine player in his own right and had

made his mark at Belvedere College. When he was 17, he broke his neck, which left him quadriplegic. The text read: 'Both of us have many things in common. Same birthdays, both stunners, both great rugby players! And we have both taken personal setbacks with honour and dignity. Despite your recent hurt you remain a living Lion legend, Donal O'Flynn.'

After reading that message, the world didn't seem such a bad place after all, and Brian knew he had plenty to be grateful for. Yes, there had been an enormous injustice and he would continue to fight to put that right, but there was little point in letting it dominate his mind for every minute of every day. It was time to move on, and to start plotting his comeback.

Chapter 7

MOVING ON

Despite being injured, Brian was not going to fly home immediately. He still had a great deal to offer as non-playing captain, and would be on hand to support the rest of the squad in the important challenges that lay ahead.

There were other obligations to fulfil, some of which Brian really wasn't in the mood for. One such instance was an official reception at the Parliament building in Wellington where Brian was booked in for a photo shoot with Tana. He decided it wouldn't be a good idea to turn up. He knew the media would be after photos of the two men shaking hands, and, since they hadn't even spoken at this stage, he decided it was inappropriate to proceed with this stunt.

MOVING ON

Later that same night, Tana phoned Brian and the now infamous heated exchange took place. Despite his obvious anger during the call, Brian did not allow himself to be overcome with fury for too long, remembering that he had made a promise to himself to draw a line under the episode.

Glenda was due to fly out to join Brian at any time. Despite his having been hostile to having her around when he was part of the playing squad, she now couldn't arrive soon enough. Having his family around him those past few days had been a source of enormous comfort and support, and having Glenda around would make him feel far happier for the remainder of the tour.

He began to reflect upon his attitude in the lead-up to that first Test. Yes, he had been right to remain focused and determined to play the best rugby of his life, but shutting out those closest to him was perhaps not the best idea he'd ever had. He had now realised just how much he valued Glenda and his family, and knew that in future he'd have to strike a more sensible balance.

Glenda had respected his decision not to have her join him in New Zealand, but he now realised that she meant too much to him to just shut her out when an important match was approaching. After all, there were many members of the squad who loved nothing more than having their wives and children around them during the build-up to big games, and Brian now thought that maybe he had something to learn from their approach.

With time on his hands until Glenda arrived, Brian decided to go for a few beers with some of the New Zealand players who would not be taking part in the upcoming Test, including Conrad Smith, Doug Howlett and James Ryan. He enjoyed spending the evening in their company, and especially enjoyed talking to Conrad, who he found to be exceptionally bright and discovered he was training to be a lawyer.

The following day, Glenda finally arrived, which helped brighten Brian's mood. She could tell how disappointed Brian was with the way things had panned out but said all the right things. He seemed relaxed as they joined his family for a meal that night and he felt as though he could spend the time that remained on tour enjoying New Zealand and spending some valuable time with Glenda.

On the morning of the second Test, the papers were still talking about the incident, even though it was no longer dominating Brian's thoughts. He read a piece by Colin Meads, which summed up exactly what he was thinking. Colin said, 'Tana should have been around the Lions team hotel on Saturday night, Sunday night at the latest, with a crate of beer. It might have been frosty to start, but the thaw would have soon started. There is a lot of merit in the old ways.'

Brian couldn't have put it better himself. He was used to settling on-the-field disputes over a few beers; it was the way he had always done things. This incident was an extreme example, but Brian freely admitted that, if Tana had behaved in the right way in the days that followed, he would soon have let it drop.

There was a series decider to be played that night, and Brian took his seat in the Westpac Stadium to watch as the Lions attempted to make amends for the previous week's disaster and level the series.

The Lions got off to a perfect start when new captain Gareth Thomas spotted a gap to score a superb try early on. Jonny was never going to miss the conversion, but a minute later he missed a golden opportunity to extend the lead further when his penalty kick hit the post.

However, it wasn't long before the hosts turned on the class through two cleanly taken penalties by an in-form Dan Carter, who went on to engineer a marvellous try for Tana, shrugging off Gavin Henson before charging 50 yards down the pitch to finish off the manoeuvre.

Jonny cut the gap with his first penalty eight minutes later but straight from the restart the Lions conceded a penalty and Carter restored the home side's lead. It wasn't long before the All Blacks scored their second spectacular try of the evening. After winning a scrum five yards out from the Lions line, they spun the ball across the width of the field allowing Sitiveni Sivivatu to score.

At half-time, the score was a respectable 21–13 but it wasn't long into the second half before Dan Carter ensured the Lions were out of the game for good. Within minutes, he had kicked a penalty, which was followed by a memorable solo try that he duly converted from the right touchline.

The Lions were deflated, although they weren't going to give up without a fight, but 10 minutes of superb pressure that followed produced nothing. The All Blacks defence was just too strong. Just before the hour mark, Jonny hobbled off after a tackle on Tana went badly wrong, causing a 'stinger' injury to his already fragile right shoulder.

They got a consolation try through Simon Easterby but in the final quarter the All Blacks turned on the class, scoring a further two tries, one coming from Dan Carter to cap off what was probably the greatest performance of his career to date, followed by a short-range effort from McCaw to seal a 48–18 victory, securing the series in the process.

It was all over. The Lions had blown it. There would be time in the weeks and months ahead for a detailed post-mortem, but, for now, everyone involved was devastated. Every single player who boarded that plane to New Zealand all those weeks before had worked hard to earn their place in the squad. The backroom staff had left nothing to chance, and it was difficult to see how they could have prepared better at this stage.

Yet, despite everything, things just hadn't clicked. There were numerous problems the Lions could look to. The line-out was generally poor, as was the scrummaging.

The defence looked brilliant in patches but poor communication often let the All Blacks through at vital moments.

Even though Brian was watching from the sidelines that night, the defeat affected him more than most. During the past week, he had taken his role as non-playing captain seriously and was on hand to give the boys guidance and advice. He had lived and breathed the Lions over the past few months, and staying in the same hotel as them and being surrounded by the same old faces meant he couldn't detach himself from them easily.

As soon as the final whistle had blown, Brian headed down to the changing room to be with his team-mates. They all felt the pain as much as he did. After all, this tour was the pinnacle of their rugby-playing careers for many of them. They could not realistically hope to collect a World Cup winners' medal before they retired, so, for them, this tour was as good as things got.

Prince William had arrived in New Zealand a few days earlier and had met Brian in the hotel the day before the game. The Prince went down to the changing room to console the Lions, where Brian greeted him with: 'Howaya, Willie!' Royal protocol was clearly not at the top of his priority list at the time.

The Prince sat down and chatted to Brian about the game for 10 minutes, and the boys generally seemed to appreciate the gesture of his coming down and consoling them.

When they got back to the hotel, the mood seemed to ease somewhat and the atmosphere was nowhere near as grim as it had been following the previous week's defeat. Many of the players had given a decent account of themselves and they were far from disgraced in that night's game. Clive said in the post-match press conference that they had just been beaten by a stronger, better side. Brian, meanwhile, had come to the conclusion that the side had not yet peaked and that they probably should have had five weeks together before the Test series began. He told his team-mates that, if the Test series was starting again right now, it would be far closer.

The media, meanwhile, were far less forgiving, and the Sunday papers were full of condemnation of the Lions. Sir Clive, who had been hailed as a national hero less than two years before, bore the brunt of the criticism for his team selection, coaching methods and choice of captain. So many prominent journalists seemed very wise after the event.

Brian decided to hit the town that night and drown his sorrows. He and several of the Lions met up with the All Blacks and they enjoyed spending some time socialising together. The spear-tackle incident was the last thing on most of their minds, and it wasn't long before Brian realised that he actually liked a lot of the All Blacks as people. At one point in the night, he caught Justin Marshall's eye and was about to go up to him and thank him for being the man who came up to see if he was OK after that tackle. But then he decided this probably wasn't the right moment. It could reignite the situation at a time when everyone was getting along well and enjoying one another's company.

Instead, the two men talked for a while about Justin's upcoming move to Leeds. Brian soon found out that Justin was a massive golfer, so he took the opportunity to invite him to stay at his house if he fancied a short golfing break in Ireland. It seemed the most appropriate thing to do at the time, and it was his way of letting Justin know that he had a great deal of respect for him as a person.

By the beginning of the following week, Brian just wanted to go home. Looking out of his hotel window, he became depressed by the grey weather and felt it was a waste of time his being there. For the first time, he felt like a hanger-on, a spare part who served no purpose. He felt a fraud for accepting payment and believed he didn't deserve to be there. The one thing he could do to put that right was head straight for the gym and train hard to make amends as soon as possible, but he could not even consider doing this until after his operation.

He also came to realise that he felt very different on this visit to New Zealand from his previous trip there with Ireland. Put simply, he wasn't enjoying it anywhere near as much. He had become increasingly aware of a

137

nasty edge to the public's passion for rugby. Every time he came out of a pub or café, he would be subjected to loutish and drunken abuse from supporters, something he didn't recall happening when he was last there three years earlier.

In Brian's view, the public's passion for rugby was bordering on an unhealthy obsession, to the extent that it dominates national life. He read that after the Christchurch Test there were 22 arrests, all of them New Zealanders. Some of the Lions fans got pretty drunk that night, but not one of them crossed the line and became nasty with it. Brian didn't think this was a coincidence.

He was also fed up with the attitude of virtually all of New Zealand's press, who seemed absurdly biased in their reporting of matches, to the extent that they were completely unrecognisable from the game he had just played in. All of this, he felt, was not a healthy approach to have. He was increasingly aware of the need to have a life outside rugby, and felt the New Zealand public could learn from his changing attitude. He thought that maybe things could be better if they had perhaps a few other national sports that captured the public's imagination.

These days, cricket came a very distant second to rugby in the minds of the people. There was very little else that the nation got passionate about apart from rugby, and this, he felt, meant that winning games became too important – it was no longer just a sport.

Brian's mood lifted slightly later that day when he read an article by Lions veteran JPR Williams, who said that the problem with the 2005 Lions was that they did not sleep together! This made Brian chuckle, but, reading on, he soon realised that there was a very interesting point behind it.

JPR was making the point that, in his day, sharing a room with a player from another country and travelling around on old planes and trains helped to create a really tight squad. Brian knew that there was probably a lot of truth in what he was saying. A close-knit squad who spend virtually every minute of the day together undoubtedly feel more like a team when out on the field.

But Brian also knew that this was the professional era, and there could be no going back to the old ways, and any attempts to deliberately make life difficult for the players would not be appreciated. He also remembered how relieved he felt on that first day of the tour when he found out that players would each be having their own room.

He began to feel a lot better about things the following day when he went with his mate, Prince Willie, to visit the Starship Children's Hospital in Auckland, accompanied by Andrew Sheridan. Not for the first time on this tour, Brian experienced something that made losing a game of rugby seem not all that important after all.

The Prince took the lead and it soon became clear that

he had inherited his mother's incredible gift for being able to communicate with children. Seeing these sick children being so positive as they fought serious illnesses came as a stern reminder to Brian that there were people in this world, not too far away from where the rugby was going on, who were going through a far tougher time than he was.

Brian spent the afternoon relaxing with Glenda, before making his way to the stadium for the Lions' match against Auckland, which was played in torrential rain. The home side put out virtually their entire Super 12 team, so this was always going to be a tough challenge. This Auckland team were by far the strongest midweek opposition they had experienced all tour.

The Lions took the lead through a Charlie Hodgson penalty after four minutes. It soon became clear that Auckland were up for this challenge when they bravely opted for tap-penalty moves rather than kicks for goal on three separate occasions in the first half, but the Lions defence just about did enough to hold up.

Charlie, who had been playing well enough to warrant a place in the Test side, was forced off injured midway through the first half, and was replaced by Ronan, who added another three points straight away. But Auckland quickly replied with three points of their own through Brent Ward.

Martyn Williams was denied what looked like a certain try when he was taken out off the ball right under the posts. Shortly before half-time, the Lions finally scored following an impressive jinking run from Mark Cueto, before crossing to Martyn to finish off a perfectly executed manoeuvre, making the score 14–3 at the break.

A penalty against Gordon D'Arcy allowed Brent Ward to kick Auckland back into the game early in the second half, which seemed to give the home side momentum as they controlled possession for most of the remainder of the match. Some clever passing by Auckland created gaps in the Lions line, and their persistence paid off when Isa Nacewa crossed for a try, which was duly converted.

The Lions were now well and truly on the back foot and had to defend manically to avoid throwing the game away. They soon conceded another penalty with just 11 minutes to go, but Ward's kick hit the post. This was proving to be a real nail-biter.

Ronan kicked a penalty with just five minutes to go which put some space between the sides, but there really was no telling which team were the club side in the second half. They were evenly matched throughout; indeed, if anything, it could easily be argued that Auckland were the stronger of the teams. Nevertheless, the midweek Lions were delighted to have won a tough battle in awkward, slippery conditions. Brian was especially happy with the result, as from where he was sitting he could see thousands of loyal Lions fans who had braved the conditions and had been soaked right through. If anyone deserved to see the team win, it was them.

Following the game, Brian joined the team in the 'Midweek Massive' party, which they had been planning for some time. It was a heavy night on the town that was well deserved. Even Prince William received an invite, though he couldn't attend due to other engagements. The Southland game aside, the midweek boys had done themselves proud throughout the tour, and coach Ian McGeechan aided by Gareth Jenkins could be very proud of what they had achieved with the players.

The following day, Brian couldn't help but think that separating the Test and midweek teams during training sessions had been a major mistake. It is true that there had been a very chaotic squad session in the first week, and that Clive had decided to split them up from then on, but by now Brian had reached the conclusion that they could learn a lot from each other and that it would have helped develop a feeling of being a complete squad.

On the evening of 7 July, Brian received yet another poignant reminder that there was more to life than rugby when he turned on the television in his room to discover that suicide bombers had struck London. He headed downstairs and met up with the rest of the squad, many of whom were frantically phoning home to make sure none of their loved ones was missing. Fortunately for them, everyone they knew was safe but as the death toll rose by the hour the whole squad got a sharp reminder that the upcoming Test was only a game.

With the relief of knowing that none of the boys had been directly affected by the terrible news, Brian proceeded with his evening's plans and enjoyed a night's social eating and drinking with some friends who had come over from Ireland, who had probably booked their tickets expecting to see him captaining the Lions in what may well have been a series-deciding Test match. Still, it wasn't to be and Brian decided to just enjoy their company for the evening and have a few drinks instead.

The following night, which was the night before the game, Brian decided that he would be doing more harm than good if he were to stay around the Test squad. He had been invited for a few 'quiet drinks' with Jason Leonard. He knew full well what this meant. Jason simply didn't do 'quiet drinks' and this would inevitably lead to a good drinking session. Brian couldn't think of a single good reason not to accept the offer, and so the two headed off.

Once again, Brian took his seat in the stand in Auckland for the final Test. Yes, the series was lost, but there was still a lot to play for in this game. Every single member of the squad wanted to avoid being forever labelled as part of the Lions squad that lost every Test match on tour. They were playing for pride, and for their reputations as world-class rugby players.

Before kick-off, there was an impeccably observed minute's silence in memory of those who had lost their lives in the London bombings. When the referee blew his whistle to start the game, it was the Lions who took the initiative, when Stephen Jones kicked a penalty after just three minutes.

They should have scored their first try early on, after a searing Josh Lewsey break down the left touchline, and a powerful run from Gethin Jenkins set up a promising position, but Irish lock Donncha O'Callaghan spurned a clear four-man overlap to his right.

Stephen Jones added another three points after their old friend Tana was sin-binned for lying on the ball, deliberately slowing down possession. If the Lions thought that the All Blacks had gone to sleep, they were about to be given a blunt reminder that they were playing the best Test side in the world.

A surge from number eight Sione Lauaki fed Conrad Smith, who beat Geordan Murphy and Mark Cueto to romp home under the posts. With Dan Carter injured, it was left to the debutant Luke McAlister to take the kick. He duly added two points with the easy conversion.

It wasn't long until the All Blacks added a second, when Dwayne Peel fumbled McAllister's grubber kick, allowing Williams in for a try. The Lions fought back almost immediately when Stephen Jones added another penalty on 23 minutes.

The opening quarter had been played in cold, but dry

weather, but all that was about to change. Without warning, the heavens opened and torrential rain poured down on Eden Park, turning the pitch into a waterlogged mud bath in no time at all. Both sides, but especially the Lions, struggled to adapt to the severity of the conditions as passes were fumbled due to the greasy ball.

A relatively straightforward Jones penalty hit the post and stayed out, and things went from bad to worse a few minutes later when a Josh Lewsey error resulted in a try for Tana right under the posts.

A passionate half-time team talk from Clive didn't have the desired effect, and their spirits were deflated still further early in the second half when Tana scored his second try of the game. Could things get any worse? The hosts soon added a fifth try, but mercifully for the Lions this was disallowed after Jerry Collins was sin-binned for an off-the-ball tackle on Jones.

This gave the Lions some inspiration, and a prolonged spell camped on New Zealand's line was eventually rewarded with a try for Lewis Moody. This was to prove nothing more than a consolation try, however, as from then on the Lions seemed tired, sluggish and eager to get on the plane home. This was capped off when Rico Gear chased a kick at the death to score one more try, bringing the final score to 38–19.

Unfortunately, any bitterness between the two camps was not eased following the final whistle. Clive and

Graham Henry had been at loggerheads since Henry was put in charge of the Lions tour four years previously. Clive had been highly critical of many aspects of Henry's preparation for that tour. In his post-match interview, Henry was clearly in no mood to extend an olive branch. He said, '2001 was a blessing for me because I wouldn't be sitting here now if it wasn't for 2001, so I should thank the people for the ribbing because it pushed me back to New Zealand quicker than I probably would have come back.'

Clive, maintaining a degree of dignity, urged caution on the part of the New Zealand rugby-loving public. He warned them not to get too carried away with this tour win, and that they could not take winning the World Cup in two years' time for granted. Clive said, 'I would offer a caution on the New Zealand team. When I see them going through the quarter-finals and semi-finals and win a World Cup, then it is time to celebrate, because it is a very tough tournament. The only time you can judge teams like New Zealand is when you arrive at World Cups when everyone has had the same degree of preparation.' Clive's words would turn out to be a sound prophecy, but they sounded like sour grapes to the New Zealanders at the time.

Brian joined the rest of the squad in attending the after-match function, but he wasn't really in the mood for polite company and left as soon as it was respectful to do so. Some of the guys, such as Gareth Thomas, had been suffering with a touch of flu and Brian felt that he might have been coming down with it.

He headed back to the hotel and turned in for the night, knowing that he had a very long day's flying home ahead of him. When he got up the following morning, some of the boys were still heading in after a wild night out with the New Zealand players. He didn't especially mind them going out and enjoying themselves; after all, the series had really been lost the week before. But, for him, there was no hiding the disappointment he felt, not just for himself but for the whole camp. A career-defining tour, one that, on paper, provided the Lions with their best hope of winning a series in New Zealand in decades, had come to nothing.

Brian had started the tour intending to mix with the All Blacks far more than had been possible, through a combination of the bad blood that had emerged between them and the constraints of time. This was just another of the disappointments he had to come to terms with. All those months earlier when Brian and Clive talked at his home in Henley, the two men agreed that they should make every effort to enjoy the experience of being in New Zealand and to soak up the culture and attractions the country had to offer.

The reality was far different. Brian had not enjoyed being there at all for much of the time. The only part of New Zealand he really liked was Wellington, which he considered a place he could emigrate to one day. He wished there had been far more opportunities to explore New Zealand's rich and ancient culture, but the sheer intensity of the tour, and his determination to remain completely focused on the rugby in the lead-up to the big games, made that impossible. There were no sightseeing trips.

He had felt humbled when visiting sick children with Prince William, and had enjoyed the precious few chances to watch the schoolchildren train, but there had been few other excursions. The way Brian was feeling now, he just wanted to get on the plane and begin the long journey home. Luckily, having an early night meant that he was in far better shape for a long flight than most of the squad were, which would involve stop-offs in Sydney, Singapore and Heathrow, before finally touching down in Dublin. Brian couldn't wait to get back home.

It was a warm summer's day in Dublin and Brian was back where he wanted to be. He organised a barbecue to celebrate his homecoming, which was attended by a select group of friends. He was feeling mighty relieved to be back home, and glad that at long last the tour was behind him. His shoulder was feeling surprisingly good, perhaps a little too good really. As he enjoyed the evening, he completely forgot about his shoulder, until he dropped a bread roll and moved suddenly to catch it, and got a painful reminder that he was suffering from a serious injury.

The following day, he did the sensible thing and saw a local specialist. The diagnosis was exactly the same as in New Zealand. Eager to get it over with and move on, Brian booked himself in for the op that coming Friday.

In the few days he had before he was to go into hospital, Brian began making preparations for his house move. He had decided to have a new house built, and, upon visiting the site, he was surprised to see the plot cleared and the foundations already laid. The plan was to move in by Christmas. He got talking to one of the builders who said that his local had put up a poster with a picture of Tana that read underneath: 'Barred for life from these premises.' Another of the workers, a real giant of a man, told Brian that he should sue for GBH, and he wasn't joking.

As Brian was about to find out, this man's strong feelings on the incident were by no means rare. With some time on his hands, Brian started reading up on the British and Irish newspapers' take on the saga. He had heard that the story had been huge back home, but it was hard for him not to become blinkered by the very biased, one-eyed perspective given by the New Zealand press. When he analysed what had been written in his absence, even he was shocked by the strength of feeling about it. That said, he was unhappy with the way in which so many articles had been mixed up with Alastair Campbell's supposed spinning of the story. In Brian's mind, nothing could have been further from the truth, as

Alastair had nothing whatsoever to do with the publicity that followed. It was Brian who decided to release a press statement on the night of the incident and it was he who showed up at the press conference the following morning and spoke from the heart. It also seemed absurd to link Alastair to any of the sentiments that came from the subsequent New Zealand press conferences where Graham Henry and his chums did everything they could to play down the incident.

Brian checked into the hospital the night before the operation. The hospital staff talked him through the procedure, and he found out that the operation was nicknamed the 'shark's bite' because it leaves a deep, prominent scar. The plan was to open up the shoulder and reset the joint before tightening it up with 16 staples, allowing the ligaments to grow in exactly the right position so that the shoulder regains full strength. The operation was deemed a success but it was clear that Brian would probably miss the autumn internationals, and making it on to the field for Leinster at Christmas was a far more realistic target.

He was home in two days and made the decision to hide from the public view until he was fully recovered. Over the next few months, he would be looking to spend more time with Glenda – she certainly deserved to be spoiled a bit by him after the few months she'd endured with him. He would also be taking a far keener interest than he otherwise would in the construction of his new home, visiting on an almost daily basis to see how it was coming along. The next few months were about sitting back and doing very little, giving the shoulder every chance to get back to full strength.

The year had promised so much for Brian, and looked set to be the most successful of his career, yet it had delivered absolutely nothing. Leinster had blown their chance of European glory, and the Ireland team had seen their prospects of winning the Grand Slam fall apart. The Lions tour, which had been planned to perfection in Brian's eyes, cruelly fell apart for him within a matter of seconds of the first Test kicking off. But there was little he could do about it now. All he could do was put his feet up, allow his body time to heal and plot his comeback at the end of the year.

Chapter 8

BACK IN BUSINESS

Brian's aim of maintaining a low profile during his recuperation didn't exactly go according to plan. In a number of interviews, he had hinted that at some point in his career he would like to play his club rugby in France. This was not intended as some kind of clue that he was in advanced negotiations with a French club, but the media, especially in Ireland, began speculating that he would be leaving Leinster when his contract expired in the summer.

In truth, Brian's reasons for wanting to move to France at some point were simple. The attacking, physical style of rugby the French clubs tend to play particularly suits his game, and he was growing a bit tired of the weather back home. Then again, he was having a brand-new home built to his specifications, so that might have been taken as a hint that he wasn't planning to move away any time soon. The speculation gathered pace in September when Brian was spotted in the crowd for a game between Biarritz and Stade Francais. There were persistent rumours that he was there to discuss a contract with Biarritz, though it is equally plausible that he was there to enjoy the rugby and kill some time as he recovered from injury.

The IRFU repeatedly stated that they wanted to keep as many of their players as possible playing in Ireland. Yes, it is true that there were several players plying their trade for English clubs and Simon Easterby was playing for Llanelli, but, as captain and their most prominent star, Brian was the jewel in their crown and it was deemed important for the good of the national game that he remained within their domestic setup.

For the next few months, Brian's club future remained in a state of limbo as he neither signed a new contract with Leinster nor committed himself to a French club. However, new Leinster coach Michael Cheika appointed Brian club captain, taking over from Reggie Corrigan for the upcoming season. He had made it clear to his new coach that he intended to be fully involved with the team despite his other commitments, and Michael couldn't hide his delight at the unveiling press conference that a man who was held in such high esteem as Brian was had accepted this honour. Brian didn't take on this commitment lightly, and from this point onwards he wanted to remain at Leinster for the foreseeable future, provided the right contract could be agreed.

Although he was obviously in no fit state to take part in day-to-day training, he was impressed with the changes Michael had brought in during his short time there and felt that after years of stalemate both he and the club were going places, and would be serious competitors for major silverware in the upcoming season.

In November, he had to settle for a seat in the stand at Lansdowne Road as Ireland took on New Zealand in the first of the autumn internationals. The Ireland squad, along with the pundits, believed they stood a chance of giving the All Blacks a run for their money to go some way towards getting revenge for the Lions tour flop. The visitors clearly didn't share the sense of occasion as coach Graham Henry fielded a completely different side to the one that had just defeated Wales, with a few less familiar names in the squad. That's not to say there weren't plenty of world-class players taking to the field to perform the haka in front of 42,000 mostly Irish fans that day.

Ireland made a strong start but soon struggled to get out of their own half, and it quickly became clear that the side was missing Brian and there was a considerable gulf in class between the sides. After just 10 minutes, the All Blacks forced a scrum deep inside Ireland's 22, which resulted in a soft try for Sivivatu. They added a second

12 minutes later when some superb long passing allowed scrum-half Piri Weepu to score. The conversion was missed, but Ireland were up against it and conceded a penalty right under the posts a few minutes later, which was easily kicked over the bar by Nick Evans. Ireland produced a rare attack of their own five minutes later thanks to a Gordon D'Arcy burst but Geordan Murphy spilled the centre's less than accurate pass. The visitors were soon awarded another penalty deep inside the Irish half, which added another three points to their tally, sealing their authority on the game. The Irish defence was poor, and Sivivatu had acres of space when he scored his second just before half-time, making the score at the break 25–0.

Eddie O'Sullivan's team talk didn't have the desired effect as the second half brought more of the same. New Zealand scored two quick penalties to rub salt in the wound, but something was about to happen that would have supporters having flashbacks to the tackle that ended Brian's Lions tour a few months ago. Ma'a Nonu performed an extremely violent tackle on Gordon D'Arcy which greatly upset the crowd, though match referee Jonathan Kaplan decided that it did not even warrant a yellow card. The incident gave Ireland a new lease of life as they sought to punish the All Blacks for the tackle, but their best opportunity to score was lost when Ronan failed to utilise a five-on-three overlap. After that, New Zealand reasserted their control of the game. The video referee was called to pass judgement on two close calls for Doug Howlett and Nonu, deciding both were not tries. Eventually, they did manage to score again through Howlett, putting the game well beyond Ireland's reach. The hosts did eventually get a consolation try through Horan that was duly converted, saving the hosts from the humiliation of failing to register a score. However, there was no denying the team's disappointment in being unable to exact any kind of meaningful revenge on the All Blacks, and seeing some of the less pleasant aspects of the Kiwi game being played out on Irish soil left a bitter taste in the mouth and did little to lift Brian's spirits.

The truth was that, without Brian, Ireland were no match for New Zealand's sheer physical presence. There was no hiding the fact that Ireland had suffered a heavy defeat by what was essentially New Zealand's second-string side. This concerned both Eddie and Brian significantly. How could a side that, at the start of the year was being touted as potential Grand Slam winners and among the world's best sides, have fallen so far backwards in such a short space of time? It could not all be put down to Brian being out injured. There were clearly a number of areas that needed reviewing.

A week later, there was a chance to put things right when they took on an out-of-sorts Australia side. Eddie decided to stick with much the same side that crashed the week before; however, he did allow the young Ulster centre Andrew Trimble the chance to make his Test debut. Once again, Eddie decided to keep faith with Simon Easterby in Brian's absence. Ireland looked the better side during the opening exchanges, although neither team produced anything approaching earth-shattering rugby. Ireland took the lead after seven minutes when Ronan kicked over a penalty. A superb Johnny O'Connor run exposed the fragile nature of the Australian defence but his pass could not find Gordon D'Arcy, blowing a golden opportunity to score the first try of the game. A heavy double-hit saw Malcolm O'Kelly knocked out for the count, but Ronan failed to make the most of the penalty that followed. His opposite number Mat Rogers gleefully accepted a quick chance to reply on 26 minutes when Ireland strayed offside, and he levelled the scores at three a piece. Shortly before half-time, Ronan made up for his earlier mistake by putting a penalty over to put the hosts 6–3 up at half-time.

It wasn't pretty, but at last Ireland were looking like a team that could beat one of the big names in world rugby. Brian would not have been satisfied with what he saw of the first half. Yes, they were winning, but the lead could – and should – have been much more convincing. Tommy Bowe missed out on a glorious chance for the first try through no fault of his own in the closing stages of the first half. A sweeping move off a set scrum in the right corner saw Ronan, Gordon and Geordan Murphy combine to arch Ireland out to the left flank and into space – a killer pass was called for but, with Bowe haring up the touchline, Murphy's offload was far too high and found touch.

Straight after the break, Rogers levelled the scores once more with a simple penalty. Just five minutes later, Ireland failed to take Drew Mitchell out of the game, and as he stayed on his feet the support players pushed him over the line for a try. From then on, the game started to slip away from Ireland. David Humphreys came on for Ronan and soon converted a penalty, but that was to signal Australia's revival. Ireland's line-out was shambolic, allowing Chris Latham to charge through a gap and score from 50 metres out. Things went from bad to worse when Humphreys saw his pass intercepted by Mitchell who ran down the field, and, although he was initially stopped by Bowe, he found his feet once more to score his second of the game. Once again, Ireland had to settle for a consolation score that finally came four minutes from the end after a promising move saw Shane Horgan touch down. However, Australia were to have the final say when Rogers converted his third penalty to make the final score 30–14, ending Australia's seven-game losing streak.

It would have been hard for Brian to put his finger on exactly what went wrong in that game. Australia looked very beatable and there were some superb individual performances from Irish players. But, as a team, they did not gel and this was to be their downfall. Key areas such as the scrum and the line-out clearly required a great deal of work before the upcoming Six Nations campaign. There was one more autumn international to come, against Romania the following week, and, despite the weak opposition, Eddie decided to stick with the same players who had failed to gel in the previous two games. This call led to his receiving a great deal of stick in the Irish media in the days leading up to the game, with numerous journalists calling for him to drop John Hayes and Shane Byrne, who many believed had been poor scrummagers for some time. However, one notable change saw David Humphreys attempt to fill Brian's boots as captain.

At a blustery Lansdowne Road, Ireland started the game poorly, failing to assert their superiority over the amateur opposition. Despite the captain successfully kicking a penalty early on, two conceded penalties of their own saw Romania leading 6–3 after 12 minutes. Superb individual performances were the order of the day when a well-timed break by Geordan Murphy, followed by a perfect pass to Trimble, allowed the youngster to score on 22 minutes, which Humphreys then converted. Neil Best, Ireland's most consistent player in the opening half, then rounded off a period of pressure three minutes before the interval when he broke through a couple of weak tackles to notch the home side's second try. The subsequent conversion gave Ireland a 17–6 lead at half-time.

Ireland made a sloppy start to the second half and it

was only a quick-thinking intervention from Geordan that stopped the visitors scoring a try of their own after Humphreys's attempted clearance had been charged down. Trimble soon notched up his second try of the game, earning him the man of the match award for his superb display in only his second Test. Two Romanian penalties in quick succession reduced the deficit to 24–12, and for a short while it looked as though one moment of good fortune for the visitors could make the scoreline uncomfortably close.

However, as the match wore on, fitness levels began to tell and Johnny O'Connor pushed through some sloppy tackling to score for Ireland. The conversion made the score 32–12 and finally there was some daylight between the two sides. The remainder of the match didn't resemble an international game of rugby as both sides were guilty of some very poor tackling. Ireland were on the defensive for sustained periods and the Romanians came uncomfortably close to scoring on more than one occasion. Poor tackling by the visitors allowed late tries from Geordan and Girvan Dempsey but in all honesty the 43–12 final score flattered Ireland, and fans would have expected a far wider gulf between such mismatched sides.

It was now time to go back to club duty until the following year's Six Nations but Brian knew that there would have to be some very hard work put in if Ireland were to be serious contenders for the upcoming Six

Nations. The Romania game had reinforced the fact that there were some brilliant individual performers wearing the green jersey, but they did not gel as a team. If they could tighten up their line-out, improve their scrummaging, pass precisely and get the tackling right, they would be one of the world's very best teams. This was clearly frustrating for Brian to watch, but only made him more determined to put things right once his shoulder was sorted out.

In early December 2005 came the news that, after months of speculation, Brian had signed a new contract with Leinster that would keep him at the club until after the 2007 World Cup. This was far from the ideal solution the IRFU had wanted, as they sought to keep him committed to playing in Ireland for a far longer period. But for Brian this was an ideal compromise. It would keep him at the province for the foreseeable future, ending the unhelpful speculation, and allow him time to settle into his new home. On the other hand, the length of this contract would allow him to fulfil his dream to play for a French club while still at his peak in less than two years' time.

Meanwhile, his recovery was going to plan and he was on course to be playing again soon. On Boxing Day, rugby fans from all over Ireland got the Christmas present they really wanted when Brian was named on the bench for Leinster's Celtic League fixture at Ulster. He came on to applause from the whole crowd after 50 minutes. He didn't get too involved in the half-hour he played, but his presence spurred on Gordon and Girvan to score a try each to turn a half-time deficit into a 24–19 victory for Leinster away from home. Brian knew that it would take five or six games for him to be completely match-fit and that he could not take anything for granted at this stage. But after months of misery and some unhelpful speculation about his future, it just felt good to be playing rugby once again.

On New Year's Eve came the traditional battle against arch rivals Munster, now coached by Declan Kidney. Brian's first start at home was greeted by a Celtic League record crowd of 14,155. These matches were always fiercely fought affairs and this was to prove no different. Leinster scored the first try when young hooker Brian Blaney got over from a line-out drive. A Felipe Contepomi penalty was soon added, but Munster were allowed back into the game when Ronan scored two penalties in quick succession. Shane Horgan scored for Leinster shortly before the break after a superb run that saw him resist tackles from Anthony Horgan and David Wallace to put the ball down in the right corner. Contepomi added the two points with a superb kick taken at an awkward angle, and added his third penalty of the game in first-half stoppage time.

In the second half, Munster stepped up the pace and reminded Leinster that these games aren't over until they're over, and on 65 minutes O'Connell spurned tackles from Easterby and Blaney, and the resulting conversion cut Leinster's lead to just six points. Contepomi was the star of the game and on 74 minutes he chipped the ball over Anthony Foley and beat the cover right beneath the posts, which he duly converted. Munster pulled one back through Trevor Halstead to make for a tense final few minutes, but Contepomi raced on to a loose ball 35 metres out and beat the covering Horgan and Halstead to score at the corner flag, making the final score 35–23.

This was a quiet game by Brian's standards. He didn't want to take any chances and so didn't become too involved. He was far from fully fit and it was left to others to take the star roles, but this famous victory over their old rivals made it a happy ending to what had been a pretty miserable year.

The New Year arrived, and inevitably attention soon turned to the 2006 Six Nations. As usual, the squad met up at the City West hotel in Dublin several weeks in advance to prepare for the long campaign that lay ahead. Brian was getting fitter by the day, and was on course to be back to full fitness when the time came to lead his men out to battle against Italy at Lansdowne Road in just a few weeks' time.

Eddie knew he had his work cut out in the weeks ahead, but it was a massive consolation to him to have a squad of players, who, as individuals, were truly among the world's best. His task was to coach them to think and play like a team, which had been their downfall in the autumn internationals. Training was well structured and intense during those few weeks. The line-out was regarded as an area where games were won and lost and in the Tests against New Zealand and Australia this was exposed as a major frailty in Ireland's armoury. The only way this was ever going to be put right was through practising the drills and learning the line-out calls by heart.

The first match was at home against Italy, but Brian and Eddie both knew only too well that the days of Italy being the whipping boys of the tournament were past and they could not afford a repeat of the previous year's sluggish performance if they were to secure victory. Brian led the team out at Lansdowne Road feeling confident that they had prepared well and this would be the year that the squad's potential would be revealed and Ireland would take the Six Nations by storm. Yes, he had felt exactly the same way the previous year, but this time he, and a few of the others, had matured considerably as players and this would show through on the pitch.

However, things didn't exactly go according to plan. A fired-up Italian side pegged Ireland back and didn't allow them to play the wide, expansive game they were looking to play. It became clear very early on that there were still serious problems with the line-out and it was going to be a tough 80 minutes.

Italy took the lead early on when the excellent Ramiro Pez tapped over a penalty. The first Ireland try came when O'Connell managed to steal the ball from the Italian line-out, before passing to the debutant Jerry Flannery, who was hauled over the line. Ronan added the conversion to put a bit of breathing space between the sides, which went some way towards making up for the 40-metre penalty he had fluffed a few minutes earlier.

The game was evenly poised and the visitors regained the lead on 29 minutes when Pez found a gap between Ronan and Gordon to set up a try for Mauro Bergamasco. Pez, who was having the game of his life, added the two points. However, he let his enthusiasm get the better of him just a few minutes later when he was yellow-carded for a late tackle, allowing Ronan to add three points from the penalty that followed to bring the scores level at half-time at 10 points a piece.

Paul Griffen edged the Azzuri ahead on the restart. It was a statement of intent, as they stretched the Irish defence in the period of play that followed. Eventually, Ireland managed to find a little more space in an often cluttered midfield and Gordon started causing problems for the Italian defence. But it was Bowe who eventually scored when he received an excellent cross-field kick from Ronan before outwitting the defence to score. Ronan converted and knocked over a couple of penalties with Pez also squeezing in one of his own as Ireland moved seven points ahead. However, the previously excellent Pez was struggling to keep his concentration and missed a simple penalty that would have made the final minutes very tense. Ronan soon made the game safe for Ireland with his fourth penalty in the 76th minute.

It was a victory, and a win is always a win, but Brian knew that this had been a quiet game by his standards and there was still a great deal of work to be done if they were to defeat the stronger sides – and, with a trip to the Stade de France just a week away, there was work to be done. If Italy's backs had been stronger, it would have been a very different story. Brian's preparation hadn't been ideal and, while he was now back in the peak of physical fitness, he lacked match practice and this showed on the field. The squad watched the video of the game with Eddie during the week and looked at the areas that needed tightening up ahead of the upcoming games. It was the same old story – untidy line-out, gaps in the defence and loss of concentration at key times.

That said, Brian was looking forward to the match against France. Their style of rugby suited his game and a strong, physical encounter was probably exactly what was needed in order for him to reach full match fitness. Brian led the team on to the field feeling geared up for the challenge. Matches away at France in front of a full house are always special occasions and Brian had been gearing himself up for this fixture all week. However, it wasn't long before things started to go wrong once more. Bowe's slip in midfield after just three minutes handed possession to the French and Aurelien Rougerie touched down in the corner after beating Geordan. Ireland didn't lie down and die and were awarded a penalty of their own, but disaster soon struck. The decision to take the tap penalty instead of kicking an easy three points rebounded disastrously when Denis Leamy and Geordan got in each other's way, allowing Frederic Michalak to grab the ball and begin a charge down the other end of the field before supplying Olivier Magne with the scoring pass.

This had been a disastrous tactical decision and meant the game was all but lost after just 15 minutes. Ronan was having a howler of a game. After missing a penalty, his clearance kick on 18 minutes was charged down by David Marty who went on to score another French try. Ireland's fighting spirit was needed if they were to get anything at all from this game and they responded convincingly just a minute later when Gordon crossed the French line, but it was correctly ruled out for a knock-on. Ronan and Jean-Baptiste Elissalde kicked penalties at either end before Ireland's first-half horror show was completed in the 35th minute when Murphy's speculative looping pass was intercepted by Cedric Heymans who ran in unopposed to score France's fourth try.

At half-time, the score was an embarrassing 29–3. All their hard work during the week had come to nothing. The same mistakes that had haunted the boys since the autumn internationals kept creeping back. Essentially, France were so far in front due to silly errors on the part of a handful of Irish players rather than some kind of huge gulf in ability between the sides.

If Irish fans had thought things could not get any worse, they soon did as France notched up two more tries through Heymans and Marty, with yet another awful kick from Ronan giving France their sixth try. The introduction of several replacements resulted in France picking up the loss-of-cohesion bug that Ireland had been suffering from throughout the game, and after three minutes of sustained pressure Gordon ran in an Irish try with Ronan slotting the conversion. Ireland's revival continued when replacement Donncha O'Callaghan notched another try in the 66th minute and the French lead was cut to 43–31. Andrew Trimble touched down with 11 minutes remaining, with Ronan adding both conversions, going at least some way towards making up for his appalling first-half performance. It was going to be a tense end to a game that was suddenly looking winnable for Brian's men. However, the French regained their composure and held on for a win.

Once again, Brian had not been the centre of attention during the game but he took great heart from his side's display in the final half-hour. The defeat definitely hurt, but the truth was that Ireland had dominated the final part of the game and Brian knew that, if they could maintain those levels of commitment and discipline for the three games that remained, they would still be in with a shout of winning the Championship. Within a day, Brian had moved on from the defeat and began preparing for the home fixture against Wales. He remembered that incredible day in Cardiff during the final weekend of the previous year's Championship and was keen to exact revenge. He was also aware that the Welsh camp had been in disarray and that this was far from being the same Wales side that had won the Grand Slam a year earlier.

Brian's old friend Mike Ruddock had resigned as Wales's coach just days after their unconvincing win at home to Scotland. Mike had cited family reasons for his resignation but there had been ongoing rumours of a rift with Gareth Thomas, who made little secret of the fact that he had been having serious clashes with his coach.

This was a difficult issue for Brian to deal with. He had a huge amount of affection for Mike from his days as a young player, yet he had also become close to Gareth during the previous summer's Lions tour and had been impressed with his captaincy when called upon, which made it very hard for him to make any kind of judgement on the issue. What was clear was that this was not the same Wales of a year before and this would prove a great opportunity for Brian and his men to shine among the disarray.

Wales were hit by a further massive blow when it was revealed that Gareth Thomas had been rushed to hospital and had suffered a mild stroke, ruling him out of rugby for the foreseeable future. The stress of the situation had clearly caught up with Gareth and just hours before he was taken to hospital he had been involved in a highly charged debate on Welsh television. Ireland took to the field at Lansdowne Road a more confident side than they had been at any time since the previous year's Six Nations.

However, any thoughts that the Welsh would be allowing their off-the-field problems to distract them from the task in hand were soon dispelled when Mark Jones scored after just seven minutes. Ronan pegged three points back 10 minutes later, but it was a shaky start by the home side. After 20 minutes, Brian's men started to gain control of the match and the lack of preparation by Wales was beginning to show when David Wallace scored a try from a five-metre scrum. Ronan missed an easy conversion but a penalty a few minutes later left Ireland leading 11–5 at the break.

Early in the second half, Brian made his first major contribution of the tournament when three minutes after the restart he found man of the match Shane Horgan, who then cut inside two defenders to score a superb try. Ronan didn't miss this time, and soon added another penalty to extend the Irish lead. Right at the end, scrum-half Stringer forced his way over for a try which Ronan converted, to give Ireland a sound 31–5 victory.

At last, Ireland were playing the sort of rugby Brian

knew they had in them, and after the game he was typically understated as he told journalists that the convincing win had not come as a surprise to him. In his view, when the pressure came on, they produced the goods and they could take great satisfaction from that. Brian soon reminded the boys that the Championship was still very much on and, although their performance was by no means perfect, they could take a lot of pride in their overall performance.

Next up was a tricky fixture against Scotland at home. The Scots had been enjoying something of a resurgence after a lean few years, and had fired a warning shot in Brian's direction by defeating World Champions England that weekend. Their defence had been rock solid and some accurate kicking from Chris Paterson had seen them win the game 18–12. In the two-week break, Eddie's task was simply to tighten up any remaining shortcomings in their game, and prepare them in whatever way he could to play to their maximum potential for the full 80 minutes. The match against Scotland wasn't just any old game of rugby. It would be the last time Ireland took to the field in a Six Nations game at Lansdowne Road before it closed for redevelopment. This gave the game an extra edge and made Brian even more focused in the days leading up to the game.

Brian led his team out in front of an emotionally charged crowd, who wanted to give the old place a good send-off. Ireland dominated possession and territory in the first half but could not break Scotland's superb defence, who maintained the same levels of focus and accuracy that had led them to victory against England. The conditions weren't ideal following a torrential downpour just minutes before kick-off, but this only seemed to strengthen Ireland's resolve not to allow any silly mistakes to creep in on this special occasion. Ronan kicked his side in front thanks to a penalty in the second minute. He added a second three points just five minutes later but Scotland were awarded an easy kick from the resultant kick-off when Malcolm O'Kelly impeded Jason White and Paterson opened his account. Another Irish infringement allowed Paterson to draw the scores level soon after.

In tricky conditions, both sides chose to kick most of their possession and, considering the strength of both defences, there never looked like being any tries. It was going to be left to Ronan's kicking to win this awkward game. He pushed one effort wide but he soon made amends by putting one straight between the posts just minutes later, only for Paterson to draw level once more shortly afterwards. Both sides enjoyed periods of good possession in the first half but yet more heavy rain made attacking and passing play difficult, and it was another penalty from Ronan that saw Ireland lead 12–9 at half-time.

They had a good opportunity to score early in the

second half when Geordan's low pass to Andrew Trimble allowed Hugo Southwell the split-second he needed to bundle the wing into touch. Another opportunity presented itself just moments later, only for Sean Lamont to pluck Paul O'Connell's pass out of the sky a metre from the line. Ireland began to dominate possession, but the Scottish defence remained rock solid and the hosts had to make do with another superbly executed penalty from Ronan to extend the lead. With seven minutes left, the visitors made what was almost their first foray of the half into Ireland's 22 but, whereas their line-out was precarious, Ireland's remained solid. This came as a mighty relief to Eddie and Brian, and at long last this aspect of the game that had gone a long way towards costing them victories over the past year finally seemed to have sorted itself out. Ronan missed one final kick, but it didn't matter and the last Championship game at the old ground ended in a 15–9 victory.

Ronan's was the only name on the scoresheet, but everyone had played their part in this victory and Brian's tactical decisions as captain had been spot on. After months in the doldrums, Ireland were on a roll. The Triple Crown was still on, and in theory they were still in with a shout of winning the Championship, although they would have to rely upon France losing against Wales for that to happen, as the points difference between them was almost certainly too great otherwise.

With one game against the World Champions to go, there was a lot still to play for.

England were coming into the game following a humiliating 31–6 defeat to France in Paris. Brian knew only too well that there would not be a repeat performance at Twickenham. Yes, England were very much in a lull between World Cups but they were at their most dangerous when wounded and Brian was expecting his type of game – tough and physical – and he knew that, once again, they would face a defence that was difficult to break down. England coach Andy Robinson knew his job was on the line and that a repeat of Paris would almost certainly cost him his job.

It was England who came out of the blocks quickest when they won a penalty from a first-minute scrum that Martin Corry took quickly, and from a smartly recycled ball Jamie Noon raced on to Andy Goode's precise pass to score in the left corner. Ireland were soon let back into the game when Ben Cohen slipped when trying to deal with Brian's kick ahead, allowing Horgan to nip in and bring the scores level after just seven minutes. This game was quickly turning out to be the tight battle everyone was hoping for. A penalty kick from Ronan gave Ireland the lead five minutes later and England missed two opportunities of their own to bring the scores level. Brian should have set up a superb try for Gordon, but his pass was too high and it was an opportunity wasted. A penalty each made the score 11–8, but another incursion into the line from the impressive Geordan should have yielded more points for Ireland, but nevertheless they still went into half-time with a slender lead.

Early in the second half, Lewis Moody conceded a penalty that allowed Ronan to extend the lead to six points, but Goode kicked one over of his own almost immediately, beginning England's best passage of play. They launched themselves at the Irish line for five minutes but appeared to have wasted their efforts when they kicked a penalty to touch and Paul O'Connell stole the line-out. But they finally found a way through when Goode's pass sent Steve Borthwick over on a great angle for his first Test try.

The game turned once more after 57 minutes when England's line-out plan fell to pieces on their own line. The throw was intended to reach the isolated Moody but Leamy intercepted to touch down, with Ronan adding the extra two points. However, two penalties in seven minutes seemed to give England the game, barring any last-minute miracles.

Cometh the hour, cometh the man, and at the very last opportunity Shane Horgan resisted Moody's attempted tackle to score right in the corner. Ireland had snatched victory from the jaws of defeat in the most breathtaking style. In the post-match interview, Brian paid tribute to his side's phenomenal spirit, saying that this was the 80 minutes of rugby he had been waiting for his team to produce. He made it clear straight away that he saw this as a stepping stone to bigger and better things and he was not prepared to rest on his laurels just yet. Yes, there would be wild celebrations that night, but already he had one eye on the World Cup that was now just 18 months away. His belief in his team's ability had proven true, and at long last the individual talents of the 15 men who wore the green jersey had gelled to create a truly world-class team.

Brian was presented with the Triple Crown trophy immediately after the game and there was no hiding the delight on his face at what had been achieved, remarkable considering the clumsy performances they had put in during the autumn internationals and in the games against Italy and France.

Upon arriving back in Ireland, Brian ended the Six Nations campaign with the traditional end-of-tournament debrief at Kehoe's bar in Dublin, which, in practice, meant a good night's drinking with the rest of the boys and a handful of specially invited guests. This was not a time to reflect upon any minor shortcomings that might still exist in Ireland's armoury, but to celebrate those all-too-rare occasions in rugby where you've achieved something quite special and are left with a memory to cherish for the rest of your life.

Chapter 9

LEADING LEINSTER

It was not long after the conclusion of the Six Nations that Brian and Glenda announced they would be going their separate ways. Their relationship had been rekindled after a previous split, but this time they both agreed that it had run its course and it was time to move on. They both led hectic lifestyles, which didn't help. Brian would be away from home for long periods with his rugby, and Glenda knew that she would not have the opportunity to spend much time with him in the upcoming summer as he would be away on Ireland's tour of New Zealand and Australia.

Meanwhile, Glenda's modelling career was going from strength to strength and she was becoming a regular fixture on Irish television. With both of them keeping busy diaries, it became increasingly difficult for them to find time to spend together.

Both parties maintained a dignified silence and there was no vicious backbiting in the press. For the time being, Brian wanted to focus solely on his rugby and, with an especially busy few months ahead with Leinster and Ireland, he needed to be completely focused on the challenges that lay ahead.

For now, his immediate priority was winning major silverware with Leinster, and, with them in contention for both the Celtic League and the Heineken Cup, he knew that his presence as a player and as captain would be vital in determining their fate. The club had come on in leaps and bounds since Michael became coach. Brian felt that his game was developing and he was improving as a player for the first time in several years. The new coaching regime had brought in a new spirit to the club, and they were seeing the fruits of their efforts on the pitch.

At the beginning of April, Brian travelled to reigning Heineken Cup holders Toulouse for a quarter-final clash. This was a chance for Brian to show off to the fans just how much the club had come on since Michael took over as coach. No player should need motivating to take on such prestigious opponents. He knew it would be a tough task overcoming the French giants, but he had faith in his own ability and felt his team were more than capable of giving them a run for their money.

Early on, a series of penalties for both sides saw Leinster leading 9–6, with Contepomi showing superb accuracy with the boot. After 25 minutes, a superb move involving Horgan and Contepomi ended with Brian bursting through the defence to score a cracking try. If the critics were in any doubt that Leinster were among Europe's best club sides, this try silenced them once and for all. At half-time, they had a 10-point lead and the three-times champions were on the ropes.

They had done everything right so far, but every player knew that a lapse of concentration or a loss of momentum could easily allow Toulouse back into the game, and there was still a tough 40 minutes to come. Sure enough, early in the second half two penalties from Elissalde and a Michalak drop goal brought the French side within a point of Leinster and suddenly they were the side in control of the game.

Just when it seemed as though Toulouse were dominating the game's possession, a loose pass from Michalak was snapped up by Cameron Jowitt for Leinster's second try. Leinster were on a roll, and more was to follow when Denis Hickie cleverly exchanged passes with Gordon and managed to squeeze over in the left corner.

Brian's men added a fourth through Horgan, and, although Yannick Nyanga and Yannick Jauzion went over for late Toulouse tries, Leinster had done enough and Brian had led his team to one of the most famous victories in their long and proud history. This was undoubtedly the proudest moment of his club career to date, and, although he wasn't going to rest on his laurels, he took time out to celebrate this win in style and reflect upon what had been an excellent season for Leinster so far. That said, there was still a great deal of work to be done and they could still throw it all away with a few poor performances.

In mid-April, Brian was to lead Leinster out in front of a packed Lansdowne Road for a Heineken Cup semi-final against arch rivals Munster. This was the biggest game of his club career to date. Matches against Munster were always special but, with so much at stake, this game had an extra edge to it. For one, Declan was returning to his own stomping ground and Brian felt that both he and Leinster had something to prove.

And, of course, the winner would have the opportunity to face French giants Biarritz to be crowned champions of Europe. However, from very early on it became clear that this wasn't going to be Leinster's day. From the kick-off, Malcolm O'Kelly failed to gather Ronan's kick cleanly, putting the Leinster defence under immediate pressure.

After two minutes, the pressure gave and Munster were awarded a penalty, which allowed Ronan to put his side ahead. After nine minutes, Ronan had the chance to kick for another three points but instead opted for the corner. It was an inspirational decision. Paul O'Connell took the ball cleanly from the line-out before passing to Leamy who drove through the Leinster defence to score. Ronan converted to give the away side a comfortable 10–0 lead.

Leinster finally managed to break out of their own half after 12 minutes when Hickie went on a superb break but Shaun Payne's tackle was just about enough to force him into touch. They finally got their first points on the board after 20 minutes when a nervous Contepomi kicked a penalty over. However, within eight minutes Ronan had kicked over two more penalties to make it 16–3.

Contepomi had been responsible for conceding one of the penalties and his nightmare continued in the 30th minute when he missed a penalty that couldn't have been easier. The first half had been a disaster, and at half-time Brian had some harsh words for his men to try to kick them into gear for the second half. This was a huge deficit, but one that could be overcome.

The beginning of the second half was scrappy with neither side able to control the game convincingly. Contepomi saw a well-taken 40-metre kick come back off the post, but, as time wore on, Munster enjoyed the lion's share of possession and Leinster didn't look like getting back into the game. Contepomi eventually added three points in the 68th minute but, in truth, the comeback never looked like coming to fruition.

The fighting spirit that had seen Leinster progress to this stage of the competition had gone. Ronan was able to add another try unopposed three minutes from time, and deep into injury time Trevor Halstead added another after strolling all the way from his own half to put the ball between the posts.

The final score was a humiliating 30–6 defeat. After the game, Michael put on a brave face before the camera and refused to blame Contepomi for his errors during the match. He was quick to point out that at the start of the year nobody had given him the time of day and now he was suddenly regarded as one of the world's best kickers.

Brian, meanwhile, was devastated by the defeat. He knew this was an opportunity lost. This was his best chance to date to win some major silverware at club level, and his side had blown it, and as captain he had to take his share of the responsibility. What's more, they would have booked their place in the final by beating their arch rivals. But that wasn't all. Declan's homecoming was meant to demonstrate that things had changed for the better at the club since he left. As things turned out, it looked as though they were missing him badly, although Brian believed that the decision to appoint Michael had been the right one and he was still far happier with the structure at the club as it was now.

With Leinster out of the Heineken Cup, Brian began to wonder how long it would be before he won some major silverware as a player. He was now of an age where he would have, at most, another five years playing rugby at his absolute peak, and there was now a very real possibility that he would be remembered not as a great player, but as a captain of his club, country and the Lions who showed so much promise but ultimately failed to deliver the goods.

For this reason, the Celtic League gained extra importance for the rest of the season. At the start, he felt that, naturally enough, his duties as Ireland captain would be his absolute priority. Second would come Leinster's progress in the Heineken Cup, with the Celtic League coming a very distant third. Indeed, he was expecting to be rested for a large number of Celtic League fixtures. After the Munster defeat, winning the Celtic League suddenly meant a great deal.

On the final day of the season, the Leinster squad travelled to Edinburgh knowing that they stood an excellent chance of winning the league. They had to beat their Scottish hosts, and hope that the Ospreys managed to beat Ulster, the team currently sitting top of the league.

Brian had kept one eye on this fixture since the Munster defeat and didn't underestimate the importance of this game to his career as a whole. Yes, ultimately their fate was out of their own hands and depended greatly on the Ospreys giving them a helping hand, but it was absolutely pivotal that they won this game.

Leinster started badly, and soon found themselves a man down when Will Green was sin-binned and Ander Monro had kicked a penalty over for the hosts.

Brian remembered all too well how he had felt in that

game against Munster a few weeks before, and how his side had blown it very early on. He was determined not to let that happen again, and led by example to put things right. He found himself in the right place at the right time to receive a perfectly weighted feed from Horgan. There was no way he was going to mess this up and scored a perfect try. Minutes later, he scored a second when he outwitted the Edinburgh defence by finding an extra yard of pace to dart between the posts when they were expecting him to send the ball wide. This was Brian O'Driscoll at his absolute best.

With his side in firm control of the game, he almost added a third try shortly afterwards when he raced after Contepomi's grubber kick, but Edinburgh fly-half Phil Godman reached it a split-second ahead of him. Four minutes before the break, Edinburgh managed a consolation try through the veteran lock Scott Murray.

Leinster were still 14–8 up going into the break, and during the interval Michael and Brian reminded the players of exactly how bad they felt after the defeat to Munster, and how important it was not to blow this opportunity to pick up some silverware. News came through from Swansea that Ulster had a three-point lead over the Ospreys. The players didn't dwell on this fact, knowing full well that a few well-placed kicks from Gavin Henson could deny Ulster the title in the second half.

Brian remained completely focused on the 40 minutes

of rugby in hand. For him, this was right up there with the most important games of his career. Get this right, and he could be parading the Celtic League trophy around Dublin on an open-top bus. This was not a time for him, or the team, to lose concentration or momentum.

Brian the two-try scorer became Brian the provider as he set up Shane Horgan, who finished it off in style. Contepomi was keen to repay Michael's faith in him, and on this occasion he didn't disappoint, bagging a typically opportunist effort late on. He added a further penalty for good measure, to give Leinster a 31–8 victory. They had done their bit, and bagged a precious bonus point along the way. Things couldn't have gone better. Now all they needed to do was to hope the Ospreys could do them a favour in Swansea.

At the Liberty Stadium, a late Jason Spice try, which an in-form Henson converted, had given the Ospreys a slender 17–16 lead. It looked like the title was going Leinster's way. Then, in the final minute, disaster struck when David Humphreys attempted a drop goal that cannoned off one post, then the other, before going over. It was one of those fifty-fifty kicks that could so easily have gone the other way, and the title would have gone to Leinster, but it wasn't to be, and the man who had captained Ireland in Brian's absence had led Ulster to the league title in the most breathtaking of games.

This was a heartbreaking way to end what had been a perfect night to date, and the whole team were shell-shocked with what had happened hundreds of miles away in South Wales. The defeat was especially hard on Eric Miller, who was retiring after 11 years' service with Leinster. For Brian, this was a difficult pill to swallow. Everything had gone right for Leinster that night, and he had played out of his skin to make sure Leinster bagged maximum points from the game. Yet events elsewhere, combined with a bit of good fortune for his Ireland colleague David Humphreys, had denied him his chance to pick up some major silverware.

It was the end of another long, hard season that had promised so much yet failed to deliver when it really counted. Yes, Brian was obviously pleased with the Triple Crown win, and he could be proud of his country's Six Nations displays after a shaky start. And, at last, Leinster were starting to look like serious competitors for the big prizes. Over the course of the season, they had beaten French giants Toulouse and had even seen off league champions Ulster in the final club game to be played at Lansdowne Road.

Yet, at the same time, they had not shown up against Munster in the semi-final. They had given up early in the second half, when there was still plenty to play for. What if they had shown some of the same spirit that had seen them destroy Toulouse at home? Things could have been very different. Again, in the Celtic League, on the big occasion against Edinburgh they had won in style, but league titles are not won and lost on a single night, and

Relaxing on the British and Irish Lions tour of Australia.

Above: Brian enjoys a round of golf in Perth.

Below: When in Australia do as the Aussies do – trying his hand at surfing with Dan Luger.

Brian breaks away to score the Lions' third try in the first test against
Australia at the Gabba (*above*) and celebrates the 29-13 victory (*below*).

Above: Brian walks off the pitch dejected after the Lions lost 35-14 in the second test.

Below: Captain Martin Johnson is consoled by coach Graham Henry after losing the final test and the series. Rumours of an unhappy camp were rife, and Brian and Graham did not enjoy an especially warm relationship.

Above: Back to his best! After something of a blip in form Brian returned in spectacular fashion in the 43-22 victory over Scotland in the 2002 Six Nations.

Below: Made captain for the 2003 Six Nations, Brian led Ireland to four consecutive victories, including this one over France at Landsdowne Road.

Above: 'Drico' goes over the line against Australia in the 2003 World Cup pool match. Ireland came agonisingly close but lost 16-15, though they still qualified for the quarter finals.

Below: Despite his best 'Superman' impression, Brian couldn't stop Ireland crashing out of the tournament against France. © *PA Photos*

Above: The captains get together prior to the 2004 Six Nations (*from left – right*): Wales' Colin Charvis, Brian, England's Lawrence Dallaglio, Italy's Andrea di Rossi, Scotland's Gordon Bullock and France's Olivier Brouzet.

Below left: Brian runs at the England back line as Ireland beat the World Champions 19-12.

Below right: Brian wins his 50th cap in the Triple Crown decider against Scotland.

© *PA Photos*

Truly an Irish legend! On 21 March 2009, Brian O'Driscoll led Ireland to their first Grand Slam victory since 1948.

© *Inpho*

Above: In action for his club Leinster in the 2005 Heineken Cup quarter final.

Above: The greatest honour and the greatest challenge; Brian with Lions coach Clive Woodward after being named as captain for the tour of New Zealand.

© *PA Photos*

there had been some poor performances against sides they should have beaten comfortably.

At times in the season, Leinster had been breathtaking and Brian had put in some of the best performances of his career, and had captained with distinction. Things were undoubtedly heading in the right direction at the club, but they lacked consistency at key times, and occasionally looked beaten in games when there was plenty of time left to claw results back. These were things Michael was going to have to look at over the summer.

For a few days, the disappointment of the last day of the season really hurt, but it wasn't long before Brian realised that there was little more he could have done in that final game. Truthfully, they had blown it long before they went on to the field in Edinburgh and their fate was out of their own hands. It was now time to enjoy the end-of-season drinks and to give Eric a good send-off after serving the club with distinction over the last decade. Eric was only 30, but had decided that a series of injuries had taken their toll and the demands of the professional game were too much for him now. He would go on to find employment at his old school, Wesley College in Dublin, where he was to become a popular rugby coach for the under-16s and senior school team.

Brian's attentions quickly turned to the tough summer's rugby that lay ahead with Ireland. Very soon, he would be joining up with the Ireland squad and they would be flying out to New Zealand to play two Tests against the

All Blacks before flying on to Australia for a further Test there.

This tour meant so much to Brian for a number of reasons. Firstly, it would be an opportunity to lay some ghosts to rest from the previous summer's Lions tour. The incident that ended his tour was gone but not forgotten, and he felt he owed it to himself to show the New Zealand public how good he was.

It was also a chance for the Ireland squad to experience playing in New Zealand and Australia, and to consolidate their excellent performances in the latter part of the Six Nations. The World Cup was a little over a year away, and Brian knew that, if his men could perform as they did in those latter games, they would be in with a serious chance of winning the tournament. This tour would give them the opportunity to pit their wits against two of the strongest sides in the world, and would also provide them with ample opportunity to make amends for the poor performances they displayed against these two rugby-proud nations in Brian's absence the previous autumn.

Eddie already had one eye on the World Cup, and he was keen to establish who his best 15 players were at this stage, to give them plenty of time to prepare, train and play together before the tournament began.

Brian left the comforts of his new home in Dublin and boarded the plane for the long flight to New Zealand believing that Ireland had what it took to beat the All

Blacks. By now, Graham Henry's men were more confident than ever and believed themselves to be invincible. Brian was keen to cut them down to size, and getting one over on Henry was enough of a motivation in itself to beat the All Blacks.

This time, though, Brian would not be coming face to face with Tana, who had retired from international rugby in January. He had cited family reasons for his decision, but he was still serving a six-month ban for that tackle and was still regarded as a villain everywhere apart from New Zealand. Brian would, however, be coming face to face with Keven Mealamu once more. Keven's role in the tackle had largely been forgotten by the world's media, who tended to blame Tana entirely, but Brian regarded Keven as equally responsible. With no real apology ever coming from him, Brian felt more motivated than usual to hit him where it hurt – by making sure he was on the losing side.

Brian led Ireland on to the pitch in Hamilton for the first Test fired up and raring to go. His preparation for this series couldn't have been better. He felt in the peak of physical fitness, and his shoulder was in as good a condition as it had been in a long while. He faced the haka in the same way he had during the Lions tour, remembering the instructions the Maori warrior had given him the previous year. Then, once more, it was time for battle to commence.

However, the game plan went out of the window

from the kick-off. Brian knew all about bad starts to tours in New Zealand. Fortunately, this time he wasn't to sustain a serious injury but what followed seemed as though all his weeks of preparation for this game had been for nothing.

Full-back Mils Muliaina surged through a flimsy tackle from Ronan, and handed the ball on to Aaron Mauger. The inside-centre sprinted deep into Irish territory before passing to the lightning Doug Howlett, who held off Andrew Trimble's dive to score in the corner. Luke McAlister missed the subsequent conversion, but the game could hardly have got off to a worse start for Brian's men.

He wasn't going to be beaten this early, and the humiliating setback only seemed to make him more focused and determined to defeat the opposition, and it wouldn't be too long before he got the opportunity to strike back in style. After 11 minutes, Gordon picked up a quick ball from the scrum, before passing to Brian who cut inside Joe Rokocoko and Ma'a Nonu to score under the posts.

At last, Brian had shown the New Zealand public what he could do, and caught two of the world's greatest players off-guard to put his country in front. There was no way Ronan was going to miss such an easy conversion, not on a night like this. A few minutes later, he added a penalty to make it 10–5 to the visitors.

New Zealand added a penalty of their own 10

minutes later, but some superb Irish defending frustrated them as the lead was maintained. Soon Ronan added another three points when debutant All Black loose-head Clarke Dermody conceded a needless penalty. He added another penalty with the last kick of the half, giving his country a comfortable 16–8 advantage at half-time.

Brian knew that the hosts were almost certain to come out rejuvenated in the second half, and did not underestimate the importance of keeping concentration in the early exchanges. There was no way they could allow themselves to go to sleep the way they had done at the start of the game.

Despite Brian knowing what was required, other members of the team failed to keep focused and the second half began with a blunder similar to the first. McAlister's initial dent saw Rokocoko, Nonu and Mauger combine before Muliaina finished the move. The conversion reduced Ireland's lead to just a point, and all of a sudden the reasonably solid lead they took into half-time looked very slender indeed.

Ireland regained composure, and a good period of attacking possession ended with Ronan lobbing a superb overhead pass at Trimble who touched down in the left corner. Ronan took his time and added a superb conversion, extending his side's lead to eight points once more. Shortly before the hour mark, two McAlister penalties reduced the lead to two points, and five minutes later Ronan's aim let him down as a chance to gain another three points went begging.

With nine minutes left, McAlister added another penalty to give his side the lead. Brian's men shared his desire to fight to the death, and it wasn't long before Paul O'Connell went on the attack. Incredibly, his pass was intercepted by Muliaina. He surged upfield, passed to Nonu, who continued the run and dismissed an attempted tackle from Stringer, before passing to Flavell who finished the manoeuvre in style. The conversion was added, giving the hosts a 34–23 victory.

There was no hiding Brian's disappointment in this defeat. He had prepared so well for this game and had played out of his skin, continuing the fine form he had shown with Leinster towards the end of the season. It was one bad mistake from Paul that had cost them the game, although it would have been crass to place all the blame on him. He had been having a superb game until that moment of bad judgement at the death.

After a day's pondering, Brian soon realised that there were many positive things that had come from this match. His country had just given the All Blacks a far tougher game than any of the Lions Tests had been. They had a far smaller pool of players to choose from, yet they played as a well-oiled unit for most of the game, and had it not been for a loss of concentration at vital times the result may well have been different.

He also realised just how hurt the players felt after the

defeat. This meant that they were not out there for fun, and that they were deadly serious about going out there and beating a team that most commentators agreed were the world's strongest. If they had gone out there playing for pride, or were expecting to lose before the whistle blew for kick-off, they would have been far less down at the end of the game.

It was clear to Brian that they had come on a huge amount in a relatively short space of time. The abysmal displays of the previous autumn now felt like a lifetime ago. This was a side that, with a year's solid preparation, stood a very real chance of winning the World Cup. As for this tour, with one more match to come against the All Blacks, there was everything to play for.

This time around, Brian had even less time to soak up the culture and atmosphere of New Zealand. The second Test was only a week away and once that was over they would be flying straight on to Australia. Yet the gloom that had dominated his mind for much of the Lions tour didn't occur this time. He was feeling far less homesick and felt far happier about being away from home. There could have been a number of reasons why this was the case.

Maybe being single allowed him not to have such an emotional tie to home and allowed him to concentrate on his rugby. The fact he was actually a part of the playing squad also helped. He did not feel like a spare part lying around looking for something to do all the time, which is how he ended up spending the majority of the Lions tour. This time, he was a playing captain who was working with Eddie and the boys on every aspect of the preparation for the big games. He had a purpose, and this made being away from home all the more bearable.

He had also changed his psychological preparations for the big games. He was no longer as obsessive about the game that lay ahead. Well prepared, certainly, but he did not 'close down' in the way he had done in the week leading up to the first Lions Test. He had remembered how unfair it had been to shut Glenda and his family out the way he did, and this time he was far more jovial to be around while he was on tour.

Having a long injury lay-off had taught him that, while winning games and tournaments was massively important, he had to learn to enjoy being a professional rugby player more. He knew that there were millions of people all over the world who would happily swap jobs with him, and it dawned on him that he was, after all, doing the one thing he had always wanted to do since he was a young child, and he had to learn to enjoy seeing the world and playing the game he loved on the big stage.

The following week, Brian finally got the chance to lead his side out at Eden Park, Auckland in the second Test. The referee was Brian's old friend Jonathan Kaplan, and he went out there as determined to win as he had been the previous week. In the intervening days, Eddie had been working with them to iron out the silly errors that had cost them victory last time around and Brian was keen to make sure they gave their absolute best.

Ireland found themselves up against it from the start as the All Blacks controlled early possession, but Ronan fell marginally short with an early long-range penalty. But the hosts were in control and Byron Kelleher burrowed over after Geordan Murphy had lost possession.

New Zealand remained in control and, midway through the first half, Chris Jack drove for the line and appeared to play the ball while on the ground, but referee Kaplan waved play on and Clarke Dermody dived in for the score. McAlister added a penalty before Brian's men struck back in style.

Paul O'Connell broke free of a weak covering tackle to charge over under the posts, with Ronan adding a further two easy points. Soon after, Ireland had the All Blacks trapped on their own line. They earned a series of penalties, but they opted for the line-out instead, so confident were they that this aspect of their game had finally been sorted out.

From the second line-out, Ireland drove for the line and Flannery was awarded a try. Ronan converted, bringing the scores to 20–14 at the break. One more converted try and Ireland would be in front.

In the second half came a traditional New Zealand downpour. Ireland's new resolve was going to be tested and they would have to succeed in difficult conditions if they were to take anything from this game.

Brian led by example and was pivotal in keeping Ireland in the game early in the half. After 10 minutes, a penalty from Ronan reduced the deficit to just three points. The rain continued to fall heavily, making the ball greasy and the surface slippery, with both sides struggling to control possession.

With eight minutes remaining, McAlister took the ball 10 metres out, crashed straight through Ronan O'Gara's challenge and touched down under the posts. He converted his own score to increase the lead to 10 points. The game was lost, but, in truth, it was far closer than the score suggested.

This time, however, Brian had few complaints. Ireland had given it their all in tough conditions, and there were no glaring errors that cost them the game. In the post-match interviews, he was full of praise for his team's spirit and resilience, saying that if one break had gone their way the result might have been different.

As the tour prepared to move on to Australia, Brian could find no major faults in his game or with his team's progress. Some of the rugby played in the two Tests wasn't pretty, but the conditions weren't easy and, in the second Test in particular, if they had been a tad more lucky the result would have been different, and Ireland would have smashed a century-old winless record against the All Blacks.

The squad touched down in Australia genuinely believing they had what it took to defeat what had been an indifferent side over the past year. On paper, the sides looked fairly evenly matched, although the Australian team were more established and one would naturally expect home advantage to count in their favour. Both had seen their share of ups and downs over the past year and both had put in some pretty half-hearted performances in the previous 12 months.

Brian was keen to display just how much he and his team had moved on since their last meeting at Lansdowne Road the previous autumn. He led his team out on to the field in Perth determined to show their class. It had been a good week in training, and they had consolidated all the good work they had put in over the previous two games. What could possibly go wrong?

The home side had the better of the early exchanges and went ahead through a Stirling Mortlock penalty on 14 minutes. They extended their lead midway through the half when Chris Latham scored to make it 8–0. Ronan and Mortlock exchanged penalties, leaving Australia with a comfortable lead at the break. Brian was furious with the half-hearted display his team had shown in the first half. This 40 minutes of rugby was a major step backwards for the side, but the lead was not large enough for the game to be dead and buried and Brian called on his men to put on a fighting display in the second half to show the Australian crowd what the new Ireland were made of.

With Brian's words ringing in their ears, they made a

far better start to the second half. Early on, Ronan's high cross-kick was caught by Shane Horgan, who fed David Wallace and his pass was well taken back by Ronan for a fine try on 47 minutes.

They struck again just three minutes later when Neil Best scored in the corner following some good work from Andrew Trimble and Denis Leamy. Ronan kicked over the conversion to put the side 15–11 in front. This was more like the play Brian expected from the team.

As quickly as the team came into form, they lost it again. Their lead lasted only five minutes, when Australian winger Mark Gerrard broke through for a clinical first-phase try. After this, Ireland went to pieces and the Wallabies added no fewer than three further tries in the closing stages. Firstly, loose-head Greg Holmes pounced on a loose ball before running half the length of the field to touch down. Further scores followed from George Gregan and Cameron Shepherd to condemn Ireland to a 37–15 defeat.

After the game, Brian cited fatigue as the main reason for his side's poor performance, especially in the final 30 minutes. He told reporters that three weeks of tough Test matches had taken their toll, and that the legs had started to get heavy. He also said that the series had taught him that, while Ireland had made considerable progress, there was still a very long way to go and there was major work to be done if they were to be serious contenders for the World Cup.

Despite the obvious disappointment Brian was feeling, he felt he could not have done much more to win the game. After all, he had been playing in tough, physical contests since the start of the year and there had been very little time to allow his body to rest and recuperate in the last six months. He knew that another tough season with Leinster was little over a month away, and that the next set of internationals were only a few months down the line.

Brian decided that, when he got back to Dublin, it would be time to take it easy for a few weeks before the next battles began. The demands on a modern professional rugby player may be high, but he knew full well that nobody could play that standard of rugby all year round without it having some kind of an impact, and that resting was actually a very important part of preparations. The next few weeks would be about taking it easy, catching up with the family and having a few good nights out with the boys.

As soon as he got back to Dublin, it was time to let his hair down and party. Being single, and on a night out with your mates, has its dangers as Brian was about to find out to his cost in what was one of the most embarrassing things that had ever happened to him.

On a night out, he got talking to a girl and they swapped phone numbers at the end of the night. Unbeknown to Brian, one of his friends had got hold of his mobile and replaced her number with his, while keeping her name. The following day, 'she' sent Brian a very interesting text and he replied in kind. The messages were quickly getting more and more spicy and Brian became quite excited. Once his friend had finished having fun, he told Brian the truth, which he later described as one of the biggest disappointments of his life.

It wasn't long before he was back in training and preparing for the long, hard season that lay ahead. As things stood, Brian would publicly say that Ireland were in with an outside chance of winning the World Cup, but he now knew who he'd be facing in the Pool stages; clashes against France and Argentina were going to be tough games in their own right and there was no point in looking beyond them at this stage.

The Ireland squad met up in early November to prepare for three autumn internationals against South Africa, New Zealand and the Pacific Islanders. It was time to test the new Irish resolve against Southern Hemisphere opposition on home soil. As an added incentive, these games were to be the last international rugby matches to be played at Lansdowne Road before it closed for redevelopment, and every player wanted to send the old place off in style.

First up came that game against South Africa, which turned out to be a classic, and one that will long be remembered in the hearts of every Irish rugby fan for all the right reasons. South Africa took first blood through an Andrew Pretorius penalty but conceded the opening try after just four minutes.

Ireland were on the attack and won a scrum 10 metres out which they used to bring Trimble in from the left wing, allowing the powerful Ulsterman to charge through to score. Ronan missed the tough conversion, but soon made up for it by adding a penalty to make it 10–3.

The in-form Trimble began the move that led to Ireland's second try in the 25th minute by breaking through several tackles before recycling. Quick hands and sharp thinking saw the ball moved right where Ireland had numbers and Horgan drew his man before supplying the scoring pass to Wallace who raced in under the posts. A surge from Marcus Horan at close range saw Ireland lead by an incredible 22–3 margin at half-time.

The Irish defence was made to work hard early in the second half, but held up well after several periods of intense pressure. South Africa finally managed to score their first try after 65 minutes when new cap Francois Steyn dived over in the left corner. Bryan Habana soon added another after the ball was swept over to the right. Brian was beginning to fear the worst, and knew that this was no time to be losing concentration.

He rallied his troops and they reacted well by hitting back immediately, when Brian's back-handed pass set up a historic try for Horgan. The conversion was soon kicked over by Ronan, making the final score Ireland 32 South Africa 15. This was one of the most famous days in Irish rugby history and Brian had been the man who captained his team to glory against one of the world's best teams, playing one of his best ever games for Ireland in the process.

In the post-match interview, there was no hiding Brian's delight when he declared that Ireland could now beat any team in the world. Eddie was slightly more modest with his reactions, pointing out that South Africa had fielded several inexperienced players. But even he was delighted with the performance his boys had put in and he finally began to see several years of hard work with this group of players coming to fruition.

Naturally, Brian and the boys enjoyed a few beers in Dublin that night, but they could not afford to celebrate for too long as they were just days away from another big game against Australia.

The tired, lethargic Ireland team that had been soundly defeated by Australia just a few months before had been replaced by a confident, attacking, well-oiled machine that was more than capable of defeating any side that was not completely on top of its game. Brian knew this was an opportunity not to be missed.

The Lansdowne Road crowd knew that Ireland weren't just there to play for pride or make up the numbers. Every Irish rugby fan knew that, if their team won, they would have proven that the previous week's win was not just a fluke and they would be right up there with the giants of world rugby.

However, it was Australia who took first blood when

skipper Stirling Mortlock kicked over a penalty after just four minutes. Not long after, Ireland thought they had scored in the corner through Murphy but the television replay showed that the Leicester full-back had not quite got the touchdown. Instead, play was taken back and Ronan kicked over a penalty which went through after first hitting the post.

Ireland enjoyed the better of the opening exchanges and controlled possession well, and they finally got the try they had been threatening for some time on 25 minutes when Ronan spotted Hickie on the left touchline and kicked cross-field. The Leinster winger caught the ball cleanly before outmanoeuvring three defenders to score an excellent try.

A minute before half-time, Ireland added a second when some superb handling from Ronan released Gordon, who rushed forward before feeding Shane Horgan, who in turn managed to pass to Geordan before he was pushed into touch. Geordan managed to finish an excellent move to put Ireland 15–3 up at the break.

It had been a classic 40 minutes of rugby from the home side and they received a well-deserved standing ovation from the 43,000-strong crowd as they returned to the dressing room.

The second half lacked the pace and drama of the first half but in the early stages Australia added another penalty score. However, Ronan hit back with two more in quick succession for Ireland.

At one stage it was 14 men against 13 as Denis Leamy along with Aussie pair Mat Rogers and Phil Waugh were sin-binned for fighting. Hickie came close to getting another try but Ireland had already done enough and Australia never looked like getting the extra points to snatch the game, leaving Ireland with a 21–6 victory – only their second victory over Australia in 27 years.

Brian had not got his name on the scoresheet, but his judgement and preparation as captain had been superb and he thoroughly deserved the vast praise he received after the game. At last, everything Brian had thought possible over the past few years had come to fruition. Brian had never doubted that this Irish squad had what it took to perform on the big stage and be right up there with the world's best, and now, at long last, they were beating the giants of world rugby on a regular basis.

Yet neither Brian nor Eddie became complacent. Both knew that there was a danger that, with the winter break from international rugby, the squad could easily take a major step backwards and all the old errors and scrappy play could return for the Six Nations campaign in February.

Another concern facing Eddie and Brian was that the squad might lack the depth required to win the following year's World Cup. Certainly, the first-choice XV had proven they were a match for any team, but, as injuries inevitably took their toll over the course of a long tournament, would they have the depth in the squad to succeed?

Eddie took the decision to make no fewer than nine changes for the final match of the autumn against the Pacific Islanders. He saw it as important to keep Brian in the squad because, as captain, he would have to work with these players. One of the changes saw Paddy Wallace coming in for Ronan at fly-half.

This was also to be the final time Ireland would play at Lansdowne Road before the old place was demolished and rebuilt. Brian shared the view of the majority of Irish fans that this redevelopment was necessary to give Irish rugby a world-class arena on the scale of the Millennium Stadium or modern-day Twickenham, although there was no denying this would be a day of mixed emotions. Yes, Lansdowne Road looked dated and the facilities and size of the ground was not as good as many others around the world, but there could be few places guaranteed to generate such a noisy, passionate atmosphere anywhere in the world and for that reason it would be greatly missed.

Ireland started the game confidently when a clever reverse pass from Wallace sent Hickie through for the first try after five minutes. Wallace added a conversion and a penalty came soon after that gave the home side some early confidence.

But the visitors struck back after 12 minutes thanks to a converted try from Seru Rabeni. Wallace added two more penalties to give Ireland a nine-point cushion but this really did look like a side with nine changes and Ireland were lacking rhythm and the class they had shown in their previous two matches.

With mistakes creeping in, the Islanders added their second try on 34 minutes when Lome Fa'atau scored after a turnover. Shortly before half-time, Ireland managed two tries in quick succession through Wallace and O'Kelly, who scored after impressively stealing the ball from the line-out.

At half-time, it was clear that Girvan Dempsey was feeling the effects of a strong first-half tackle from Rabeni and was replaced by Gordon. Ireland then started the second half much more brightly and they managed to score another two tries in quick succession. Brian set up the first one when his off-load sent Easterby through, while Horgan bounced off a tackle to race to the line. Both tries were converted by Wallace, who was proving he was more than capable of filling Ronan's boots if called upon.

Brian went off injured after 58 minutes with what appeared to be a recurrence of his hamstring injury, although his removal from the game was really little more than a precautionary measure.

He watched from the stand as Ireland added further tries through Easterby, Rory Best and O'Connell, but Wallace spoiled his excellent form early on by fluffing the final two conversions. But he had already done enough to win the man of the match award, in a match Ireland won 61–17. The win may not have been as classy as in the previous two games, but the new boys had done well in their first game together and it was a fitting send-off for the oldest rugby ground in the world.

After the game, a contented Brian reflected on the achievements over the last three matches, which reinforced his belief that this side was now the greatest in the Northern Hemisphere at least. He had been generally impressed with what he had seen from the second-string players and was confident that they would gel as a team if they were given sufficient time to train together.

He was, however, slightly frustrated that the squad now had to break up until mid-January when they had been in such full flow. Of course, there was nothing he could really do about that, and the reality was that he and everybody else had club commitments in the few months that lay ahead.

Brian broke with his usual routine of heading off for a few beers at the end of a series. Instead, he headed straight to a local hospital to visit his sister and new niece who had been born two days earlier.

There was hard work ahead, but right now life couldn't be better for Brian.

Chapter 10

A DATE WITH DESTINY

The year that would define Brian's career had almost arrived. Everything looked perfectly placed to put him at the centre (in more ways than one) of the greatest year Irish rugby had ever seen. By now, Brian was considered by many pundits to be the greatest centre in the world, and, among Irish fans, as one of the best of all time. 2007 could prove to be the year that sealed Brian's place in history.

On paper, things couldn't be better. Although things hadn't quite materialised with results on the pitch at Leinster, Brian was more than happy with the progress the side were making since Michael took over as coach. With Ireland, things really couldn't have been better after the autumn they had just experienced, although Brian and Eddie were both wary of the trap of complacency.

For the time being, though, Brian needed to focus on his club duties. Leinster had made an indifferent start to the season in Brian's absence, having suffered three defeats and one draw in their opening nine Magners League fixtures. Over Christmas, Brian took to the field at Thomond Park, Limerick, for the traditional derby against Munster.

Matches against the old enemy still meant as much to Brian as they ever did and he still absolutely hated losing to them. He took to the field determined to give his best and to lead his men by example. However, they would have to do without the services of the excellent Contepomi, who was out injured, which allowed Jonathan Sexton to make his Magners League debut.

The new boy made an impact within five minutes when he kicked a penalty over but Munster soon responded with a period of concerted pressure that led to them being awarded a penalty try following a collapsed scrum after 13 minutes, which was soon converted by Ronan.

Leinster responded in style with Girvan Dempsey scoring in the corner just five minutes later. Ronan soon put another penalty over to give Munster a 10–8 lead but it would be Brian's men who would have the upper hand at the break, when Munster flanker Frankie Sheahan was sin-binned for a professional foul in added time and Sexton converted the subsequent penalty.

Only three minutes after the break, Ronan added a penalty for Munster, and added a further two within a short space of time, while Sexton pushed a long-range effort wide. As the second half progressed, the home side reinforced their dominance as their forwards pressurised Leinster who became increasingly prone to mistakes.

Despite bringing on a half-fit Contepomi late in the game, he was not able to make much of an impact and Munster won the game 25–11.

Although Brian always hated losing to Munster, this defeat hurt more than most. He had failed to get into the game and penetrate the Munster defence, and the rest of the team had not managed to get into gear and confront a well-oiled Munster unit. However, he had been impressed with Sexton's debut and knew he would have plenty to offer the side at some stage in the future. A few days later, Leinster managed to go some way towards making amends for the defeat when they beat Ulster at home, 20–12, ending 2006 on a high.

In mid-January, Brian met up with the rest of the Ireland squad at the City West hotel in Dublin to begin preparations for the upcoming Six Nations campaign. From the outset, Eddie and Brian both knew exactly what they expected from this campaign, and that was to achieve the Grand Slam. After all, there was no reason why they shouldn't.

The three autumn internationals had been a huge

success, but the reality was that in a few years' time nobody outside Ireland would remember just how good they had been in those games. For this team to be remembered throughout the world, they had to pick up a major trophy. Brian believed his task was to beat every major nation in the Northern Hemisphere, achieve the Grand Slam and hold up the Six Nations trophy in March. For this side, anything else would be a disappointment.

Yes, they had achieved the Triple Crown this time last year, playing some breathtaking rugby in the latter stages of the tournament, but Brian knew that the side had come on a great deal since then. He also knew that other nations had upped their game in the intervening 10 months.

England could well return to form with the recent appointment of the experienced Brian Ashton as coach. Scottish rugby was still on a high after the previous year's success, while Italy would inevitably continue to improve, as they had done every year since joining the tournament. France, meanwhile, were rarely poor for any more than the odd game here and there and were always likely to prove tough opposition.

In the weeks leading up to the first game, Eddie focused the training on making sure they were as well drilled as they had been in the autumn, and were ready for the long campaign that lay ahead. The build-up to the tournament couldn't have gone better. Brian was confident that the preparation had once again been spot on and they would continue their run of fine form.

The first match was away to an out-of-sorts Wales side that was still feeling the ramifications of the debacle that erupted during the previous year's tournament. However, Brian knew their new coach Gareth Jenkins well from the Lions tour and had a great deal of respect for what he had done with the squad in New Zealand, and also admired what he had achieved with the Llanelli Scarlets side. As Simon Easterby would be quick to point out, Gareth was a passionate man and no team he coached would lack commitment, and therefore they could not take this game for granted.

Brian led his team out at the Millennium Stadium for their first match in front of 74,000 noisy fans. This was it; the start of the year when Brian would show the world what he and the Irish team were made of.

Things couldn't have got off to a much better start when, after just 46 seconds, Brian blocked Stephen Jones's kick, allowing Rory Best to gather the loose ball and flop over the line. Ronan missed the subsequent conversion, but the breathtaking start had left the Welsh crowd shell-shocked.

Wales soon fought back into the game and made some good ground, which resulted in a penalty opportunity for Jones, which he kicked over the bar with ease.

The pace of the game was electrifying and the crowd produced deafening volumes of noise, with both sides playing exciting, attacking rugby in the opening 20 minutes. Ronan missed a difficult penalty kick and then had to watch Jones kick one of his own over to give the hosts a 6–5 lead.

A period of fierce Welsh pressure followed, which eventually resulted in Jones kicking over another penalty, while Hickie spilled blood and had to go off for stitches. This left Geordan replacing him temporarily on the left wing.

However, Ireland soon fought back and Wallace skilfully burst through several Welsh tackles before passing to Brian, who scored his 17th Championship try in the right corner. Ronan kicked the conversion that followed, and Ireland were back in business thanks largely to Brian's sharp judgement. They had a 12–9 lead at half-time.

Ireland nearly lost the lead shortly after the break when Chris Czekaj broke clear down the left, sent a grubber past Andrew Trimble and seemed destined to gather and score. But Simon Easterby clipped the Blues wing just enough to slow him, the infringement going unpunished, allowing Ireland full-back Girvan Dempsey to get back and slap the ball away.

In the 64th minute, James Hook had a kick charged down by Ronan that led to him claiming a third Ireland try. Gordon made the decisive break, brushing through Czekaj too easily to get to within inches of the Welsh line and Ronan was on hand to dive over despite Hook's despairing tackle.

With the game almost certainly won, Ireland felt things had gone more or less to plan on the day. However, disaster struck five minutes from the end when Brian hobbled off with a recurrence of his dreaded hamstring injury and was now a real doubt for the upcoming big clash against France.

This was a real worry for Eddie and the boys and they all felt nervous about losing their captain and star player for what was likely to be a Championship-deciding game. For the whole squad, this twist of fate took the gloss off what had been a well-earned victory.

As the week progressed, it became clear that Brian wouldn't be able to lead his side out against France. This was a double blow for him. Obviously, he had wanted to play in the big game. Matches against France suited his style of play and he always gave his absolute best for these games. They meant a huge amount to him and being injured came as a bitter blow.

Secondly, this was Ireland's first match at Croke Park, where they would be playing their home matches while Lansdowne Road was being redeveloped. There were massive historical and political connotations associated with this occasion and Brian had been looking forward to leading his team out in front of an 82,000-strong crowd since the announcement had been made to play the matches there.

Paul O'Connell was to captain Ireland in Brian's absence. Brian was sure this was the right decision and had every confidence in his ability to lead the team on this big occasion.

Brian took his seat in the stand for the game, knowing full well the significance of this game. The hairs stood up on the back of his neck as he soaked up the unique atmosphere of Croke Park. He had long been a fan of Gaelic sports and had visited the stadium many times before, but to have Irish rugby internationals being played in this huge arena meant a great deal to him. He was desperately sorry he wouldn't be leading the boys out himself, but he had to put those thoughts to the back of his mind and think of the team as they prepared for battle.

The match was every bit as physical and demanding of the players as Brian had expected it to be. Just three minutes in, O'Connell was penalised for killing the ball, allowing David Skrela to kick France into a three-point lead. Six minutes later, the fly-half added another three points from in front of the posts when Rory Best was adjudged to have interfered at a ruck.

Ronan got a penalty back for Ireland in the 14th minute but it was becoming clear that they were going to be up against it for the rest of the game. French captain Raphael Ibanez soon broke through a weak tackle from Geordan, and ploughed passed the challenges of Marcus Horan and John Hayes to cross the Irish line.

However, Ireland fought back in style and Ronan soon added another penalty. They kept the momentum going and on 32 minutes Ronan scored a try in the corner following an impressive run of play involving Hickie, Horgan and Wallace. However, the kick was at a difficult angle and he failed to add a further two points. Skrela missed with two penalty attempts before half-time, leaving his side with a two-point advantage at the interval.

Early in the second half, Geordan sprinted towards the line after France lost possession but referee Steve Walsh had already blown his whistle for a knock-on without playing advantage. Despite this setback, Ireland seemed to be controlling the game and Ronan kicked his side into the lead for the first time on 56 minutes.

The game continued at a frantic pace and was a fitting curtain-raiser for life at Croke Park. Replacement Lionel Beauxis hit the post with a long-range drop goal attempt which would have put France ahead again.

Ireland looked to have won the game when Ronan added another penalty to give the side a four-point lead with two minutes remaining, but right at the end of play Vincent Clerc ran through the Irish defence for a French try, with Beauxis converting to make the final score 20–17 to France. The crowd, who had been so vocal throughout the game, sat in stunned silence. Ireland hadn't been at their brilliant best but they had controlled the game for much of the second half and the game looked in the bag right up until the last play of the game. In truth, the team were probably missing Brian's influence as captain and, had he been on the field, the result may well have been very different. The confrontational style of the game would've suited him perfectly and there was no hiding his disappointment at being forced to sit helplessly in the stand as his team crashed to a last-minute defeat.

The defeat was a bitter pill to swallow, but Brian knew that another massive game against England was just a fortnight away and he began looking forward immediately. He was highly likely to be back fit for the game and preparations had to begin now if they were to defeat a rejuvenated England side.

Eddie and Brian made sure that all the boys were looking forward, rather than backwards. The Grand Slam was gone but there was still every possibility of their winning the Championship, and the Triple Crown was still very much on. In training, they focused on sorting out their defensive line, which had been a substantial weakness in the game against France, while Brian spent the first week of the fortnight gap doing some gentle exercise. He didn't want to overwork the hamstring as he knew from past experience how fragile it was, but by the end of the first week it was clear he was fit and able to lead the boys out against England.

At last, Brian's chance to take to the field at Croke Park had arrived. Once again, the place was buzzing and the crowd expected nothing but the best from Ireland now that Brian was back and in top shape. He got the physio to give his hamstring a rub shortly before kick-off. He knew there was a chance that, if his hamstring got cold during the anthems and presentation to the dignitaries, it could give way early in the match. Spending so long out in the cold standing still before the game wasn't ideal preparation for him, but decorum and tradition dictated it had to be done.

It was England who struck first through a Jonny Wilkinson penalty, but Ronan replied in kind soon afterwards. The opening quarter of the match was fairly even but two further penalties from Ronan saw the Irish leading 9–3 after 26 minutes. Both sides struggled as a massive downpour fell on Croke Park making conditions difficult with a boggy ground and slippery ball. However, it was Ireland who adapted best to the conditions and after 30 minutes came a moment that would swing the match firmly in their favour.

England just about managed to stop the rampaging Simon Easterby but Danny Grewcock cynically went offside at the ruck and was yellow-carded. From the resulting penalty, Ronan kicked the ball into the corner. The visitors managed to hold back the initial driving maul, but, after a poor pass from Stringer, some quality passing from Gordon and Brian rescued the manoeuvre, before passing to Dempsey who touched down in style, with Ronan adding the extras.

Shane Horgan nearly added another but a last-ditch tackle from Mathew Tait denied him, though Ireland remained firmly in control of the game. A period of sustained pressure resulted in a try from Wallace after 38 minutes, with an on-form Ronan adding the conversion to give Ireland a 23–3 lead at the interval.

The game looked firmly in the bag, although Eddie and Brian were quick to remind the team that complacency had cost them dear before and they could not afford to lose concentration for a moment as the game could still be snatched from them as it had been against France.

Ronan stretched the lead further with a penalty shortly after the break, but England hit back in style when the debutant David Strettle slid over in the corner. Jonny added the conversion and a penalty followed soon after. Ronan restored Ireland's 16-point advantage when he struck back with a penalty of his own after Julian White was punished for illegal use of the boot in the ruck.

From then on, it was Ireland all the way as they launched a series of threatening attacks on the England line, which were in no small part down to Brian's efforts. His best attempt nearly saw him cross the line but he was narrowly held up by Mike Tindall. From the resulting scrum, Ronan cross-kicked and Horgan towered above Josh Lewsey to claim a superbly executed try.

In the dying moments of the game, replacement scrum-half Boss claimed a late interception try to finish off what had been a superb display by Ireland, giving them a 43–13 victory. This was England's heaviest ever defeat in the history of the Championship. The Croke Park crowd gave Brian's men a standing ovation as they left the field.

This was the Ireland side that had looked like world-beaters the previous autumn, and this match proved just what an important part Brian played in the team. It was as though his presence could turn a talented but disorganised group of players into one of the most disciplined and focused rugby teams in the modern era. Right now, though, Brian's priority was capturing the Triple Crown which was very much still on.

Next up came Scotland, a side that had blown hot and cold during the Championship so far. They went crashing to an away defeat to England in the first week, but had gone on to thrash Wales at home a week later, before being on the receiving end of a 37–17 drubbing by Italy in the previous round of fixtures. Eddie and Brian both knew that this Scotland team were capable of providing tough opposition, but they were terribly inconsistent, a bit like the Ireland team of 18 months previously. They realised that in the intervening fortnight they had to prepare thoroughly and remain disciplined and well drilled as a team.

Brian arrived at Murrayfield knowing that this was a golden opportunity to retain the Triple Crown. To win it once was impressive, but to win it two years in a row, and three times in four years, showed the squad had true class. They may have blown the Grand Slam for another year, but the Triple Crown was no easy feat and a win here would see the current Ireland squad go down in the record books as one of the Championship's all-time great sides.

Brian led his warriors on to the field, backed by a massive Irish contingent who had made their way across the sea for a weekend in Edinburgh, hoping to paint Prince's Street green that night. Ronan kicked a penalty over to give Ireland the lead after seven minutes, but, despite some powerful Irish surges, Paterson scored the first try of the match for Scotland just eight minutes later, the circumstances of which will not be remembered as Brian O'Driscoll's finest hour.

The Scotland skipper was caught by Hickie while on a run and, when he was on the floor, Peter Stringer caught him in the head. A minor brawl ensued, and Brian was very lucky to get away with a warning from the referee when the situation had calmed down. Ireland had seen many examples of fine team leadership from Brian in recent times, but this wasn't one of them.

Ireland hit back when a Dan Parks kick was charged down by Ronan, who passed to Gordon, who exchanged passes with Easterby, before passing back to Ronan who touched down. In truth, it was a soft try caused by some sloppy Scottish defending of the sort that had caused them to be thrashed by Italy two weeks earlier, but Ireland were back in the game and, for Brian, that was all that mattered. Paterson added two penalties and Ronan added another before the half-time break, which Ireland went into leading 13–9.

Brian made up for his silly antics early in the second half when he sprang two great breaks, but the rest of the team failed to give him the support he deserved to make the most of it, most notably when Shane Horgan was guilty of a poor forward pass when a try looked certain.

Scotland fought back and scored another penalty to reduce the deficit to just one point. Suddenly, Ireland had to be on their guard. On the hour, Paterson kicked over another penalty to give the home side the lead. However, the hosts were just as jittery as Ireland had been and Ronan hit back with a penalty of his own to give Ireland a 19–18 victory, with him scoring all of Ireland's points.

That was it – another Triple Crown in the bag. It wasn't Ireland at their most fluid and eloquent, but rugby isn't always pretty and Brian was more than aware that sometimes you just had to knuckle down, get stuck in and grind out results, and this was just one of those occasions. However, celebrations were muted following a nasty incident that could have left the hero of the hour, Ronan, seriously injured.

In the closing seconds of the game, Ronan found himself at the bottom of a ruck that somehow left him choked. According to Eddie, someone had their arm around his neck, cutting off his air supply, and he went blue. The doctor came on and soon made sure he was all right, but that could have been a very serious incident. After looking at the replay, the independent commissioner found no blame with any Scottish player and nobody was punished.

Going into the final day, no fewer than four teams could theoretically win the Championship. Ireland's task was to beat Italy in Rome in the first game of the day and hope Scotland did them a favour against France.

Brian led his team out on to the pitch at the Stadio Flaminio not underestimating the size of the task ahead. Italy had just been through their best ever Six Nations Championship, and they were now a team that did the basics very well and were more than capable of beating any of the traditional five nations on their day. The Ireland team had prepared seriously in the week leading up to the game, knowing they might not be able to afford the sort of errors that had crept in during the match against Scotland.

After Ronan put Ireland in front through a penalty, Pez equalised with a drop goal before putting another penalty over soon after. Any ideas the Irish fans had about this being an easy game to win were soon dispelled.

However, this Ireland team were back on top form and their first try of the afternoon came after Gordon and Brian had done some good build-up work to allow Dempsey to score in the left corner with 16 minutes played. Five minutes later, Horgan sent Easterby wide to score Ireland's second. Italy needed to hit back fast, and the superb Pez soon added another penalty and drop goal to cut Ireland's lead to just one point. Ireland scored a controversial try to end the half when Hickie's scoring pass to Gordon was clearly forward but he was allowed to play on and score Ireland's third.

After the break, Ireland were keen to remind the world of the sort of rugby they had been playing the previous autumn, and managed to put through four tries in 13 minutes. Dempsey charged through a large gap over the line, with Ronan adding the conversion. The floodgates had opened when Hickie danced through Italy's midfield before passing to Horgan who finished off in style. Hickie crossed himself following a crafty dummy and then O'Gara was over, chasing a kick after D'Arcy had broken from his own half.

With Ireland seemingly unstoppable, Brian's Championship came to an unfortunate end when the dreaded hamstring gave way once again completely out of the blue, and he had to be helped to hobble off the field. He was obviously disappointed that his game was to end early, but he had captained his team with distinction and there was no way they could lose it from here.

Marco Bortolami got Italy's first try on 74 minutes but Ireland replied with Hickie's second of the game. A stoppage-time touchdown from Roland De Marigny in the corner made the final score 51–24 to Ireland, but little did they know that the late consolation try for Italy would cost them the Championship just a few hours later.

The Ireland team returned to the hotel to watch France take on Scotland in Paris, knowing that the title was on a knife-edge. The first half was very close, with Scotland at their best, forcing France to push very hard, but in the second half the difference in power began to tell and the home side scored a few tries to stretch their lead. After 80 minutes, they were three points behind Ireland, so they pushed forward.

A try was awarded to Elvis Vermeulen following a decision by an Irish Television Match Official, which was highly controversial because it could barely be seen on the replays. The match referee asked him if there was any reason why he thought the try shouldn't be awarded, implying that he had already decided that it should be given.

This close call had deprived Ireland of the Championship in the most cruel way imaginable. It had been the most dramatic and nail-biting conclusion to a Six Nations Championship ever, and, as with all tense sporting dramas, one side was left on the receiving end of a painful and bitter defeat. Brian and the boys were stunned into silence. As the clock ticked down in Paris, it looked as though they had done enough. Indeed, many of the players could justifiably think they had the Championship in the bag. Few would argue that Elvis

Vermeulen had been on the receiving end of a very fortunate refereeing decision.

It turned out that, for the thousands of Irish fans watching the France match on big screens and in cafes, bars and restaurants in Rome, there had been an extra cruelty for them to endure.

Because the match had over-run its allocated time slot, French television had cut the feed to other countries, meaning that a large number of Irish fans lost pictures from Paris a few moments before the end, and had naturally assumed Ireland had done enough and began celebrating. It was some time before news filtered through of what had actually happened right at the end of the game.

This had been one of those 'what if' occasions. What if Ronan had landed his goals? What if Brian hadn't been forced to go off injured? What if Andrea Scanavacca had missed his conversion? What if Paterson had landed his? Brian's men had come so near, and yet the atmosphere at the end of the game in Rome some-how implied that Ireland hadn't quite done enough.

To make matters worse, Brian's injury was more serious than he had first feared and Eddie was worried he might be facing a lengthy lay-off. Despite this, Eddie made it known in the interviews that followed that he would not be allowing his squad to dwell on this painful setback for too long because the opportunity to grab a far bigger prize was only a few months away.

It wasn't long before Brian's mood was lifted when he discovered he had been named RBS Player of the Tournament for the second year running following a fans' poll on the official tournament website, with over 10,000 votes cast for him. This was a testament to the high esteem in which he was now held not just in Ireland, but also by rugby fans the world over. Despite Ireland falling short of expectations, few now doubted that Brian was one of the best centres, if not the very best, in the world.

Meanwhile, with the press unable to talk about Brian's rugby performances, they soon turned their attentions to the latest goings-on in his private life. The press were speculating that he was dating actress Amy Huberman, probably best known for her role in RTE's *The Clinic*. As with previous relationships, Brian was keen to keep things as low profile as possible. They both had careers of their own and it soon became clear that neither of them wanted to be part of some sort of celebrity golden couple. However, they had now been together for several months and a certain amount of press attention was inevitable.

It soon became clear that Brian wouldn't be returning to club duty with Leinster for the remainder of the season. The priority now was getting him fit for the World Cup in the autumn and there was no point in risking him in these comparatively minor games.

The club, meanwhile, were experiencing a disappointing climax to the season. After being thrashed by Wasps in the quarter-final of the Heineken Cup, their only hope of winning any silverware came on the final day of the season when a win away at Cardiff would give them the Magners League title.

Brian travelled to Cardiff to give his men moral support for this vital game. As with the previous season, the league had gone down to the final week of fixtures. Leinster entered the match knowing that a win plus a bonus point for scoring at least four tries would secure the title, regardless of whether the Ospreys managed to win their final game.

However, after just six minutes, Nick Robinson made the crucial break, accelerating past a surprised Keith Gleeson before swinging a superb pass to Robin Sowden-Taylor to score a textbook try as he sucked past Denis Hickie.

Felipe Contepomi, who earlier in the day heard he had qualified as a doctor, got Leinster on the scoreboard with a brace of penalties, bracketing one from Blair for the home side. Both sides struggled to cope with the pitch, which had become sticky after several days of heavy rain in the Welsh capital. It therefore came as no surprise that the next try was a forward effort for the home side finished off by hooker Gareth Williams, giving the Blues a 13–6 lead at half-time.

Michael knew at half-time that Leinster were in danger of throwing it away at the last minute once again, and that a massive effort in difficult conditions was needed in the second half. Unfortunately, they were unable to click into gear and the Blues added two further tries in quick succession. The first was engineered by Nick Robinson whose fine cross-kick was fielded by Chris Czekaj on the right to send full-back Rhys Williams over, with Nick Robinson converting.

Not long after, Marc Stcherbina benefited from a crucial error when Horgan muffed a chip, allowing him to gather the ball and take it over the line. Horgan managed to make amends on 55 minutes when his grubber was mis-fielded by Rhys Williams, allowing the Ireland back to hack on and touch down. Contepomi missed the subsequent conversion and then found himself sin-binned for out-jumping Jamie Robinson in mid-air. This game was turning into a disaster for Leinster exactly when they didn't need it.

Hickie and Gordon continued to make decent breaks but they lacked support and there were handling errors at key times, condemning Leinster to a 27–11 defeat. The title was lost to the Ospreys, who got the win they needed at Netherdale the following day. Although he was not on the pitch that day, there was no hiding Brian's disappointment at coming so close, yet being pipped at the post once again, for the umpteenth time in his career. The lesson of the season for both club and country had been that, while both sides were packed with talented players, Brian's presence on the pitch, both as a player and leader, added an extra dimension to the side that turned them from losers into world-beaters.

In his personal life, in June, Brian attended the wedding of Ireland's fitness coach Michael McGurn. For once, he and Amy made little effort to hide from the waiting press as they posed for photographs, complete with trendy sunglasses, outside the church in Enniskillen. This was taken as a clear sign by the press that this was now a long-term relationship and that things seemed to be going well.

With the domestic season over, attention soon turned to Ireland's preparations for the biggest tournament of Brian's career to date – the Rugby World Cup 2007.

Chapter 11

THROWING IT ALL AWAY

One thing that had become clear over the last six months was that, while Ireland's strongest XV were capable of beating any side in the world, there were real concerns that the squad lacked the strength in depth required to win the World Cup.

It was inevitable that, during the long World Cup campaign, injuries would occur to key members of the squad and backup in all positions was needed. With Brian out injured, and Eddie concerned about key players becoming injured at this crucial time, he decided to take a largely second-string squad for the two-match tour of Australia.

The results were clearly not Eddie's main objective, but getting squad cohesion and injecting some competition to avoid complacency from the first-choice XV were right at the top of his priority list. Yet, even so, the performances were disappointing. In the first game, Ireland crashed to a 22–20 defeat thanks largely to Contepomi's superb kicking, and in the second they lost by an embarrassing 16–0 scoreline. This was hardly the message they wanted to be sending to Argentina, who they would be facing for real in the group stages of the World Cup.

In early August, the squad met up at the City West hotel to begin preparations for the World Cup. This was it – the time had arrived when this squad, who had proven they could beat any side in the world, set out to prove they really were the best rugby team on the planet. The early signs were encouraging. Brian had recovered from his hamstring injury and was now at the peak of his physical fitness. There were no major long-term injury concerns in the squad and there was no obvious reason why this side wouldn't win the tournament, or at least come very close.

Their first of two warm-up games would come away at Scotland in mid-August. Eddie knew the time for experimenting was over and his first-choice men needed a chance to get match-fit. Brian led his men on to the field expecting nothing less than a convincing win. Scotland had gone backwards in the last year and, while spectacular at times, had not had as good a Six Nations campaign as they would have hoped. A victory here was the minimum requirement.

However, it took just three minutes for Ali Hogg to break through the Irish defence to give the home side the lead, with Paterson adding the conversion. Paddy Wallace cut the gap for Ireland but the Scots were in full control and it came as little surprise when they added a second soon after when Andrew Henderson muscled his way over for his sixth international try, which Paterson duly converted once again to make it 14–3. This looked like a very different Ireland side to the one that took the world by storm the previous autumn and the alarm bells started ringing for Eddie and the fans.

Geordan added a penalty but Ireland just never looked like getting into the game and were guilty of making silly errors, and shortly before half-time Scotland added a third try when Ewan Murray crossed the line to make it 19–6 at the break. Needless to say, Eddie made his views abundantly clear in the dressing room.

With Eddie's scathing words ringing in their ears, the boys came out for the second half determined to put things right. The game was still winnable and there was no reason why, with discipline and concentration, they could not still grab a victory from this mess.

Yet it was Scotland who struck first with Henderson's second try of the game. But after this they began to become complacent and Ireland started to work their way back into the game. Tommy Bowe's break led to the ball reaching Isaac Boss who evaded both Lamont brothers – Sean and Rory – to score his team's first try of the afternoon and spark Ireland into life. Trimble added another in the 55th minute before Wallace added a penalty to make it 24–21 at the midway point in the second half. Ireland had got stuck in and fought their way back into the game. This was more like it from Brian's men, but, once again, concentration seemed to slip and this allowed Scotland to creep back in and score one more try through the superb Henderson, to give Scotland victory by 10 points.

Brian had come off in the second half with a tight hamstring and sore wrist but this was little more than a precautionary measure. However, there was no ignoring the fact that Ireland had once again slumped to a defeat when he wasn't on the pitch and it may not have been entirely coincidental that they lost concentration at around the time he was replaced. However, the main injury concern that arose from the game was Shane Horgan, who twisted his knee and was now a serious doubt for the World Cup. Shane had been instrumental in Ireland's successes over the last few years and Brian feared, with some justification, that losing a player of his calibre for the World Cup would leave Ireland a significantly weaker team.

As the evening progressed, it became clear that Shane would be out of action for roughly four weeks. When the squad was officially announced the next day, his name was included, meaning he was in with a chance of making the second Pool game against Georgia. The main omissions from the squad were Trevor Horgan, Mick O'Driscoll, Keith Gleeson and Jamie Heaslip, while Eddie decided to choose Brian Carney, who had only converted from rugby league a few months earlier, over Tommy Bowe.

At midweek, the squad travelled to France for a match against Bayonne that Ireland won 42–6. Brian had recovered from his hamstring injury and captained the side to a comfortable victory. However, a nasty incident took place during the game that threatened to jeopardise Brian's participation in the World Cup. What should have been a minor warm-up game had turned into a game Irish rugby fans would long remember for all the wrong reasons.

During the second half, he was punched by lock Mikaera Tewhata as he approached him to break up a row, in what was a blatant act of violence that brought back memories of the Tana incident on the Lions tour two years earlier. The impact of the punch fractured Brian's sinus. He required nine stitches just below his right eye, and the doctors warned him that there was a danger of infection due to there being pockets of air in his battered eye socket. There were even fears for Brian's sight in that eye, let alone whether he'd be able to play rugby again. This was not what the Ireland squad needed so close to the World Cup. Once again, Brian had been on the receiving end of an unsporting act that would threaten to rule him out of what should have been one of the highlights of his career.

With just one more game to go before the World Cup started, it was important Ireland put in a strong performance in their final warm-up game against Italy, which was the first international to be played at Ravenhill in Belfast in half a century. The ground played host to many Ireland matches until 1954, when it was abandoned for internationals in favour of Lansdowne Road. Yes, they would have to do without Brian, Shane Horgan and David Wallace, but this needed to be the game where they proved that there was depth in the squad and they could cope without Brian, as it seemed likely they would have to do without him for the first few games at least.

The 14,000 full house watching should have witnessed a try in the third minute after Denis Leamy's break but Denis Hickie opted to go it alone instead of passing to Girvan Dempsey and was bottled up by the Italian defence.

Ronan managed to kick the first Irish penalty after six minutes, but, instead of building up momentum, they started to lose their way somewhat. In the 21st minute, Ronan's loose clearance was gathered by the Italian full-back David Bortolussi, who took the opportunity to kick a superb drop goal from 10 metres out. Shortly afterwards, a brawl broke out between a number of players after Sergio Parisse had thrown a punch at Peter Stringer.

Ireland regained composure and Stringer gathered

Ronan's superbly placed kick to score a try. Ronan added a conversion but Bortolussi added a penalty to narrow the gap to just four points. In the closing minutes of the first half, the strong Italian scrum exerted pressure and Ireland finally lost the lead when a tap-penalty saw Alessandro Troncon charge through for a try, with the video referee giving the correct decision in Italy's favour. Bortolussi added the conversion to give his side a 13–10 lead at the interval.

Geordan was prominent as Ireland made a rousing start to the second half, and Ronan eventually kicked a penalty over after an earlier attempt just moments earlier had hit the woodwork. However, Ireland's attempts to break down Italy's robust defence came to nothing. Trimble's break in the 72nd minute after an Italian fumble set up a chance for Hickie but the Irish wing didn't have the legs to get past Kaine Robertson. However, Ronan restored Ireland's lead in the 74th minute with a superbly taken long-range drop goal. In injury time, Matteo Pratichetti notched a breakaway try after Peter Stringer had fumbled the ball in the Italian half. Geordan claimed the try-scorer had impeded him in the build-up but the try was awarded and the conversion duly followed.

Ireland looked beaten. But deep into injury time Trimble's forward-looking pass sent Ronan charging towards the line. There looked to be major doubt over whether Ronan had grounded the ball after being challenged by Kaine Robertson but the score was awarded, much to the relief of the Ravenhill crowd, giving Ireland a 23–20 victory.

After the game, Eddie told reporters that he was disappointed with the team's stop-start performance, but praised their character in getting back into the game. However, this wasn't good enough for much of the Irish public, who were rightly furious as they had witnessed an embarrassing display that was disjointed and lacked rhythm. This certainly didn't look like a side that was going to beat the world's greatest teams within a few weeks and Eddie's statement that they were not 100 miles away from clicking didn't go down well with many people.

The game had highlighted once again the importance to the team of having Brian on the field. As had been the case before, without his leadership and commitment they soon fell to pieces and wouldn't threaten an average Six Nations team, let alone the world's best.

To the astonishment of many, within days of the embarrassing victory the IRFU announced an extension to Eddie's contract that would see him remain in charge until 2012. This decision was criticised by many within the Irish media, who saw this as taking much-needed pressure off him to deliver a strong performance at the World Cup.

Meanwhile, as the days passed by, it became more and more likely that Brian would be able to play in all of

Ireland's Pool matches. However, the squad remained tight-lipped on his progress. After all, what would be the point in letting their rivals know that he would be OK when they could surprise them with his inclusion in the squad and ruin their game plan in the process?

By the end of August, Brian had regained 80 per cent of his vision in his right eye and he was expected to fully regain his sight in time. He was also back in training and his stitches would be out within days. Brian couldn't hide his delight at the astonishing progress he had made and was getting himself into shape for the most important tournament of his career.

Brian boarded the plane with the rest of the squad as they flew to France in early September. But it wasn't long after landing that the problems that were to haunt the squad for the duration of the tournament began to come to light. They were taken by coach to a hotel in a dreary part of Bordeaux. At first sight, many of the players couldn't believe how little research the IRFU had put into choosing the hotel. This was not the sort of place Brian or any other professional rugby star was used to. Yes, there was a video room and a 'private sport room', but the facilities just weren't up to scratch and there was very little to do in the surrounding areas. This did not compare to the sort of places Brian was staying in during the Lions tour of New Zealand. This stark 1970s concrete block did not feel like the sort of place Brian would want to spend a month living in.

More bad news was to follow when the camp was rocked by reports in the French media that Ronan had racked up gambling debts of more than £250,000 and that he had separated from his wife Jess. Ronan angrily denied the accusations, describing them as 'despicable' and reassured his team-mates that, while he clearly enjoyed gambling on horses, he had not been an excessive gambler and was fully in control. He was furious with the suggestions that he had been kicked out of his home and made it clear that they were still very much in love.

As for the rugby itself, there was no denying the scale of the challenge that lay ahead. The media had dubbed the Pool 'The Group of Death', with Ireland having to face Argentina and France in the weeks ahead, with other, supposedly easy matches against Georgia and Namibia to play as well. Indeed, it would be Namibia who would be Ireland's first opponents. Brian had by now made an excellent recovery and was named in the starting line-up. The circumstances were far from perfect and the preparation had been terrible in so many ways, but Brian remained keen to prove that his was still one of the best sides in the world and his ambition of leading his country to World Cup victory remained very much alive.

Brian led his men on to the field in front of 32,000 fans at Stade Chaban-Delmas in Bordeaux expecting nothing other than a clear, convincing victory against one of the tournament's supposedly lesser sides. It didn't take long for Brian to make a statement of intent when after just four minutes he scored a try, running on to his own chipped kick and shrugging off Ryan Witbooi to make himself Ireland's sole leading try-scorer of all time. Ronan then added the conversion and a penalty followed soon after.

Ronan was clearly keen to silence those who had made such hurtful comments in the press, and set up Ireland's next try on 29 minutes by taking a tap penalty and kicking to the right corner where Trimble gathered before touching down. On the stroke of half-time, Namibia fly-half Emile Wessels landed a long-range penalty.

Early in the second half, the referee rightly awarded Ireland a penalty try following two collapsed scrums, and Namibia could have few complaints, securing the Irish a bonus point in the process. Yet, in the final quarter, Ireland fell to pieces and Namibia managed to play some decent rugby, and in the 61st minute big blindside forward Jacques Nieuwenhuis thundered over for a try. Another soon followed when Piet van Zyl touched down. However, Ireland scored one more when Flannery was a tad fortunate to be credited with a try in the left corner, and Ireland had a 32–17 victory.

Yes, they had won, but they had been truly awful on occasions. That said, Brian led by example and seemed to be the only player on the pitch worthy of wearing the green shirt for much of the game. His commitment levels were exemplary from start to finish. If the reports of complacency within the squad were to be believed, Brian would be the name right at the bottom of the list of players on the field that night who were taking their selection for granted.

Following the game, Brian didn't mince his words, describing it as a really awful display that started badly and got worse as the game went on. There were no excuses. It was a victory, but it really felt like a defeat. There was a huge amount of work to be done before the next game.

Just six days later, Ireland returned to the Stade Chaban-Delmas for what should have been a straight-forward game against Georgia. Brian had shrugged off a minor elbow injury sustained in the match against Namibia and it was clear both he and the squad had to give their absolute best in this game to look like serious competitors for the tournament. After all, it was less than a year since this group of players had been beating some of the world's greatest sides. Where had it all gone wrong? Surely they still had it in them to do it – there was no logical reason why they shouldn't be able to.

Ireland took the lead after 16 minutes when the pack grabbed a line-out and drove through the Georgian forwards, before Ulster hooker Best got over the line. Ronan added a difficult conversion. Ireland failed to improve on this try and for much of the first half there were elementary mistakes, with only Brian threatening the Georgian defence, but he couldn't do it all by himself and his team-mates let him down throughout the rest of the first half. Late on in the half, a powerful charge from George Shkinini swept Georgia out of their own half and, when openside David Wallace had been sin-binned for killing the ball, Merab Kvirikashvili stepped up to slot the three points.

The stadium was stunned shortly after the break when Georgia took the lead. Peter Stringer sent a looping pass in Brian's direction but it was intercepted by Shkinini. The Blois winger galloped home under the posts with Kvirikashvili landing the conversion. This was turning into a humiliating and shameful performance. However imperfect their preparations had been, there was no excuse for struggling against such lowly opposition.

It took 10 minutes for Ireland to work their way back into the game when Gordon ran through midfield before passing to Dempsey who managed to score. Panic over, but this did not disguise the fact this was turning out to be one of the worst performances in Irish rugby history, and even now a Georgian fight-back wasn't out of the question.

Georgia dominated for long periods in the second half, and the stadium was on tenterhooks when Denis Leamy denied Georgia late on, with referee Wayne Barnes seeking confirmation from the video referee that the ball had been held up. Ireland had won the game 14–10, but this was another truly awful display, and they risked being thrashed by the more renowned opposition in the two games that remained.

Georgia had given a good performance, but Ireland should have played far, far better. After the game, both Brian and Eddie were incredibly upbeat considering the unconvincing nature of the win. Ever the gentleman, Brian praised the Georgian performance but he knew that Ireland would now have to win their matches against France and Argentina to progress beyond the Pool stage. Eddie, meanwhile, told the press that there were a lot of positives they could take out of the game and that Georgia played really well. This angered many rugby writers and supporters back home. There was no doubt that many players had been fed up with staying at the hotel and preparations in training had not been ideal, but, even so, the exact reasons why the side had declined so much so quickly remain a mystery. What was clear was that Brian was the only player on the pitch who looked truly world class and dedicated during the tournament so far.

As the week progressed, it emerged that Geordan seemed to be inexplicably out of favour. This was the man who, a few years previously, had been described by the Irish media as the 'George Best of rugby' and was now felt by many to be the man who could turn Ireland's fortunes around, and end their dependence on Brian to turn on the class against quality opposition. Thus far, his only appearance in the tournament had been as an 80th-minute replacement against Namibia.

When Eddie named his squad to play France, Geordan's name was completely omitted, with his place on the bench being taken by Gavin Duffy. Eddie's team selection had not gone down well with Irish fans. Whatever the ins and outs of what went on, this was not the kind of pressure they needed with their crunch match against France just a few days away.

As they failed to secure a bonus point against Georgia, they needed to beat the French to stand a realistic chance of progressing to the quarter-final stage of the tournament. Brian led his men out in front of 80,000 passionate fans knowing that this game was just as important for the host nation, who had experienced an earlier slip-up against Argentina. This was one of the most important games, if not the most important, of his career to date. He knew full well that the Irish public expected nothing less than 100 per cent from the team and there would be no excuses if they failed to deliver.

Yet it was the French, buoyed by the home crowd, who took the lead through a penalty after Ireland failed to retreat the full 10 metres following an earlier infringement. Shane Horgan was back at long last, and he soon made his presence felt, when in the 18th minute his superb tackle denied Clement Poitrenaud a certain try. However, Ireland were adjudged offside in that move and Elissalde knocked over a simple penalty. This was not a great start, but Ireland were looking far more committed than in the earlier two games.

Just four minutes later, Elissalde knocked over another penalty to extend the French lead. Ireland, meanwhile, seemed to be relying heavily on Ronan's up-and-unders, but they failed to materialise into anything approaching a try, although he did manage an impressive drop goal from 25 metres out in the 36th minute. The last act of the half saw Elissalde boot his fourth penalty of the night to make it 12–3 to the hosts.

This Ireland side was the best that had taken to the field since the Six Nations, but they still looked a long way from the team that were defeating the Southern Hemisphere giants less than a year ago. They made an encouraging start to the second half with Brian clearly showing that he did not think the game was lost yet, but after 55 minutes Elissalde added another penalty to make it 15–3. The deficit was now looking large, though not unassailable. Yet just two minutes later the French scored their first try of the match when Michalak put through a kick with the outside of his right boot to the right corner and it fell perfectly for Clerc.

Brian's men never looked like recovering from this major setback, and more was to follow when Paul O'Connell was sent to the bin. His absence seemed to deflate Ireland's spirits and France soon scored their second try when Clerc collected Elissalde's chip and forced his way over for a second score in the corner, the Television Match Official confirming the score.

What started out as an evenly matched contest had turned into a battering and Ireland didn't manage to add any further points, the final score being a 25–3 drubbing. After the game, Eddie citied lack of discipline, especially in the first half, as the main reason for the team's defeat. He was the first to admit that there could be no excuses and the better team had won. As for Brian, he had shown commitment and leadership throughout the game but had never been allowed the chance to make a game-changing contribution.

With one group game against Argentina left to play, Ireland had their work cut out. Their opponents had been playing some of the most impressive rugby of the tournament so far, and their brand of well-disciplined, flowing and exciting rugby had led many to believe that they were now serious contenders for the tournament. Few would now argue that Argentina were among the world's leading rugby teams and Ireland would have to give their absolute best to beat the South American giants.

However, Brian knew that, to progress in the tournament, a win alone would not be enough. Their failure to pile on the points against Georgia meant that his side would need to score four tries to progress to the quarter-final stage. Brian obviously knew Felipe Contepomi well from Leinster, and understood fully the mammoth task that lay ahead of him. Yet he also knew that this was an aim worth pursuing. Four years was a long time to wait for another opportunity. By the time the next World Cup came round, it was unlikely he would still be Ireland captain, and age would dictate he would be lucky if he was still playing international rugby at all. Even so, there was no way of knowing how naturally gifted the Ireland squad of four years' time would be. This huge task, although daunting, was also a once-in-a-lifetime opportunity he could not afford to miss.

The match took place at the historic Parc des Princes, which was the home of French rugby for many decades, and, sadly, also the scene of many an Ireland thrashing. It was time to make this a place for Irish rugby fans to remember for the right reasons. Geordan was back in the starting line-up, and there were no major injury worries. This was Brian's big chance to put things right.

The game started promisingly as Ireland controlled possession in the opening 10 minutes, but they failed to make the pressure count and it was Argentina that made the opening breakthrough. After a solid scrum, the ball was worked to winger Lucas Borges who ran over with the Irish defence in a muddle.

Ronan kicked a penalty to bring Ireland back into the game but Argentina replied almost immediately with a drop goal from Juan Martin Hernandez. Despite Ireland being behind, Brian was showing signs of being at his most dangerous, and eight minutes before the break he brushed aside some tame Argentinean tackling to score a memorable try. Ronan added the conversion to give Ireland the lead.

However, it was just four minutes later that Hernandez produced his second drop goal to give Argentina the lead once again. Brian, Ronan and Geordan were having superb games but the Irish defence looked shaky and this allowed Argentina to add their second try through Horacio Agulla just before the break, with Contepomi adding the conversion to give the Pumas an 18–10 lead.

Brian was not giving up yet. He had led by example by scoring that try, and, if by sheer hard work and dedication they could somehow tighten up their defence and score another three in the next 40 minutes, they would be in the quarter-finals. It was a tall order, but not an unassailable one.

Seven minutes after the break, Geordan scored a 47th-minute try after the ball was swung out to the right flank from a line-out. He was having a great game, and was showing just what a class act he was. His absence in Ireland's earlier games was now looking like an extremely poor piece of judgement on Eddie's part, and all those who had voiced astonishment at his absence from the team sheet were proved right. Nobody will ever know what impact Geordan could have made to the team if he had played in those earlier games, but it is not inconceivable that he could have turned the matches in Ireland's favour.

Ireland failed to add to the momentum and two Contepomi penalties and a third Hernandez drop goal sealed Argentina's emphatic victory, 30–15. Despite Ireland not being at their best, it was clear that Argentina were going to have a big role to play in the World Cup.

After the game, Brian was deflated, but dignified in defeat. This was the second time his side had been knocked out of the World Cup by the Pumas. He made it clear to reporters that, in his view, the blame lay squarely with the players, believing that there was only so much coaching that could be done, and ultimately it was up to the 15 men who wore the green jersey on the pitch to deliver the goods.

This was a once-in-a-lifetime opportunity lost forever, and was undoubtedly a bitter pill to swallow for him. In truth, they had probably left too much to do against one of the tournament's best and most exciting teams. They were beaten by the better side, but why were Argentina the better side? It had been less than a year since Ireland were giving master-class performances against the giants of world rugby.

Eddie made it clear that he would not be walking away from the job, but was lost for a valid explanation as to why the team had declined so much in such a short space of time. The only possible explanation from him was that the team had not had enough match practice leading up to the World Cup, yet they played no competitive matches at all in the weeks before the Six Nations, in which they played so well.

Chapter 12

GETTING BACK ON TRACK

Brian had led Ireland through a miserable 2008 Six Nations campaign, in which every match, except the game at home to Scotland, had ended either in defeat or in a narrow and unconvincing victory.

The first match against Italy at Croke Park saw Ireland win 16–11, in which they were effectively saved by a Girvan Dempsey try in the 18th minute.

The 26–21 defeat away at France was less humiliating. Losing to hat-trick of tries from Vincent Clerc was no disgrace, and an Ireland try from David Wallace, along with some sharp kicking from Ronan O'Gara, added some respectability to the scoreline.

The 34–13 victory over Scotland in week three was undoubtedly the highlight of the campaign. David

Wallace scored his second try of the campaign on 22 minutes, and Brian's Leinster colleague, 21-year-old Rob Kearney got his first international touchdown just four minutes later. Marcus Horan got Ireland's third early in the second half, and despite a Scottish consolation try from Simon Webster, Ireland struck back with two more tries from Tommy Bowe in the final quarter of the game.

However, from Brian's perspective, the victory was tainted by the fact he had to be substituted after receiving treatment for a calf injury. Fortunately, he would have a fortnight to recuperate before the trip to Wales, and it proved long enough for him to recover sufficiently for him to lead his side out at the Millennium Stadium.

Wales were on course for their second Grand Slam in four years, and a win against Ireland would give them the Triple Crown. Most people agreed that Wales weren't playing with the same flair and zeal as they were in 2005, and this team looked beatable. In the event, Ireland went down to a 16–12 defeat, thanks largely to a Shane Williams try. All of Ireland's points came from Ronan's boot. Eddie O'Sullivan said afterwards that the match 'went down to the wire', but even he must have known that he was running out of chances by now.

A bigger concern was the fact that Brian had limped off with ten minutes to go. It transpired that he had suffered a hamstring tear, and would not be able to lead his country out in the final match, playing England away. Ronan captained in Brian's absence, and although the match started brightly with a Rob Kearney try after four minutes, Ireland were simply overpowered, as tries from Sackey, Tait and Noon helped England on their way to victory. The real star, however, was 20-year-old Danny Cipriani, who was making his England debut, replacing legend Jonny Wilkinson at fly-half. He kicked seven out of seven in the game, getting his international career off to the best possible start.

Losing three of the five matches, and finishing fourth in the table wasn't good enough for the IRFU. It wasn't good enough for the fans. It certainly wasn't good enough for Brian O'Driscoll, or for the standards he expected from himself and from the team he led. It was clear that the World Cup hangover wasn't cured, and that some kind of changes needed to be made.

Brian had a quiet, disappointing tournament not just by his own standards, but also by the standards the fans had come to expect from him. Allowing for the fact he didn't play against England, he didn't manage to score a try in the tournament and his influence on the matches that he did play hadn't been as great as it had been in previous years.

Just four days after Ireland's loss to England, Eddie O'Sullivan resigned as Ireland coach. He did so with dignity, and with his reputation as the most successful coach in Ireland's history secure. During his seven-year tenure, Ireland had won 50 of his 78 games in charge, including three Triple Crowns. What a difference six months made. Before the World Cup, Eddie had been awarded a four-year deal worth somewhere in the region of £1 million, but the governing body had their backs well covered by the small print in the contract, and Eddie walked away with a performance-linked pay-out in the region of £500,000 following a meeting shortly after the end of the Six Nations campaign.

In hindsight, Eddie probably did the right thing. If he had stayed on, the IRFU would have held a Six Nations review in the near future, and probably forced him to resign. By jumping before he was pushed, he maintained his dignity, and when the dust had settled on the disastrous World Cup and most recent Six Nations campaign, Irish rugby fans would generally look back on his tenure with pride and affection.

For the time being, all Brian could do was get himself back from injury and concentrate on leading Leinster for the remainder of the season. He was now three years into his time as captain, and despite being more than happy with the vision and leadership being shown by coach Michael Cheika, there was no denying his frustration at not having some major silverware to show for the club's efforts. Yes, he had played his part as a youngster in Leinster's victory in the inaugural Celtic League in 2001/02, which culminated in a 24–20 victory over arch rivals Munster in the final, but that was a long time ago now, and more recent memories, such as in

2006 when David Humphreys' extraordinary drop-goal for Ulster against the Ospreys to deny Leinster the title, were more prevalent.

Despite the lack of silverware, there was no doubt that the Leinster brand was growing. At the start of the season, they had made the 18,500 capacity RDS Arena their official home, since Donnybrook Stadium was too small to accommodate all those who wanted to watch the team's matches. From now on, the RDS would be Leinster's official home ground, with Donnybrook only being used for friendly games to maintain a sentimental link with the past.

This year, their Heineken Cup campaign had brought disappointment when they were knocked out in the pool stages in mid-January following a 25–9 defeat against Leicester. Their pool stage campaign hadn't been a complete disaster. They won each of their home fixtures against Leicester, Edinburgh and Toulouse, but they lost each of the reverse away fixtures, and this simply wasn't good enough to progress to the knock-out stages.

All Brian's efforts were now geared towards delivering Leinster the Magners League title. However, injury meant he would play no part in proceedings until the beginning of May. He would watch from the sidelines as the team recorded a 21–12 victory over Munster, thanks largely to Contepomi's boot, to give them their tenth league win in a row.

Brian made his return to the fold when he captained

the team in the following game against Edinburgh, knowing that a bonus point would be enough to give them the title, but he couldn't complete the full 80 minutes and was substituted with 67 on the clock. For a team in such good form, Leinster found it difficult to break down a well-organised Edinburgh side, even though they were without their influential skipper Mike Blair.

Surprisingly, they looked to be out of the game until Luke Fitzgerald's late try, and Contepomi's conversion, brought the scores to 15–13 in Edinburgh's favour. However, there was late drama around the corner when Edinburgh were penalised for handling on the deck in stoppage time. This was it. An easy kick for Contepomi, and they'd win to get the bonus point they needed. Yet it wasn't to be. His effort crashed straight off the wood-work, and the champagne was going to have to be kept on ice for the time being. Leinster fans generally knew they'd have to quickly forgive Contepomi for this embarrassing miss. He'd saved their bacon on plenty of previous occasions, and even in this match he'd kicked two penalties and a conversion, which made this final kick significant in the first place.

More than a fortnight would pass before the next round of Magners League fixtures, so the wait to finally get their hands on the trophy was all the more frustrating. That said, it helped to focus the mind. Perhaps they had taken that last game against Edinburgh for granted, and the defeat had come as a sharp reminder that they couldn't afford to take their foot off the gas until they'd crossed the winning line. The next game, a home fixture at the RDS Arena against the Newport Gwent Dragons, required everyone to be on top of their game, so Michael Cheika and Brian took no chances with their preparations. Surely, this time, Leinster would do it.

Prop Ollie le Roux seemed determined to make the most of his final outing for Leinster and he barged over for his first try in the fourth minute after taking a quick tap penalty following a good period of pressure from his team.

The burly South African did it again five minutes later when he broke through some more feeble Dragons tackling. Leinster had got off to the perfect start, but, as Contepomi's penalty against Edinburgh had shown, they could afford to take nothing for granted.

Sweeney replied with a Dragons penalty two minutes later and there followed a lull in the scoring as a number of over-ambitious Leinster moves broke down.

However, Leinster were back in the groove on 33 minutes when Brian's superb off-load enabled Shane Horgan to score. Contepomi converted, and a penalty shortly afterwards left Leinster 20–3 ahead at the break. Surely they weren't going to let this lead go. Brian took time at the interval to remind his players not to throw away all their hard work now. He needn't have worried.

Leinster cut loose after the break with Contepomi's superb angle setting up Jennings for a simple finish on 44 minutes.

Jamie Heaslip's 60-metre run set up Australian scrum-half Chris Whitaker's close-range finish for Leinster's fifth try and a turnover in their own 22 culminated with Cameron Jowitt notching another touchdown just after the hour.

Keith Gleeson, playing his final home match for Leinster before his retirement, received a rousing farewell from the large home crowd as he was replaced with 12 minutes to go.

The great le Roux was also afforded similar treatment as he departed the field in the final quarter.

Brian was slightly frustrated at only having played a bit-part in Leinster's success in the Magners League throughout the season, and he was understandably eager to make his mark in this historical game. He looked to have scored a classic, individual, characteristic Brian O'Driscoll try, but he failed to get the ball down after charging over the Dragons line.

As Leinster eased off, Adam Black pinched a late try for the Dragons, but Leinster had done enough, and won the game by a resounding 41 points to 8.

The crowd erupted: victory was theirs, as was the Magners League title, which they'd won with a game to spare. Brian's efforts as captain under Michael Cheika's guidance had paid off. The fans had been rewarded for their loyalty and for forgiving the near-misses of recent years. At long last, Brian had a trophy to his name that was worthy of his ability as a player, and of his leadership skills as a captain. This was obviously not a trophy on the scale of the World Cup or the Six Nations, and was not held in the same level of prestige as the Heineken Cup (by far the Northern Hemisphere's biggest prize in club rugby in the modern era), but it was an important piece of silverware nonetheless.

Following the final whistle, Brian couldn't hide his delight at what the team had achieved, saying, telling the post-match interviewer, 'We've been close the last few years but no cigar so we'll go in and smoke a few cigars in the dressing-room now! Ollie [le Roux] was out doing his own thing but thankfully they were two great decisions and he got the tries. This title is a stepping-stone hopefully. Now we want to go out and chase the big one in Europe.'

It was clear that just moments after this victory, his mind was already beginning to focus on bigger and better things. One thing's for sure – this victory made people realise that Leinster had earned their seat at the top table of European club rugby – a place they intended staying.

Within weeks of winning the Magners League title, Brian's life was shaken in a way that put all the ups and downs he had gone through on the rugby field in recent months into perspective. Barry Twomey was Brian's best friend, with whom he shared a house for three years when they were both younger. Brian had described Barry as 'a modern-day Del Boy'. He was a popular young socialite, known for his cheery manner and sense of humour. Wherever he was seen in public, he was the life and soul of the party.

He was from a well-known Dublin business family who owned a large shop in Deansgrange, and his father was also a director of Ely wine bars. Barry had many friends who were sports stars and models, and was one of those characters it was impossible not to like. In 2005 he had set up the social magazine 'Bash' with Brian's friend and colleague Shane Horgan, aimed at 18 to 29-year-olds. A large section of the free magazine featured photographs of people out partying in the capital. It later ceased publication.

On the evening of Tuesday 27 May, Brian had been due to lead Ireland in an international friendly match against Barbarians at Kingsholm in Gloucester, but pulled out when he received the devastating news that Barry had been found dead in the isolated woodlands of Enniskerry, and there were no suspicious circumstances. It quickly became clear that Barry had taken his own life.

The news came as a massive shock to everybody, but it affected Brian more than most.

Less than 48 hours earlier, the 29-year-old had been walking around the VIP section of Krystle nightclub in Dublin, smiling brightly and greeting friends with big bear hugs. Brian had every reason to believe that Barry was happy and enjoying life. Just nine weeks earlier, he proposed to his girlfriend Barbara Matthews, and had been talking with great optimism about the future. It was around this time that Brian and Barry were seen out together in public for the last time, celebrating the engagement at the very same Krystle nightclub. Brian was even rumoured to have been named Barry's best man for the wedding.

On the Thursday evening, Barry's uncle, the respected theologian Fr Vincent Twomey, said during the removal service that his nephew was a 'bundle of joy' and went on to say, 'What Barry did caused devastation. He didn't foresee the devastation, he didn't want it – it was the opposite. Nor should he be blamed for it, and nor should we blame ourselves or think what could we have done.'

Barry's funeral service took place at Church of our Lady of Perpetual Succour in Foxrock, Dublin. Brian turned up with a rugby ball to symbolise his friend's love of the game. Indeed, he had been an accomplished player in his own right. At the service, Brian paid a moving tribute to his dear friend, before breaking down in tears. He described their relationship as being similar to that of an 'old married couple'. He talked of how, during their three years sharing a house together, he would come home at the end of the day and shout, 'Hi honey, I'm home.' Brian said, 'We'd speak three, four, maybe five times a day, often with the last conversation beginning or ending with: So hun, what's for dinner?'

Brian then admitted that he was struggling to get his head around what had happened, saying, 'In a situation like this it's hard to make sense of anything. The one thing for absolute certain: Barry loved his family, he loved his friends, and he deeply loved his Barbara.'

This was undoubtedly one of the lowest points of Brian's life. He had been incredibly close to Barry for a long time, and although they were no longer living together, they still spoke on a regular basis and remained best friends. In the years since, Brian has supported Barry's parents at suicide awareness events, but he has always been reluctant to talk about what is essentially private grief. One thing was clear: whatever success Brian was to enjoy on the pitch for the remainder of his career, things would never be quite the same again.

Chapter 13

GRAND SLAM GLORY

Despite having ended the 2007/08 season with domestic glory with Leinster, there were plenty of people echoing concerns about Brian's long-term future. At twenty-nine, injuries had taken their toll, he seemed to have lost a yard of pace, and there seemed little prospect of a return to the sort of form he showed during the back-to-back Triple Crowns of 2006 and 2007.

Disappointment and frustration are two things every sportsman has to cope with at one time or another, but Brian has had more than his fair share of setbacks in his career. The biggest disappointment of all came in 2005. He was bestowed one of the greatest honours in rugby when he was awarded the captaincy of the Lions squad for the tour of New Zealand. It was a role that would be cut all too short for Brian as his tour lasted barely a minute in a storm of acrimony and agony, his shoulder dislocated after a dangerous spear tackle by Tana Umanga and Keven Mealamu.

At the end of the 2008 Six Nations, it was entirely possible that Brian's international career was winding down. If this had been the end, his epitaph would have written about a man who epitomises everything the ideal professional rugby player in the modern era should be. His uncompromising and committed approach to the game and his lifestyle away from the pitch ticked all the right boxes. However, his outstanding ability and strong leadership were not matched by the amount of silverware a player of his calibre deserved.

In the summer of 2008 the outlook did not look good. He had gone through a disappointing Six Nations campaign by his exceptionally high standards, and had missed most of final few months of Leinster's Magners League campaign through injury.

Just days after Barry's funeral, Brian travelled with Ireland as they embarked on a short early-summer tour of New Zealand and Australia. The team was being managed in this interim period by Connacht's director of rugby, Michael Bradley, now the head coach of Edinburgh.

Brian and the rest of the Ireland team had genuine hopes of ending their 103-year wait for a win against the All Blacks as they took to the pitch at the Westpac

Stadium in Wellington under a backdrop of freezing conditions and heavy rain.

New Zealand opened the scoring on 14 minutes with a try when Conrad Smith superbly wrong-footed Brian, before charging through the gap and firing the ball out to Sitiveni Sivivatu. Paddy Wallace put Ireland ahead after 20 minutes, and the sides went into the break level at 8–8.

A series of silly errors and poor discipline cost Ireland in the second half, and Ma Nonu's try on 61 minutes put his side comfortably clear, and New Zealand went on to win 21–11.

The following Saturday's match against Australia at the Telstra Dome in Melbourne was an entirely different encounter. Berrick Barnes put the Wallabies ahead after six minutes, but Denis Leamy scored one of his own on 15 minutes, and a conversion from Ronan put Ireland ahead. James Horwill touched down after 21 minutes, with Matt Giteau converting and then adding a penalty to give Australia a 15–7 lead at half time.

The second half began poorly when Giteau extended Australia's lead with a penalty on 42 minutes. Michael Bradley tried to freshen up the side soon after by bringing on Jerry Flannery and Eoin Reddan for Rory Best and Peter Stringer.

Brian brilliantly intercepted an Australian pass on 55 minutes, but his attempted pass to Paddy Wallace went astray and the chance was lost.

With 62 minutes gone, Tommy Bowe collected an offload from Rob Kearney, broke clear and then passed to Brian who crossed the line to reduce his side's arrears to six points.

Brian had to leave the field with an injury soon after, with Geordan Murphy taking his place, and despite periods of pressure from both sides, the scoreline remained unchanged, with Australia winning 18–12.

This was a spirited display from Ireland, and Brian could take some satisfaction with the way he and his team had played. Whoever became the new coach would have to change certain aspects of Ireland's game, yet despite the defeat against Australia, being able to beat the big southern hemisphere sides in their own backyard didn't seem too far off the radar.

In July, Declan Kidney was appointed coach of the Ireland side. Brian and Declan had previously worked together at Leinster during the 2004/05 season, and their working relationship had often been difficult. Brian had been frustrated by the lack of progress in his game during Declan's tenure, and he wasn't happy with the manner in which he left for arch-rivals Munster at the end of that season, or the fact that he had released several prominent players from the club.

The early signs when Declan took over at Ireland weren't good. He initially refused to reappoint Brian as captain for the autumn internationals, instead preferring to see how things panned out at the start of the domestic season. At the time, there were serious question marks as to how well the two men could work together following their previous, well-publicised difficulties. In August, Brian decided to step down as Leinster captain.

Although his exact reasons were not specified, there was a certain logic to his decision. His own personal form had taken a slight dip in the last 12 months, and it would give him the opportunity to focus on himself during the early months of the new season.

There was also a strong argument for giving the Leinster captaincy to somebody who would be a more full-time presence at the club, to help them take the next step forward following their Magners League success. Brian would inevitably be away with Ireland for the autumn Tests and the Six Nations campaign, meaning there would be a disruption in continuity with regards to the Leinster captaincy through no fault of his own. On that basis, it was decided to award the captaincy to the experienced lock Leo Cullen, who had represented Ireland, but had not featured in the side during the most recent Six Nations campaign. Although he would eventually make a successful return to the international fold, for the time being he could focus on taking Leinster on to the next level.

A number of rugby pundits read too much into this development. There were those that took this as a sign that Brian was looking to relinquish national armband as well. Nothing could have been further from the truth, but the decision was ultimately Declan's, and at that moment in time, nobody really knew whether the two men would be able to put past differences behind them.

Having been relieved of the Leinster captaincy, Brian's return to form at the start of the season was spectacular. It was as if the injuries that had slowed him down over the past twelve months had never happened. He was fitter, stronger and faster than he had been for quite some time, and had the added bonus of being a more experienced player. With all these factors combined, Brian was now playing better than ever.

In mid-October, Declan decided to offer the captaincy to Brian after all. He could have chosen one of two men he knew well from his time at Munster in Paul O'Connell and Ronan O'Gara, but Brian's return to form had persuaded Declan that he was still the most capable member of the squad to lead the team. This was a chance for both men to make a fresh start, and to move forward together in the best interests of Irish rugby.

The autumn internationals were a mixed bag for Ireland at Croke Park. Following a 55–0 thumping of Canada, they failed to compete against an extremely strong All Blacks side, losing 22–3. Respectability, as well as Ireland's competitive reputation was restored in the final match of the series against Argentina, thanks largely to some superb kicking from the boot of Ronan O'Gara, securing the team's place among the second tier of seeds for the 2011 World Cup in the process.

There was a considerable change of emphasis in the way Ireland played their rugby under Declan. Under his predecessor Eddie O'Sullivan, the team aspired to play a high-risk, offloading game. Declan's way was markedly different; Ireland now played in a manner similar to the Munster way of soaking up pressure, kicking penalties and striking at a critical moment. Ireland under the new coach played pragmatic rather than progressive rugby. Declan's key principles were for the team to be solid at the set-pieces, strong in defence, disciplined and organised. This approach appeared to bring out the best in Brian and was more suited to his game.

Brian's return to form meant that 2009 was likely to be the most important year of his career. At the start of the year, Leinster were making good progress in the European Cup and the Magners League. On the international front, there was a Lions tour to South Africa in the summer, where Brian could be given the chance to lay the ghosts of 2005 to rest once and for all.

First, though, came the challenge of captaining Ireland in the Six Nations. The expectations of the Irish public were higher now than they had been for some time. Most were prepared to write off 2008 as a blip, following the Triple Crowns of 2006 and 2007. The consensus was that this year, Ireland could go one better and actually win the Championship.

The high expectations were well-founded. The Ireland team was well-balanced and had re-discovered their confidence following the disappointing final six months of Eddie O'Sullivan's time as coach. Their opponents in the tournament all looked beatable. The Wales side that had won the Grand Slam in 2008 were strong, but not without frailties. England, under Martin Johnson, went into the tournament after a disastrous autumn international series that had seen them suffer heavy defeats against all of the big three Southern Hemisphere teams. The consensus was that England had over-achieved in reaching the final of the 2007 World Cup, but in the twelve months since they had gone backwards and it seemed unlikely that early 2009 would produce a sudden return to form. France were in better shape than a year ago, but were terribly inconsistent, while Scotland were playing better than for many years under Frank Hadden. All of Ireland's opponents had weaknesses, and, on paper at least, they looked more than a match for any of them. Brian went into the Championship genuinely believing this was the best Ireland team he had been a part of.

Ireland's first opponents were France. With no wins against the French in eight attempts, they had been Ireland's bogey team in recent years, and had been the side that had stopped them winning the tournament in the otherwise successful campaigns of 2006 and 2007.

The 80,000-plus crowd at Croke Park gave Brian's men the best possible welcome as they took to the field, for what many pundits already considered a title-deciding match.

Strong early running yielded a penalty for Ronan and Ireland were also able to take comfort in their early defence with Sebastien Chabal flattened by swarms of tacklers. But France's game plan was clear; they were determined to run at the Irish defence and the home side were spared in the seventh minute when Thierry Dusautoir knocked on just short of the line.

France got their reward as another typically sweeping move was finished off by the recalled Harinordoquy in the fourteenth minute, although there was a possibility of a forward pass by Julien Malzieu. The conversion duly followed, but a penalty kick from Ronan straight after the re-start narrowed the gap to just one point.

France seemed in control of the game, leaving Brian's men living off scraps. The Croke Park faithful could be forgiven for thinking this game was turning into a repeat of previous encounters between the two teams in recent years.

The game suddenly changed on thirty-four minutes as Bowe's break put the French defence on the backfoot.

Paul O'Connell's quick pass kept the move going and the impressive Jamie Heaslip weaved his way past two challenges to charge over the French line. A conversion from Ronan followed to extend the home side's unexpected lead to 13–7.

France maintained their dominance of play a minute later when a typical Chabal charge kept the Irish defence on their toes. On the stroke of half-time, Lionel Beauxis struck a drop-goal which cut the Irish lead to three points. The second half would be a very different story.

The first score after the interval went to Brian, who brushed past Beauxis' poor tackle to score the kind of try which had been missing from his armoury in recent times. Most people had thought that he no longer had the pace to play like this any longer, although he had been threatening to do something like this all season. Ronan's conversion extended the lead to 20–10.

Ireland lost the momentum as France hit back when Harinordoquy pounced on some scrappy Irish play to set up an attack finished off by Medard's try. Beauxis missed the subsequent conversion but soon made up for it with his second drop goal of the day, to cut Ireland's lead to just two points.

Ireland seemed in serious danger of throwing it all away at the vital moment, but they re-grouped thanks to a forwards drive that saw the home side move deep into French territory. The attack was finished off by replacement Gordon D'Arcy sniping his way over the line, celebrating his return to international rugby in style. Gordon, a Leinster team mate and close friend of Brian's, had been out of rugby for nearly a year after fracturing his arm in Ireland's opening match of the 2008 Six Nations against Italy. His return saw him and Brian re-create one of the most successful centre partnerships. The crowd were delighted with his try not only because it extended their team's lead, but also because Gordon is hugely popular public figure in Ireland known for his affable personality and generosity.

Ronan's conversion extended Ireland's lead to 27–18 but there was only a score between the teams when Beauxis landed a penalty four minutes from time. Memories of Vincent Clerc's late try two years earlier loomed large for Irish fans but O'Gara's immediate penalty eased home nerves.

Ireland had done it, winning 30–21. At last, they had held on to beat France, despite some scary moments and some sloppy play, especially in the first half. The fans were left with plenty to celebrate, but Brian warned against euphoria. He had been around long enough to know that you cannot win the Six Nations in your first game, but you can lose it. This was not a time for the Ireland team to get ahead of themselves.

A lot had been written about Brian, about him being the captain, and about his future with the team. On this day, he had answered his critics by playing a huge part in a massively important win. However, it was only one game, and Brian knew that they could only afford to enjoy the win for a few hours before knuckling down the following day to prepare for the next match against Italy.

Trips to the Stadio Flaminio in Rome were becoming notoriously tricky. Italy were gradually strengthening as rugby became an established sport in the country, and had made real progress under coach Nick Mallett. They now needed to be treated with a great deal of respect, and no-one knew, better than Brian that victory here couldn't be taken for granted.

Ireland looked unsettled early on and gave away two penalties which fly-half Luke Mclean landed for a 6–0 lead.

But after that sloppy start, tries from Tommy Bowe and Luke Fitzgerald saw the Irish assume control by half-time.

The visitors added a third try when flanker David Wallace got over early in the second half. In the last five minutes, Ireland got two more tries to give the final result a one-sided look. Fitzgerald's nice exchange with Leinster team-mate Gordon D'Arcy gave the winger his second try. Then skipper Brian ran away for an intercept try – his nineteenth in the Six Nations and thirty-fourth for Ireland overall.

Italy had put in a spirited and courageous performance, and the scoreline was if anything a little flattering. Brian left Rome knowing there were a number of positives he could take from the game, but with a home match against England up next, his team would have to up their performance. England had lost to Wales the previous day, and would come to Croke Park wanting to exact revenge for the 43–13 drubbing they took on their previous visit to the ground.

With Wales having lost to France the night before in Paris, Ireland went into the home game against England as the only team still able to win the Grand Slam, which would be their first in sixty-one years. For now, Brian wasn't thinking about that. At this moment in time, all that mattered was beating England.

On the eve of the match, a press conference was held that resulted in one of the most bizarre moments in Brian's career to date. He was asked what it was like to have played with the England coach, Martin Johnson, during their time together with the British and Irish Lions, and now to be on opposing sides. His reply has become legendary: Knowledge is knowing that a tomato is a fruit; wisdom is knowing not to put it in a fruit salad.'

Brian could normally be relied upon to stay on message, play by the rules, and generally behave like a safe pair of hands in his dealings with the media, to the point of being a little too predictable for some people's tastes. This response was not what people were used to. It was quirky, profound, and humorous. Putting it into context was far harder. Comparisons were made to Eric Cantona's press conference in 1995 when he said, 'When the seagulls follow the trawler, it is because they think sardines will be thrown into the sea.'

Yet upon closer examination, Cantona's observation made perfect sense: he was referring to his own relationship with the press – they were following him around intensely, because they knew it was likely that he would give them a story. On the other hand, Brian's quote lacked context.

In fact, Brian's quote can be traced back to the late

journalist, musician and broadcaster Miles Kington, who used it (with a very slight variation) as his response when asked 'what is wisdom?' Assuming Brian is a fan of Kington's, we may yet be treated to more of his quotes in future press conferences, such as 'An upside-down wheelbarrow is no good to anyone, but at least it is dry on the inside', 'You cannot make an omelette without breaking a bird's heart' and 'There is no such thing as bodybuilding. Your body is already there. The most you can do with it is put on an extension, lag it, or add another small eating area'. Satirically, Kington claimed they were all Albanian proverbs. Truthfully, he made them all up himself.

This episode, which has gone down in Irish rugby folklore, provided a temporary, amusing distraction to the task which lay ahead. It also gave fans and journalists a rare glimpse of Brian's sense of humour. He is more than aware that jokes can be misinterpreted or taken out of context all too easily, but on this occasion he decided to give reporters something different to talk about. Long afterwards, he admitted he'd done it for a bet. Yet this didn't detract from the fact there was serious business ahead.

The match got off to a nervous, scrappy start, with plenty of unattractive play that saw possession repeatedly being kicked away. Ronan seemed in poor form with the boot, missing his opening two penalty chances before succeeding with his third in the twenty-ninth minute. England levelled the scores just before half time thanks to Toby Flood.

The second half started off as scrappily as the first when Ronan missed another penalty opportunity. It was left to Brian to lead by example and a superbly-taken drop goal restored his side's slender advantage.

There was momentary concern for Brian after a nasty-looking clash of heads with Riki Flutey. After treatment, he was able to continue, but was soon flattened again by a late body check by Delon Armitage who escaped a yellow card.

None of these setbacks knocked Brian's confidence, and he began to mount some pressure on the English line by ordering his team to decline penalty goal opportunities in favour of lineout ball, and this wasn't in any way due to Ronan's poor form on the day.

With such sustained pressure, it was only a matter of time before someone crossed the line. In the end it was Brian who got it when he powered over in the fifty-seventh minute.

England reduced the deficit to just five points when Armitage assumed the kicking duties to land a well-struck penalty. Indiscipline had been a major feature in England's game during their opening two matches, and this continued at Croke Park when Care was given a yellow card after shoulder-charging Marcus Horan. Ronan rediscovered his form to add three points from the subsequent penalty to extend Ireland's lead to eight points.

The game took another late twist when England replacement Goode kicked the ball through for an Armitage try. Goode's conversion cut Ireland's lead to just one point, but England ran out of time to mount another meaningful attack, and the Millennium Trophy was returning to Irish hands. Ireland had a famous and hard-earned victory under their belts, and Brian was awarded man of the match, which he richly deserved not only for his performance with the ball, scoring eight of Ireland's fourteen points, but also for the way in which he captained his side in the second half, taking positive decisions which piled on the pressure for the English defence.

Afterwards, Brian expressed his relief at the way his side managed to hang on for a one-point victory. He had played against England enough times to know that they were always a hard team to beat. It wasn't always pretty, and this wasn't a day for fancy rugby. It was a case of 'job done', and another important step towards the Grand Slam had been taken. Even now, it was a time for moving one step at time and not thinking too far ahead. Brian and the team allowed themselves to enjoy the celebrations in Dublin that night, but it would soon be time to knuckle down and prepare for the trip to Edinburgh in two weeks' time.

Scotland had suffered heavy defeats to Wales and France in their opening two matches, before inflicting a 26–6 victory over Italy in their most recent match.

However, one factor that had been present in all three matches to date had been their ability to score tries, and this was a threat Brian and his men had to take seriously.

The Scots led 12–9 at half-time as Chris Paterson traded penalties with Ronan, who became the leading Six Nations points scorer in the process, with 481, overtaking Jonny Wilkinson with 479.

After the break, Ireland raised their game and upped the intensity. As the second half progressed, their superior fitness began to show. Replacement Jamie Heaslip's try turned the match and gave Ireland the lead for the first time. Ronan's conversion, a drop-goal and another penalty were enough to give Ireland a 22–15 victory, winning their eighth consecutive Centenary Quaich in the process. Brian's main contribution to the game had been to tackle Scotland fly-half Phil Godman just a few metres short of the Irish line to deny the home side a vital try.

Following this round of matches, the calculations were clear. Obviously, an Ireland win against Wales in Cardiff the following weekend would give them their first Grand Slam in sixty-one years. Wales couldn't retain the Grand Slam they won in 2008 after losing their game against France in the third round of matches, but if they beat Ireland by thirteen points, they would retain the Championship. A Welsh victory of less than thirteen points would still give them the Triple Crown, and put a huge dampener on Ireland's Championship victory celebrations.

Brian was adamant that Ireland should not change their preparations for the final, vital game against Wales, despite the enormous weight of expectation that would be on his shoulders over the following week. He knew he could expect a tough, physical encounter, and didn't allow himself to be drawn into a false sense of security by the fact that Wales under-performed in their five-point victory over Italy in their last match.

The week that followed was like none other Irish sport had ever seen. Momentum built up on a daily basis before reaching a crescendo on the Saturday of the match itself. It gave the Irish public a welcome break from the very real problems they faced in their daily lives as the country was in the deepest recession in living memory.

The game made the front pages on more than one occasion that week. It was being talked about in every bar, every office, on every bus and on every train. TV news bulletins put the nightly build-up high in the pecking order. It seemed that wherever you went in Ireland, you could not get away from the game. However, for Brian, the priority was to keep things as normal as possible. Whatever hype surrounded it, this was after all a game of rugby, and it had to be approached and prepared for in exactly the same way as it normally would.

Brian kept a largely low profile during the week, except for one interview when he fired a warning shot in Wales's direction. He stated that he thought it likely that the best was yet to come. They had shown glimpses of what they were capable of, and now it was about trying to put it together for the full eighty minutes.

A lot of people said a lot of things in the media that week, but one man's comment stood out above all others. The Wales coach, Warren Gatland, had said that out of all the teams in the Six Nations, the Welsh players dislike Ireland the most.

His comments only served to spur on the Ireland team, including Brian, making them even more determined to do their talking on the pitch and hit Warren and his team where it hurt.

Nobody knows for sure what motivated Warren to say this. Certainly, the manner in which he was sacked as coach of Ireland early on in Brian's international career in 2001 had been controversial. The comments had left many Welsh fans feeling angry and embarrassed. The two sets of supporters had always enjoyed a warm relationship and had treated one another as Celtic brothers. Warren could in no way claim to be speaking for them. Apart from a few isolated incidents, the matches between the two teams had always been played in a competitive spirit of mutual and healthy respect for one another. Many of the players knew their opponents very well, having faced each other on a regular basis in the Magners League.

There was also the added dimension of the upcoming Lions tour. Most people expected Warren to be named as Head Coach, and there would inevitably be a large number of Welsh and Irish players taking part. If what he was saying was true, how on earth could they be expected to work together? And could Warren command the respect of the Irish members of the squad after speaking about them in such a way? There was talk that Brian would be given another crack at the Lions captaincy. How would he feel working for a man who made such a comment?

The situation was perhaps best summed up by Lawrence Dallaglio, who was Warren's captain when he was coach at Wasps. Lawrence said that the Wales players wouldn't thank him for the remarks, and it was they, not he, who would bear the brunt of it, because they were the ones who had to face the Irish team on the pitch. Few would argue that his comments were crass and inappropriate, but it only served to give Brian and his men an extra incentive to win at the Millennium Stadium.

Some 20,000 Irish fans made their way to Cardiff for the title decider, and the streets of Dublin and Cork emptied as people gathered around television screens hoping to witness what would arguably be the greatest day in Irish sporting history.

Early in the game, Donncha O'Callaghan objected to Ryan Jones's actions and a minor tussle between the players earned an early warning from the referee, but Ronan failed with the long-range penalty attempt.

Ireland had the better of first half possession as the Welsh defence and line-out allowed errors to creep into their game. Mark Jones's tackle on Brian forced him to knock-on in a passage of play that led the referee to warn both captains about off-the-ball incidents. For the majority of the first half, Ireland were happy to kick for touch in the belief they could successfully attack Wales's line-out.

This worked well until the thirty-third minute when Lee Byrne departed with an ankle injury, and Gavin Henson switched to full-back to accommodate Jamie Roberts. Denis Leamy held on too long in a tackle on Martyn Williams at the back of a line-out and Stephen Jones kicked the subsequent penalty. Another penalty from a line-out gave Jones the chance to make it 6–0 to the home team at half time. Thus far, the match had been every bit as tense and as nerve-wracking as the occasion merited.

In the dressing room, Declan told his players that they were still in it, but they hadn't converted their pressure into points. They returned to the field with all guns blazing.

Ireland began the second half with a Bowe burst down the right from Brian's pass and a cross-kick from Ronan that Mark Jones made safe, but failed to mark before he stepped into touch. That gave the Irish forwards the territory they craved and after a series of close-quarter drives, Brian's good leg strength and body angle was enough for him to cross the line and score a try that would change the course of the game.

Two minutes later Bowe claimed Ronan's chip and raced away from the pursuing Shane Williams to score under the posts. Ronan converted both tries for a 14–6 lead, but Wales were far from out of it. The thirteen point victory needed to win the Championship might have been out of reach for the home side, but they certainly remained determined to spoil Ireland's party.

Stephen Jones hit back with a penalty after O'Callaghan pushed Mike Phillips after the scrum-half knocked on.

Brian made another huge contribution to Ireland's cause when he tackled Tom Shanklin to thwart a dangerous Wales attack.

Declan brought on Peter Stringer at scrum-half for O'Leary for the final ten minutes. And that is when the drama really began to unfold.

Wales's strike runners really made their presence felt for the first time in the game. Wing Williams slipped to end one attack, but after Phillips's thunderous charge through the Welsh defence, Jones dropped the goal that put his side back into the lead.

Ronan hit back three minutes later with a drop goal of his own to give his team a slender, two-point lead going into the final tense moments of the game.

Then, after sixty-one years of waiting, it came down to the last two seconds of the match. Jones had a penalty kick for Wales from just two metres inside the Ireland half. The Irish fans inside the Millennium Stadium, and all those back home held their breath. Many were unable to look at all. Could Stephen Jones, one of the world's greatest kickers, ruin Ireland's dreams with the very last kick of the tournament?

From the moment the ball left Jones' boot, it was in the air for only a matter of seconds, but for many Irish fans it felt like an eternity. It was high, it was long, but, ultimately, it was two metres short. Ireland had done it; after sixty-one years, they were Grand Slam Champions.

After everything he'd been through, after all the oh-so-nearlys, and after all the injuries that happened at the worst possible time, Brian finally had an achievement to his name that matched his outstanding talent as a rugby player and team leader. Unsurprisingly, he was awarded the man of the match once again.

In the post-match interview, he was typically humble and dignified, paying tribute to Declan's work as coach and Ronan's courage with the boot. Back home, an almighty party was well underway that would go on well into the early hours. This was a day that Irish rugby fans had waited their whole lives for, and it was now time to make the most of it.

Brian and the team returned from Cardiff on the following afternoon to a ticker-tape reception in front of tens of thousands of fans in the capital. It was billed as the 'Grand Slam Homecoming', and fans at the very front had queued for almost three hours before the players took to the hastily arranged stage at Mansion House on Dawson Street. By the time the players arrived, there were tens of thousands of people cheering on their new national heroes.

The players looked slightly embarrassed standing

there in their civvies, as Irish sports broadcaster Des Cahill pushed a microphone under their chins. They were understandably awkward with nothing to tackle but a few anecdotes and, they admitted later, just a bit overwhelmed by the whole occasion. Paddy Wallace, who conceded the penalty that allowed Stephen Jones the chance to steal the game in the dying seconds, joked that he would have shot himself had it gone over. Asked why he conceded the penalty in the first place, he joked that he felt the game just lacked a bit of excitement. Twenty-four hours later, the Irish public could laugh, just about. Ronan freely admitted that he'd have killed Paddy if Jones had succeeded with his kick.

Then came Brian's turn to speak, and he paid a heartfelt tribute to the fans who had given the team their wholesome support during this long and arduous journey, and heaped praise on his teammates and Declan Kidney. Their previous difficulties in working together now felt like a million years ago – they had worked together in the best interests of Irish rugby and it had paid off with this incredible achievement. Declan was a private man who didn't enjoy the limelight very much, but he had quietly and diligently built up a team that had finally made its presence felt at the top table of world rugby. The public event was followed by a civic reception held by Taoiseach Brian Cowen inside Mansion House.

At long last, Brian O'Driscoll's years of hard work had

paid off, and he had earned his place in history as the man who captained the Irish rugby team to its greatest ever achievement.

Chapter 14

SUCCESS IN EUROPE

The Grand Slam victory undeniably raised Brian's status, both as a rugby professional and as a celebrity in his native Ireland. This private man, who takes little interest in mixing in celebrity circles and drawing attention to himself for its own sake, had to face up to the reality that media interest in all aspects of his life would, from now on, become far more intense. Going out partying in Dublin, without attracting unwanted attention would now be far harder than before. His success on the field had made him into a superstar well beyond the level normally enjoyed by successful rugby players.

His private life continued to be stable and happy. His girlfriend, Amy Huberman, who he had now been with for two years, was a successful, down-to-earth girl who had seen her acting career develop to include a role in the BBC drama Inspector George Gently, among other things.

Around this time, she was putting the finishing touches to her first novel Hello, Heartbreak, which was published later that summer and went on to be a number one bestseller in Ireland. The Irish Daily Mail described it as 'A funny romantic comedy – a bit like Bridget Jones on Viagra'. It's primarily aimed at a younger, female audience, but Amy knew her market well. She had shown herself to be an engaging, funny writer and it seems likely there will be further novels from her in the years ahead.

Brian was now in no doubt that Amy was the girl for him, and that he wanted to spend the rest of his life with her. The weekend after the Grand Slam victory, and the day after Amy's 30th birthday party, Brian popped the question by reportedly spelling out 'Will you marry me?' in flowers in their back garden. She texted her pals to thank them for her 30th birthday party the previous night and the 'continued celebrations because we've just got engaged'.

The news came as little surprise to their tight-knit circle of friends. They had always seemed very good together and were similar characters in many respects: successful at their careers, determined, focussed, yet private and loyal to their families and the people closest to them.

Amy is a very level-headed person – down-to-earth, intelligent and able to handle the inevitable press interest in her life. In an interview with Sunday Independent shortly before her book launch, Amy explained, 'When I see myself and Brian's world it is our little world. Other people's opinion on it, and the papers' stuff, is so unimportant. There are little layers and that is like the peripheral. Sometimes that doesn't even come into it.... Our world is our friends and our family and we can handle it. Brian is very protective of me. I think at the beginning he was kind of going: "I'm so sorry for the photographers and everything" which wasn't, of course, his fault.'

She also admitted that she didn't know who he was when they first met, nor did she know anything at all about rugby. She said, 'I had been living in London for two years and I was all in the world of the arts and I was like, "Oh that's what he does. Good for him." Brian is so chilled, so relaxed. He can read people so well. It kind of took off for us when we met. He is incredibly funny. Very low-key. Very chilled. Rational. When I met him, of course I believed the stereotypes of these rugby players and he is just this incredibly low-key guy – not a shouty, screamy, look-at-me person. He is humorous and very smart.'

The news of their engagement reached the press very quickly, but the happy couple were, as usual, keen to keep their privacy and not give too much away. No concrete plans had yet been set for the date and venue of the wedding, but even so, they were keen to keep gossip surrounding it to a minimum. On the Sunday, Brian made an appearance at the RDS to watch Leinster trounce Ulster. Brian was characteristically shy in giving too many details away, but, sporting a Leinster hoodie and a pair of glasses, simply smiled and told reporters, 'I'm delighted, I'm delighted.'

Back on the field, some poor results in April had pretty much seen Leinster's Magners League campaign crash and burn, and the title went to the old enemy Munster, who had been superb in the league all season and won it by some distance. The Heineken Cup was a different story, and Leinster's quarter-final encounter away at Harlequins would go down in rugby folklore for all the wrong reasons.

In the match itself, two Felipe Contepomi penalties gave Leinster a 6–0 interval lead, but full-back Mike Brown's try with 14 minutes remaining finally breached the superb Leinster defence, only for Chris Malone to miss the conversion to hand Brian's men a 6–5 victory.

However, this match wouldn't be remembered as a thrilling, tight match, which, in truth, Harlequins largely dominated, but struggled to get through the Leinster defence. Instead, it will be remembered for an incident that happened with eight minutes remaining, when Harlequins wing Tom Williams came off with a 'blood injury', to be replaced by the already-injured Nick Evans, who was clearly limping due to thigh problems.

It transpired that the 'blood' from Williams' injury was, in fact, from a capsule. Obviously, what looked like a blood injury meant he had to go off, but it allowed director of rugby Dean Richards to bring Evans back on as a tactical substitution. Club doctor Wendy Chapman subsequently cut Williams' lip to make the injury look real.

Harlequins were soon found out, and in the investigation that followed, the ERC and the RFU revealed that blood injuries had also been faked by Harlequins to enable tactical substitutions on four previous occasions. These findings resulted in a twelve month ban for Tom Williams – reduced to four months on appeal, a three year ban for director of rugby Dean Richards, and a two year ban for physiotherapist Steph Brennan as well as a £260,000 fine for the club. The club chairman, Charles Jillings subsequently tendered his resignation, while the club doctor Wendy Chapman was suspended by the General Medical Council for cutting Williams's lip. Richards subsequently admitted he had orchestrated the incident. The IRB confirmed they would apply his ban to rugby worldwide.

This disgraceful episode, humorously-named 'Bloodgate', was one of the biggest scandals to occur in rugby since professionalization in the mid-1990s. This soured what should have been remembered as a famous win for Leinster, to set up a potentially thrilling semi-final encounter with Munster. The match should have gone down in history as one where Leinster's defence kept Harlequins at bay for most of the match, but unfortunately events entirely out of Brian and Leinster's control meant the match was to be remembered for altogether less happy reasons.

Munster went into the semi-final encounter as reigning Heineken Cup champions and having already won the current season's Magners League title, therefore they were inevitably heavy favourites to beat Leinster. On top of that, Munster had already beaten Leinster twice during the season.

Days before the match, the Lions squad for the summer's tour to South Africa was announced. There was some speculation that Brian may be allowed a second chance to captain a Lions tour, but coach Ian McGeechan ultimately decided to award the honour to Brian's Ireland teammate Paul O'Connell. Brian was not unduly disappointed by Ian's decision – it would give him the opportunity to focus on his own game and establish himself as a Lions legend in what would very likely be his last Lions tour.

The semi-final against Munster was, without doubt, Leinster's most important club match in living memory, arguably of all time. Fittingly, it was played at Croke Park in front of a crowd of 82,208, a world record for a club game. All matches against Munster were important, but the magnitude of this game made gave it that extra edge.

Few people gave Leinster a serious chance, and Brian knew it was up to them to prove the pundits wrong.

The contest started at a ferocious pace, and Leinster had the first chance to put points on the board, but Felipe Contepomi missed a penalty and the unpredictable Argentine endured a nervy few moments as a woeful pass in midfield put his defence under pressure with Brian's attempted clearance being charged down.

Unsurprisingly for the occasion, tempers then flared after Gordon D'Arcy slapped out at Keith Earls, who earlier in the week had pipped the Leinster and Ireland centre for a place in the Lions squad.

However, Earls reacted in the best possible fashion by producing a stunning break into the Leinster 22 after a slip pass by Lefeimi Mafi and only a massive hit by Australian flanker Rocky Elsom on Ian Dowling averted the danger.

Contepomi regained his composure to stroke over one of his trademark drop-goals in the 16th minute but Ronan O'Gara levelled two minutes later after Cian Healy's silly sin-binning for a late tackle on Dowling.

Elsom was leading Leinster's charge and his break had the Munster defence backpedalling furiously in the 25th minute.

Soon afterwards, Leinster suffered a massive blow when Contepomi was forced to depart after appearing to twist his knee on the seemingly-immaculate Croke Park turf. Jonathan Sexton was the replacement and his first action was to coolly knock over a penalty to restore his side's lead.

Any suggestion that Leinster were going to be streamrolled as they were in the 2006 semi-final was ended when Gordon D'Arcy slid over for a tremendous try in the 31st minute after Fijian star Isa Nacewa's burst into space in midfield. Sexton missed the conversion but Leinster were 11–3 up and seemed in control of the match.

Rocky Elsom, who had been a formidable presence in the Leinster team since he joined the previous summer, was having a superb game but he gifted Ronan O'Gara three points four minutes before the break after a cynical obstruction on Doug Howlett.

A big Munster effort seemed inevitable after the interval but instead it was Brian's men who struck a decisive blow in the 44th minute. Yet again, Nacewa was involved in the flowing move and another of his perfect passes reached a charging Luke Fitzgerald who broke through Paul Warwick's feeble attempt of a tackle.

Sexton added the conversion from near the touchline and suddenly the lead was 12 points.

The Munster machine inevitably clicked into gear with a bout of sustained pressure before the hour mark, but Leinster refused to yield with the great Nacewa producing a superb tackle to prevent a Howlett try.

As Munster became increasingly frustrated, Lions selection Alan Quinlan eye-gouged Leinster's captain

Leo Cullen, although the match officials took no action against the flanker. However, this would catch up with him after the match when he was cited and given a 12-week ban which saw him miss the Lions tour. The incident was deemed to be in the low-range of seriousness, but he needed to be punished and made an example of for what is a stupid and potentially dangerous thing for a sportsman to do.

With 61 minutes gone, Brian gave the Leinster supporters something they would never forget. He ran 70 metres to touch down under the posts after he had nipped in ahead of Lions captain Paul O'Connell to intercept a looping O'Gara pass to complete a famous victory.

The Leinster defence held out for the remainder of the match, and a convincing 25–6 victory was theirs. Brian, who picked up the man of the match awards for his efforts, clearly felt a sense of relief at having finally beaten Munster, saying, 'It wasn't just 2006. We've lost twice to Munster this season as well so we really felt we owed them one.'

Brian appeared embarrassed at having picked up the man of the match award, and was the first to acknowledge that despite his spectacular try, there were a number of people in the side who were worthy of a mention. He said, 'I'll certainly accept it on behalf of them – they set the platform for us to get our tries. People had questioned our integrity, our pride, our passion, but we produced a big passionate performance today. Games are won and lost at ruck time. The speed of ball is critical. We managed to get some quick ball ourselves when we were going forward and managed to slow them down which was exactly as we wanted it.'

He went on to pay a warm tribute to 23-year-old Jonathan Sexton, who had stepped up to the mark following Contepomi's injury. Contepomi had already announced that he would be leaving Leinster to join French side Toulon at the end of the season, and, although the extent of his injury wasn't clear at this stage, it was quite possible he had already played his last game for the side. Brian made it clear he had 'complete faith' in Sexton. It was clear from his short career to date he had a bright future ahead of him, and was a more than worthy replacement for the Argentinian.

Leinster's opponents in the finals would be the Leicester Tigers, who had beaten the Cardiff Blues on penalties after a 26–26 draw at the Millennium Stadium. As the final at Murrayfield grew nearer, it became clear that Contepomi would not be fit to take part. An MRI scan confirmed he had torn his anterior cruciate ligament and was expected to be out of action for 6 months post-op. His Leinster career was at an end, but although this was an unfortunate way for a man who had been a faithful servant to the club for six years to finish his tenure, to be able to replace him with a player of Jonathan's calibre meant his loss was not quite as

Above: Brian in Rotorua at the opening ceremony of the 2005 British and Irish Lions tour of New Zealand.

Below left: Facing up to the haka with Dwayne Peel at the start of the first test.

Below right: Brian's tour is cruelly brought to an end within seconds of it beginning in earnest, the victim of a controversial spear tackle by Tana Umaga and Keven Mealamu. © *PA Photos*

Above left: Tana Umaga faces the press for the first time since the tackle on Brian, professing his innocence.

Above right: Clive Woodward makes his feelings on the tackle clear to the assembled press.

© *PA Photos*

Below: BOD's 'bod' as he shows off the scar from the dislocated shoulder he sustained in the incident.

© *Inpho*

Above: By Royal appointment? Despite his injury Brian stayed on with the Lions squad in New Zealand to play an important off-field role (*left to right*) – Sir Clive Woodward and players Will Greenwood, Prince William, Gordon Bulloch, Gareth Thomas and Brian.

Below left: Alastair Campbell, the political spin doctor turned controversial media advisor on the tour.

Below right: Offering consolation to Shane Byrne (*centre*) and Shane Horgan after the the third and final test, a 38-19 defeat to end a disastrous tour.

© *PA Photos*

Above: Celebrating winning the Triple Crown in 2006 after a dramatic victory over England.

Below: Brian is ecstatic after Leinster win the last ever club game to be played at Lansdowne Road.

© *PA Photos*

Above: The cream of British and Irish sportsmen (*from left-right*) – Brian, Phillips Idowu, Alastair Cook, Micah Richards and Marlon Devonish.

Below: Triple Crown victory once more in 2007 – though the Irish were to be cruelly denied the Championship.

© *PA Photos*

Above: Brian scores a try against Namibia in a shaky start to Ireland's 2007 World Cup campaign.

Below: And the tournament doesn't get much better as Ireland are eliminated by Argentina.

© *PA Photos*

In July 2010, Brian's married his long-term girlfriend, actress Amy Huberman, at St Joseph's Church in Aughavas, Country Leitrim.

©Julien Behal/PA Wire

Above: Breaking through the English defense to score a try in the 2011 Six Nations. ©*ADRIAN DENNIS/AFP/Getty Images*

Below: Celebrating with Leinster team mate Jamie Heaslip at the final whistle of the match against Northampton Saints in the 2011 Heineken Cup Final. © *PA Photos*

great to the team as it might have been a few years earlier. Brian was suffering from nerve trouble in his shoulder, and although he was well enough to play, there were concerns he could be deprived of some of his usual power during the game.

The semi-final against Munster had, by many people's judgments, been the biggest match in Leinster's history, but this was about to be eclipsed by the final against the Leicester Tigers. For Brian, this was a test of just how far the club had come in the four years since Michael Cheika became coach. They had succeeded the previous year against their fellow Celts in winning the Magners League title, but a win here would show they were European giants. The fact that Munster had won the Heineken Cup twice in the past three years rankled with Brian and everyone connected with Leinster. It was time to show they weren't the junior partner in Irish club rugby. However, Brian was only too aware that Leicester was a formidable team in their own right, having won the Guinness Premiership title the previous week. This was inevitably going to be the toughest challenge of his club rugby career.

Rocky Elsom has been an was prominent in the opening stages as Leinster, after nearly conceding an early lead, took the upper hand.

Leinster's flanker Shane Jennings, playing against his former club, conceded two early penalties and from the second of them the Tigers had the chance to take the lead, but scrum-half Julian Dupuy could not hit the target with an awkward kick.

Leicester then failed to claim a high kick in midfield and when Jennings released Elsom he powered 40 metres before charging through the attempted tackle of Leicester's powerful winger Alesana Tuilagi.

The Tigers ultimately brought him down, but Leinster recycled possession and when they fed the ball into midfield, Brian took his chance popped over a drop-goal to open the scoring.

Leicester immediately went on the attack and a quick break from centre Dan Hipkiss led to Leinster infringing and Dupuy knocked over the resulting penalty to level the scores.

However, Leinster were soon assuming control and they edged back in front when Sam Vesty failed to find touch with a clearance kick and was duly punished. Jonathan Sexton, seemingly undaunted by having to step into Contepomi's boots on this massive occasion, banged over a gargantuan effort from the halfway line. Two minutes later Leinster came within inches of scoring the first try of the match as Gordon D'Arcy was desperately hauled down in the shadow of the posts.

By now, Brian and his teammates had put the Tigers under huge pressure and when Leinster mounted another strong attack they fell offside and Sexton gave his side a six-point lead. The Tigers were clearly shaken but the English champions soon proved their resilience, and after weathering the storm they managed to get on the front foot courtesy of a couple of fine Hipkiss breaks.

The Tigers, who lost Jordan Crane to a knee injury, mounted a surging attack just after the 30-minute mark and Leinster prop Stan Wright cynically tackled Vesty off the ball.

The Cook Islands international was sin-binned and Dupuy's penalty kick cut the Tigers' deficit to three points.

With Leinster down to 14 men Leicester began to dominate and after Hipkiss and Ayoola Erline had made the initial dents in the Leinster line, Woods took a pass from Vesty and scored a try to the right of the posts. Dupuy converted and the momentum was now firmly with the Tigers. They soon edged further ahead after the restart through a third Dupuy penalty.

During Wright's absence Leicester scored 10 unanswered points but an Elsom rampage down the wing lifted the Leinster and they were given a further boost when Brian's Ireland and Lions colleague, the Leicester captain Geordan Murphy, was forced off after 46 minutes.

Leinster soon seized control of the game and Jamie Heaslip powered over to finish off a sustained attacking period, and Sexton's conversion levelled the scores at 16-16 with half an hour to play.

A rare mistake from Sexton saw him miss the chance

to put them back in front as he pushed a penalty wide, but when he was handed another chance with ten minutes to go he guided it just inside the right-hand post to put Leinster back into the lead.

The remainder of the game saw the Leinster defence hold back some late attacks from the Tigers, but they held on to claim the greatest prize in European club rugby for the first time, winning by 19 points to 16.

Leinster had done it. Brian had known since his appointment that Michael Cheika was making the side stronger and better year on year, and now they had shown they were the best side in Europe. Not only had they won it, but they had won it the hard way. In the semi-final, they had beaten reigning Heineken Cup champions and newly-crowned Magners League winners Munster, and in the final they had beaten Guinness Premiership champions Leicester. This was no fluke; nobody could seriously dispute they were the deserved kings of northern hemisphere club rugby.

After the game, a delighted Brian emphasised that the win had been a team effort, saying, 'This means so much to me, it means so much to a lot of guys. Ten years of playing in this competition, and losing in the semi-finals a couple of times, has been very frustrating. To reach a final, and finally win one, it feels very, very special, and I'm very, very proud to be a Leinster man today.'

Brian then went on to pay a heart-felt tribute to the Leinster players who had been part of the journey of the club's growth, but couldn't be part of this match either through injury or because they had recently retired: Denis Hickie, Victor Costello, Reggie Corrigan, Felipe Contepomi, Shane Horgan, Malcolm O'Kelly and Girvan Dempsey.

After years of frustration and a lack of silverware to match his talent, Brian, now aged 30, had won three major trophies in the space of 18 months. The saying 'good things come to those who wait' had never been more fitting.

Chapter 15

UNFINISHED BUSINESS

Brian didn't have long to celebrate Leinster's Heineken Cup triumph – just 24 hours later he joined up with the rest of the Lions squad as they flew out to South Africa. After an extraordinary few months, which had easily been the most successful and rewarding of his career, he wasn't underestimating the importance of this tour.

He was now 30 and this would therefore quite probably be his last Lions tour. This was his big chance to lay a few ghosts from 2005 to rest once and for all. Brian was rightly regarded as the greatest outside centre in the world, and his status as a legend at both Ireland and Leinster was secure, but despite having been on two Lions tours before, he had not yet truly established himself in the famous red jersey, albeit through no fault of his own.

The highlight had probably been that try he scored in his first ever Lions Test against Australia as a 22-year-old in 2001, but that was a very long time ago now and, for most rugby fans, the words 'Brian O'Driscoll' and 'Lions' inevitably brought back unpleasant memories of the Tana Umanga/ Keven Mealamu spear tackle in 2005.

Head coach Ian McGeechan had a difficult choice to make with regards to who to pick as captain. Was he to give Brian a second chance to impress as Lions captain, or should he go with Munster skipper Paul O'Connell? In the end, he chose Paul. Brian took the decision very well, and after speaking to Ian, he warmly congratulated Paul over the phone upon his appointment. Paul had been an outstanding captain for Munster and he deserved the respect and support of the entire squad. Not being named captain may have been a blessing in some regards. Brian could focus on his own game rather than have to think about every aspect of the tour.

Ian's pedigree as coach was undoubted. This was the 62-year-old's fifth Lions tour as a coach and his seventh in all, as he also represented them twice as a player.

In 1997 he famously led the side to a 2–1 series win over a strongly-fancied South African side. Tour manager Gerald Davies' appointment was particularly poignant. As a player, he had turned down the chance to tour South Africa with the Lions because of his disapproval of apartheid. For a player to do that in 1974 was a very profound step indeed. He had been there twice before, with Cardiff in 1967 and the Lions in 1968, but he had felt very uncomfortable. He had a friend living in Cape Town who he had known since their time together at Loughborough University. He was a Cape Coloured and Gerald knew he wouldn't be able to socialise with him.

The squad contained 13 Irish players in total – a measure of how far the side had come, and of the esteem in which they were held following their Grand Slam victory. Along with the obvious selections like Brian, Paul and Ronan, there were a few surprises, such as Tomas O'Leary at scrum-half, squeezing in ahead of more experienced candidates such as Mike Blair and Dwayne Peel.

Circumstances meant that preparations for the tour weren't as thorough as they had been in 2005. Ian had wanted to take the Lions squad to the Spanish city of Granada, at the foot of the Sierra Nevada mountains for a high-altitude training camp, but he was forced to abort these plans at a few weeks' notice due to problems with player availability. The Magners League, Guinness Premiership and Heineken Cup were all reaching their conclusions in May, and the clubs were understandably unwilling to release their players for this purpose. Most of the squad met up, minus those involved in the

Heineken Cup final, met up in Surrey for a training camp the previous week.

Brian travelled with the rest of the squad on board a plane named 'Air Force Scrum', fully aware that they were embarking on a massive challenge. South Africa were the reigning world champions, and now, 18 months after lifting the Webb Ellis Cup, it was clear they were still in very good shape, both in terms of the calibre of the players and the coaching setup.

Brian's mind-set was somewhat different to the last Lions tour. Back then, he and Clive Woodward had placed a lot of emphasis on the players enjoying the tour and New Zealand as a country. This time, Brian's ambition was purely to win a Test series. He made it very clear in an interview that this wasn't about being involved in the squad or touring South Africa and having a great time: it was about winning a Test series – that was the bottom line. This isn't to say that he wasn't looking forward to playing alongside great players from England, Wales and Scotland, and building some friendships in the process, but enjoying the South African tourist attractions or going on nights out wasn't a priority.

One big difference between this Lions tour and the one four years earlier was that on this occasion the players would be sharing hotel rooms. Paul O'Connell was particularly keen on this. Although England players were used to having their own rooms, and had been for some years, sharing was still very much the norm at Munster and Ireland, and as far as Paul was concerned, this was a brilliant way for players who didn't know each other that well to build up a rapport, in the hope that there would be more of a 'team' feel to the squad.

Brian was rested for the squad's opening tour game against Royal XV, which saw the Lions launch a late fight back to win 37–25, saving them the embarrassment of their first defeat in the opening tour match since 1971. However, in the second game against the Golden Lions, Paul was rested so Brian finally had the chance to captain the Lions and last the full 80 minutes. It resulted in an emphatic 74–10 victory, which included a try for Brian when he profited from a Tommy Bowe break to open his account for the tour.

The Lions won all of the remaining four warm-up matches, albeit by some very narrow margins against the Free State Cheetahs and Western Province, and it was time for the serious business of the tour to begin.

The first Test took place at ABSA Stadium, Durban, in front of more than 47,000 people. The match got off to the worst possible start when Stephen Jones pushed a penalty wide after just two minutes. It was a sign of things to come. Boks captain John Smit scored a converted try with five minutes on the board. The Lions had the chance to hit back almost immediately when Francois Steyn dropped the kick-off, giving them an attacking scrum in a promising position.

After two re-sets, Mike Phillips feigned right before number eight Jamie Heaslip went left, and then Jones and Brian combined to send Ugo Monye into the left corner. The winger landed short but his momentum appeared to carry him over. However after several tense minutes, the television match official Christophe Berdos ruled he had not grounded the ball after a brilliant covering tackle from Jean de Villiers.

The scrum, which had been a particular strength for the Lions during the warm-up matches didn't transfer into this Test, and there was a general nervousness about their play.

With the score at 13–0, the Lions finally managed to gain a foothold in the match when the hosts fumbled a line-out and Jamie Roberts barged straight through Adrian Jacobs and JP Pietersen. The Wales centre fed the supporting Brian, who cut back against the grain before releasing Croft to stretch over, Jones converting.

Suddenly the Springboks were making errors, Ruan Pienaar fumbling Monye's kick, and the Lions had a second try ruled out for crossing when Jones and Brian combined sweetly to send Tommy Bowe over. At half time, the score was 19–7 to the hosts. It was a big ask for the Lions to win from that point, but not impossible by any means. However, Tom Croft's converted try had kept them in the game.

Just one minute after the break, Heinrich Brussow scored for the Boks, making the mountain the Lions needed to climb even bigger.

Later in the second half, South Africa kept conceding penalties, the Lions kept kicking to touch or running them, and eventually Brian put Croft over for his second try with 12 minutes left. Jones's conversion reduced the deficit to 12 points, and the Lions should have scored again when swift hands put Monye clear, but replacement Morne Steyn forced the ball out of the wing's hands in the act of touching down.

Incredibly though, amid high drama, Mike Phillips arrowed through a gap to score with five minutes left, Jones converting to make it 26–21. The Lions had their chances in the closing minutes, but replacement Jaque Fourie gathered Bowe's pass in full flow, and a spirited comeback stalled agonisingly short.

In truth, the match was probably lost due to the sloppiness of the first half, and they'd left themselves too much to do. They also missed three or four other potential scoring chances in the second half. Speaking after the game, a disappointed Ian McGeechan said, 'We need to be a bit more disciplined, a bit more patient, and certainly we can't afford to let them get a nice comfortable lead.' Brian had given his all in this game, but as a team, there was work to be done in the week before the second Test. Ironically, the man who got both Lions tries, Tom Croft, was only called up to the squad when Alan Quinlan's ban was announced.

Brian played no part in the midweek game against the Emerging Springboks, which ended in a 13–13 draw when Emerging Springboks wing Danwel Demas went over in the corner for a try, which was converted by Willem de Waal. Their hopes of ending the tour with a 100% record in non-Test matches was over, and whilst Brian could not be in any way held responsible for this draw, it was nevertheless bad for squad morale.

The importance of the second Test in the context of Brian's career could not be underestimated. The Lions were one down with two to play. If they were to lose this match, Brian may well have had his last chance to win a major series with the Lions.

A crowd of 52,000 gathered at Loftus Versfeld, Pretoria to witness what was to be a memorable and extraordinary game of rugby. The match got off to an explosive start when Schalk Burger, who led his side onto the field on the occasion of his 50th cap, was sent to the sin bin within the first minute. The Lions had conceded a penalty but it was reversed when touch judge Bryce Lawrence adjudged the celebrated flanker had raked his finger across the eyes of Luke Fitzgerald. It was difficult to see why referee Christophe Berdos did not produce a red card, but Jones knocked over the penalty to give the Lions the early momentum.

The Boks were clearly rattled and the encounter became bad-tempered, with Brian caught up in the middle of it. Victor Matfield shoved Brian, and Juan Smith swung an arm at him. Brian, clearly buoyed up by the scuffle, shouted, 'Bring it on!' at his would-be assailants.

The Lions' try in the seventh minute featured a brilliant offload from Stephen Jones out of the back of his hand to Kearney, who left Frans Steyn unsure whether to make the tackle with Bowe lurking, allowing the full-back to reach over in the right corner.

Jones converted superbly from the touchline to make it 10–0 in eight minutes.

South Africa were quickly back in the game upon Burger's return to the field, with Pietersen scoring a try, although an out-of-sorts Pienaar missed the conversion. A Stephen Jones penalty a few minutes later helped give the Lions a more comfortable lead, and five minutes before half time Brian was denied the chance to give the Lions a second try when Pierre Spies brought him down with a superb tackle after he had released Fitzgerald down the left wing and raced up in support to take the return pass. However, the Lions recycled patiently and took play through 13 phases before Jones, in acres of space, landed a simple drop-goal from 15m to extend the lead to 18–5. The Boks narrowed the gap with the last kick of the half when Francois Steyn kicked an incredible 55-metre penalty.

The third quarter of the match was a boisterous affair which featured a litany of injuries, the most important of which saw prop Adam Jones depart with a sprained shoulder, which resulted in uncontested scrums for the remaining 35 minutes. Despite some close shaves, the scoreline reminded unchanged until the final quarter.

Shortly after Stephen Jones extended the Lions' lead with another penalty on 61 minutes, Brian was involved in a sickening collision that which saw both he and Danie Rossouw crash to the ground, with no prospect of either being able to play any further part in the match. Brian was suffering from concussion, and already there were serious doubts as to whether he could continue on the tour at all.

In Brian's absence, the Lions collapsed, and it wasn't long before a classic Bryan Habana try put the Boks right back into the game, and substitute Morne Steyn added the extras. A centre partnership of Stephen Jones and Tommy Bowe was formed for the last 13 minutes, with Ronan coming on at fly-half.

It proved an unfortunate cameo for Brian's Ireland colleagues. Jones kicked his fifth penalty to make it 22–18 to the Lions with 10 minutes left, but Ronan then missed a tackle on the powerful Jaque Fourie.

Mike Phillips's last-ditch tackle ultimately proved unsuccessful and after several minutes of deliberation, television match official Stuart Dickinson awarded the try, with no decisive replay that could either confirm or rule out whether he had gone into touch in the act of scoring, so therefore the South African was given the benefit of the doubt. Morne Steyn's touchline conversion suddenly left the Lions five minutes to manufacture a score to keep the series alive.

A high tackle by replacement Boks lock Andries

Bekker on Stephen Jones saw the Welshman step up to the mark to level the scores. But it was South Africa who were handed a chance to win the match, and Morne Steyn landed the winning penalty with the very last kick of the game.

Even though he had not been on the field for the closing stages of the match, this had been an agonising defeat for Brian to take. The Lions had played with heart, courage and skill against a team consisting of some of the best rugby players in the world, but as captain Paul O'Connell admitted, some crucial mistakes had been made at important times. The series was lost, and Brian knew that his last chance to be part of a winning Lions tour may well have gone forever.

In the days that followed, it became clear that Brian's involvement in the remainder of the tour was over. The following Tuesday, the decision was made by Brian and the medical team that he and Adam Jones were to fly home the following day. It would have been reckless to risk him in the third Test under any circumstances, but it was especially pointless considering the fact that the series was lost.

Brian's departure was a blow to the squad, because his centre partnership with Jamie Roberts had been one of the Lions' major strengths, but he had to put his health first. As a team player, Brian was naturally disappointed to be leaving the tour early, even though the series was already lost. Shortly after he arrived home, he said,

'Being a part of the 2009 British & Irish Lions squad has been one of the highlights of my career. We were unbeaten leading into the Test matches and it is a shame that the results in the Tests did not go our way, but sport comes down to fine margins at times. We could easily have won the first two Tests but it wasn't to be. I have decided to return home to my family this week after a very long season and to ensure I give myself every opportunity to recuperate.'

However, this wasn't quite Brian's final word on the tour. The following day, Brian was outraged when South Africa coach Peter de Villiers made some disgraceful comments about Schalk Burger's contact with his fingers on the eyes of Luke Fitzgerald, for which he had just been banned for eight weeks after being cited. It appears that the match referee didn't fully appreciate the seriousness of the offence when he only sent him for the sin bin for ten minutes. After examining the video evidence, most people agreed that the ban was fully deserved.

The one person who didn't see it that way was de Villiers, who said he felt the incident didn't even warrant a yellow card. He said, 'I don't think he should have received a card at all. I did see the evidence. If you ever sit through and dissect the game you'll see other yellow cards that could have been missed.' How on earth an experienced rugby man like de Villiers could reach such a conclusion after having seen the video evidence was beyond most people. Brian is normally a mild-mannered man who rarely courts controversy when interviewed.

However, he was so disgusted by de Villiers' comments that he felt compelled to speak out, saying, 'When I heard those comments yesterday I wondered how someone can get away with something like that. Irrespective of any apology, I find it an absolute disgrace that a coach of a national team can make comments as he did about gouging being part of the game. Someone made a really good point to me that kids or parents watching an interview like that, questioning whether they should have their kid play rugby or soccer, that's their decision made right there. To hear a national coach saying in any shape or form, gouging is acceptable in the modern-day game is despicable. I find that mind-boggling that you can have a national team coach saying something like that. Essentially, it brought the game into disrepute.'

For the record, the Lions won the third and final Test 28–9, thanks largely to two tries from Shane Williams. It was now very likely that Brian's last chance to impress with the Lions was gone forever. It was theoretically possible that he could be part of the next Lions squad in 2013, but he would be relying on a lot of good luck to remain injury free and still maintain a reasonable amount of pace at 34 years of age. If 2009 was to be the end, his Lions obituary would be one of being cured by bad luck, and never really having the opportunity to show his full potential in the famous red jersey.

Chapter 16

SWEET REVENGE

Ireland had come a long way since those dark says of late 2007 and early 2008. During their 2009 Six Nations campaign, they often looked like a side that could give the big three southern hemisphere sides a run for their money. Despite a rocky summer with the Lions, everything felt good about the Ireland setup. At the age of 30, Brian was in the form of his life. As being an outside centre went, he had everything, and now he had years of experience to go with it, which made him rightly regarded as the greatest leader in world rugby.

As far as Brian was concerned, there was no reason at all why Ireland couldn't beat Australia and South Africa in the autumn Tests. The opening match against

Australia at Croke Park was Brian's 100th Test appearance (including Lions matches), and it proved to be a day to remember.

Australia led 10–6 at half-time, with Drew Mitchell scoring a try, but Tommy Bowe touched down for Ireland in the second half and then Rocky Elsom scored another. Matt Giteau kicked 10 points to put the Aussies 20–13 ahead and they looked on course for victory until the very last minute, when Brian, who had been having a quiet game by his standards, proved Ireland's saviour as he caught Australia's defence napping to cruise through under the posts without a finger being laid on him. With Ronan's conversion, the game was drawn.

If they were honest with themselves, Ireland were completely outplayed for the first hour and were only allowed back in to the match to get the draw due to some late lapses by the Wallabies. It was clear that work needed to be done if they were to give South Africa a serious challenge in two weeks' time. Brian knew he needed to get more involved with proceedings and he couldn't afford to have another quiet game.

Ireland were expected to win the following week's game against Fiji, which was to be the first major international to be played at the RDS. This was a much more impressive display, and Brian was back to his old self, as Ireland produced five tries, including two from Keith Earls and one from Brian, to record a

41-6 victory. Jonathan Sexton, making his Ireland debut, kicked five conversions and two penalties to earn the man of the match award. He was starting to look like a very special player who would have a big role to play with Leinster and Ireland over the next few years.

Brian's mind was now focused on the final match of the autumn series against South Africa back at Croke Park. He maintained a low opinion of Schalk Burger after his appalling behaviour in the second Lions test, and he certainly had not forgotten coach Peter de Villiers' disgraceful comments in the aftermath. It's fair to say there was still plenty of bad blood between the two sides, as a number of Irish players had either been on the pitch with the Lions that day, or had been part of the wider squad. Even those who weren't on the summer tour all shared Brian's view of the episode. A victory over the world champions would not only be a measure of how far the Irish side had come in the last 18 months, but on a personal level it would be a case of revenge being a dish best served cold. Brian knew putting in a second-rate performance on this occasion wouldn't be an option.

There was a certain arrogance about this South African side, and this was epitomised when, with 16 minutes gone, they found themselves 3-0 down, and when they were awarded a penalty, instead of taking the three points, they went for the try. Some quick hands from Morne Steyn and Wynward Oliver saw the ball end up in Burger's hands, and he charged over the line. As soon as he scored, he aggressively punched the ball into the Ireland supporters, which did little to endear him to the crowd or indeed to Brian. If any of the Ireland players needed any extra incentive to give their all for the remainder of the game, that was it.

This was a disciplined, composed performance from Ireland, despite the inevitable bad blood between the two sides. They didn't try to chase the game too much, but what they did, they did extremely well. The star of the Ireland team was Jonathan Sexton, who kicked five of his seven attempted penalties. After being dominated during most of the final quarter, the Boks produced frantic late pressure with Tendai Mtawarira charging to within inches of the Irish line. Brian's massive hit on Zane Kirchner ensured the vital injury-time turnover, and Ireland had completed a famous victory by 15 points to 10. The significance of this victory could not be underestimated. Brian had led his men to victory over the world champions, and against the team that had beaten the Lions over a series just a matter of months earlier. To get revenge for what had gone on in the summer was a welcome added bonus.

Ireland had now gone 11 matches unbeaten – a new record. Brian had made an important piece of history as Ireland captain. He was quick to heap praise on everybody involved in the Ireland setup following the game, saying, 'You always know you are going to get a physical game against South Africa. It was good the way the boys hung on at the death and didn't give up. We weren't stepping back. When people come to our patch, you don't want them pushing you around. The team has come full circle in the last year. Our unbeaten run is a credit to all the players, management and everybody involved. We're far from the finished article but we're going in the direction we want to go.'

That same day, Brian missed out on being named IRB Player of the Year by a solitary point, with the award going to All Blacks flanker Richie McCaw. The voting system was controversial, and by most people's reckoning, utterly baffling. One of the nine judges, Paul Wallace, explained to the *Sunday Times* journalist Peter O'Reilly that the problem was very much with the system itself. There was no round-table discussion, he said. The way it worked was that each of the judges was responsible for every Test match that took place in their jurisdiction. After every Test in Ireland that year, Wallace texted the names of the best three players on the pitch, regardless of nationality. Each nomination was worth a point, and at the end of November, someone in the IRB added up all the points. As it turned out, McCaw pipped Brian by a solitary point.

Brian could have justifiably felt aggrieved at missing out on this prestigious award after the way he had played throughout 2009, along with the brilliant leadership he had given Ireland, but there was little he could do about it. However, he certainly wasn't going to let a thing like this spoil his memories at what had been an absolutely phenomenal year for him – easily the most successful and rewarding of his career to date. With the World Cup now less than two years away, the big challenge was to maintain the momentum, focus on areas of improvement and lead Ireland onto the next level. For all their achievements, he knew that neither he, nor the rest of the Ireland team could afford to repeat of the display against Australia where they went to sleep for long periods of the game if they were serious about keeping their seat at world rugby's top table.

Early in 2010, Brian was voted Player of the Decade (2000/09) by readers of *Rugby World* magazine. This award was being voted for by genuine rugby fans, and Brian felt honoured that they were acknowledging his achievements in this way. Despite all the heart-breaking setbacks along the way, he had achieved a huge amount in the game, from his impressive hat-trick of tries in Ireland's Six Nations victory against France in Paris back in 2000, to finishing the decade by captaining Ireland to their first Grand Slam in 61 years and playing an instrumental role in Leinster's long-awaited Heineken Cup triumph. This had been rugby union's first full decade as a professional sport, and there were a number of worthy contenders for this honour. For Brian to win it was a measure of the esteem in which he was now held by genuine rugby supporters.

Chapter 17

A REALITY CHECK

Brian was fully aware that 2010 was likely to be a much harder year than 2009, for one simple reason: both Ireland and Leinster were now champions, and with this came prestige and status. There was no doubt that their biggest rivals would be more motivated and better prepared whenever they met. Furthermore, the upcoming Six Nations campaign would inevitably feel harder in 2010 because it involved away matches at the Stade de France and Twickenham.

Their first opponents in the Six Nations were Italy, who they would be playing host to at Croke Park. Ireland laboured to a comfortable win over the unambitious Italians in what was ultimately a scrappy encounter.

Brian's quick hands helped produce and early try for

Jamie Heaslip and Tomas O'Leary put Ireland 23–3 up, but Italy responded when Kaine Robertson charged down Rob Kearney's kick to score. O'Leary's try came about when Leinster captain Leo Cullen made the most of his late call-up into the Ireland squad when he stole the ball from an Italian line-out, before passing to the scrum-half.

The Irish produced little purposeful play in the second half as the match petered out in disappointing fashion. Ronan O'Gara had a 100% record with the boot as he landed 16 points, and Ireland eventually won 29–11. For Brian, this was a match he would remember for Gonzalo Garcia's cynical spear tackle on him in the 32nd minute, which amazingly only resulted in a sin-binning.

Despite the comfortable victory, this was a miserable match and Croke Park was incredibly muted in the final whistle. After the match, Brian vented his frustration at the way things had gone, saying, 'We had a reasonable first half but never really got out of the blocks in the second half. They put up more of a fight and made life difficult but we didn't really string things together. We didn't get any fluidity into our game. We were glad to hear the final whistle – it got a bit frustrating. Our ability to create fast ruck ball is the winning and losing of games against sides like France. We need to work on that.'

Brian also admitted that it had been hard to carry on from where they left off in November after only having a fortnight to prepare for the tournament. Declan took more of a 'glass half full' approach in his post-match interview, but admitted that every area of the game needed working on. The one thing that was blatantly obvious to all concerned was that they couldn't afford a performance like this against France in Paris the following week. The French looked a better, stronger side than they had done for some years, and to win on their patch looked like being a very tough ask.

The match against France was billed as a Six Nations decider beforehand, and with good reason. France looked every bit like champions in their 18–9 away win over an improving Scotland side. France produced an impressive display to defeat Brian's men 33–10. In short, they had been completely outclassed. Morgan Parra kicked a penalty, and tries from William Servat and Yannick Jauzion, both converted by Parra, helped the home side to a 17–3 lead at half-time. A further try by Clement Poitrenaud, plus eight more points from the boot of Parra, and a Frederic Michalak drop-goal made the win comfortable.

David Wallace scored Ireland's try, with Ronan O'Gara kicking five points.

The dream of back-to-back Grand Slams was dead, and this had been a massive wake-up call for the entire Ireland squad. This wasn't a narrow defeat by any stretch of the imagination, and they had made plenty of mistakes throughout the game. After the match, Brian was irritated and annoyed at the sheer number of errors Ireland had made in the game. He said, 'It is one thing losing close games but being beaten badly is hard to take. We made some very silly unforced errors and bad defensive reads while the French took their opportunities. They were good but we helped make them look good. We must turn it round the next time we put on the green jersey.'

With England and France having won both of their opening games, winning the Championship didn't look likely, and it was already clear they may have to settle for the Triple Crown. To make matters worse, the next match was away to England at Twickenham, who had already beaten Wales and Italy in the campaign so far, despite having problems of their own.

This was a very special day for Ireland prop John Hayes, who became the first Irish player in history earn 100 caps for his country. John had received some criticism in recent times, much of it unfairly, for Ireland's ills at the scrum, which had been considered the team's Achilles heel. In truth, most, if not all members of the team had to accept their share of the responsibility for the team's recent problems. Brian, who was just one cap behind John on 99, willingly allowed his colleague to lead the team out at Twickenham to mark the occasion.

John was an unbelievably shy, quiet man, who was never happier than when he was home on his farm in

Cappamore, Limerick, milking the cows. A true gentleman and all-round nice guy, who always maintained a balanced outlook on rugby and life, he would never have been up for having some kind of presentation on the pitch – he would have found the attention too embarrassing. John received a standing ovation from both sets of supporters when he led his side out. The Munster veteran had earned the respect and admiration all true rugby fans for his services to the game, and the ovation was a fitting tribute to him.

The Twickenham pitch was soggy and this wasn't going to be a day for fancy, free-flowing rugby. It quickly became clear they had to take a pragmatic approach to the match and not worry about playing too much crowd-pleasing rugby. Instead, they had to focus on the result.

That said, this performance was much more like the Ireland of 12 months earlier, especially in terms of discipline and determination. They made a brilliant start with Tommy Bowe's early try and a penalty from Jonathan Sexton gave the Irish an 8–6 half-time lead. A Keith Earls try with 56 minutes gone saw Ireland lead by seven points before Wilkinson converted Dan Cole's try to make it 13–13. Two minutes later, Brian was accidentally kneed in the head by Paul O'Connell and needed to be stretchered off, but fortunately his injury wasn't as serious as first thought and his participation in the remaining two matches was as good as certain. It looked a nasty injury but in reality he had just been stunned.

Wilkinson then put England ahead with a drop-goal but Bowe's late try and Ronan's conversion saw Ireland home to make it a 20–16 victory, in what was a thrilling end to an often dogged match.

By the end of the match, Brian appeared to be fine and was up and celebrating with the rest of the boys. This wasn't the most technically brilliant performance from Ireland but they were the more creative side and most neutrals agreed they deserved their victory. They had beaten one of the world's greatest sides on their own turf, and there was a feeling in the camp that their blip was over.

Their next opponents were Wales at Croke Park. It was hard to know what to make of this Wales side. They certainly weren't playing to the same standards as two years earlier when they won the Grand Slam, but in the campaign so far, they had been outplayed by England in the opening game, but had gone on to beat Scotland and had given France a good run for their money despite losing.

This was Brian's 100th cap for Ireland, and this inevitably meant he would receive more media attention than usual in the build-up to the game. Ironically, Brian was the 13th international rugby centurion, matching the number on the back of his shirt. Brian has never been a man for grand gestures or extrovertism, but he was genuinely taken aback by how emotional he felt leading Ireland onto the pitch on this occasion. Although many people now regarded Brian as Irish rugby's greatest ever servant, he considered the accolade of representing his country 100 times to be a massive honour which he could not really put into words, and, as always, he was determined to give his very best once the whistle blew.

The Ireland who took to the field in this match looked very much like the Grand Slam winners of twelve months earlier. There were no problems with the pitch on this occasion, so they could play their usual brand of rugby without having to worry about external factors. The Irish took advantage of Lee Byrne's sin-binning with two tries which established a 16–6 half-time lead. Earls scored in the 26th minute from Brian's off-load and O'Leary touched down soon after. Earls got over again midway through the second half to finish Wales, whose 12 points were Stephen Jones penalties.

The 27–12 scoreline was an accurate reflection of the game. This was a comprehensive win for Ireland, and the defence deserved particular praise for the way in which they prevented Wales from crossing the line. After the match, an upbeat Brian was sure that Ireland were back on track after a wobbly start to the tournament, saying, 'We played very well, clinically, and took our chances. It's been a brilliant place for us and losing here to Wales two years ago wounded us. We have put that right. We now have the Triple Crown to play for and maybe even the Championship.'

France's 46–20 victory over Italy the following day effectively ended any hopes of Ireland winning the Championship. They would have to beat Scotland by a massive margin and hope England would thrash France in Paris. More realistically, they remained on course for the Triple Crown. Their final opponents, Scotland, had gone through a disappointing tournament, losing each of their first three matches, but the boot of Dan Parks had seen them hold on for a 15–15 draw in their last game. Brian knew full well that Scotland's performances in the tournament to date had not been a fair reflection of their players' ability, and they would more than likely be coming to the match as wounded animals eager to prove a point.

Ireland were going for their fifth Triple Crown in seven years. If Brian and Ireland needed any extra incentive going into this game, this was the last match to be played at Croke Park before they moved to the new Aviva Stadium at Lansdowne Road. After three and a half years of some quite remarkable rugby, they naturally wanted to end their tenancy on a high.

Scotland exerted early pressure as the hosts looked nervous and made several handling errors. Dan Parks kicked a sixth-minute penalty after Paul O'Connell had been penalised for not rolling away from the tackle. Four minutes later Jonathan Sexton showed characteristic pace and invention to loop around Gordon D'Arcy and cut through the Scottish defence before his inside pass, which looked forward, released Brian for his 39th try for Ireland, which he placed under the posts. Johno added the simple conversion to make it 7–3 with 12 minutes on the clock.

The visitors hit back just four minutes later with a Johnnie Beattie try, and they went into the break with a 14–7 advantage, aided by a Parks drop-goal. Parks and Sexton exchanged penalties early in the second half before a fine manoeuvre involving Brian and Gordon D'Arcy resulted in a Tommy Bowe try.

Parks and substitute Ronan O'Gara then swapped more penalties, before man of the match Parks emerged as the match-winner, his long kick deep into Ireland territory putting replacement Rob Kearney under pressure. The full-back opted to try to run the ball out as Simon Danielli and Nick de Luca closed him down, and was penalised for holding on in the tackle. Up stepped Parks, who took his time despite a chorus of boos from the Ireland supporters angry at the time he was taking with just two minutes left on the clock, to convert the winning penalty inches from the left touchline.

Ireland had ended their campaign, and indeed their tenancy at Croke Park with a miserable 23–20 defeat. The Scots, especially Dan Parks, had played a good game, but Ireland at their best should still have beaten them. They made too many errors and failed to execute some of their manoeuvres in the way that they should have. For the record, France completed the Grand Slam with an exciting 12–10 victory over England later that day.

Brian knew it was important to remember that Ireland hadn't become a bad side overnight, and their problems were largely to do with consistency. At times, they had shown flashes of the brilliance that had seen them win the Grand Slam twelve months earlier, and to have Ronan O'Gara and Jonathan Sexton competing for a place at fly-half was certainly an exciting development. However, at the end of the tournament, they looked a very, very long way from a side that had a chance of beating New Zealand and Australia on their tour in the early part of the summer. For now, all Brian could do was return to Leinster, and when they regrouped in the early summer, they could begin to analyse what went wrong and work hard in training to put it right.

Domestically, things were going well with Leinster, albeit with the inevitable absence of Brian, captain Leo Cullen and the other international players for a large chunk of the season. However, Michael Cheika had announced in October that he would not be renewing his contract with Leinster and would be seeking pastures new at the end of the season. There was no doubt whatsoever that Michael had taken both Brian and Leinster's games onto a higher level, and for that he had the respect and admiration of the players and supporters, but it came as a disappointment to some when in March he announced that he would be moving to another European club in the shape of French giants Stade Francais. However, Leinster were keen to keep the disruption caused by Michael's departure to a minimum, and in mid-December they announced that 44-year-old Clermont backs coach Josef Schmidt, originally from New Zealand, would be taking over in the summer. He had some connections with the province, having played a year with Mullingar in the early 1990s.

In the Magners League, they were making good progress, and Brian had been part of the side that had beaten Munster 30–0 earlier in the season, although the reverse fixture at Thomond Park in early April, which Brian missed through a fairly mild knee injury sustained against Scotland, saw Leinster win by a single point at 15–16. The following week, Brian was fit enough to take part in Leinster's Heineken Cup quarter-final against Clermont at the RDS Arena, in front of an exceptionally noisy crowd on a Friday night. They had been progressing well in the competition, topping their pool, and in this match, Brian created space with a trademark jink and passed to Jamie Heaslip who showed power and pace to surge through attempted French tackles and score the first of his two tries in the corner, which was the major force behind an exciting 29–28 victory.

Inevitably, a semi-final away at Toulouse was always going to be a tough test, but Brian, coach Michael Cheika and Leo Cullen were all aware that as reigning

Heineken Cup champions, their opponents would be that extra bit determined to beat them. This wasn't to be one of Leinster's better days, and it turned out to be an unusually quiet game for Brian. The home side took a 9–0 lead with three David Skrela penalties but Leinster battled back with two penalties from Australian Shaun Berne, who was taking the kicks in Jonathan Sexton's absence, to make it 9–6 at the interval.

The game opened up after the break and quickfire tries from Yannick Jauzion and Skrela put Toulouse in control. Jamie Heaslip's try gave Leinster hope but Skrela added another penalty and Toulouse closed the game out, winning by a comfortable 26–16 margin. They would go on to win the Heineken Cup with a narrow victory over Biarritz in the final. Leinster had let themselves down with some sloppy knock-ons, and poor management of possession. Michael Cheika also made it clear in his post-match interview that he thought they let the ball go too easily and probably kicked it away too much. Brian knew this had not been one of his better games, but, as with Ireland, there were wider problems that needed looking at.

With their European ambitions over for the season, Brian and Leinster approached the remainder of the Magners League campaign with renewed energy and vigour. The competition's profile had risen due to the introduction of a play-off system to determine the overall winner similar to that of the Guinness

Premiership in England. Leinster qualified for the play-offs after coming from behind to beat Edinburgh 37–28 in a nail-biting encounter at the RDS Arena. They finished top of the Magners League table, which would have landed them the title under the old system/

The cut-throat nature of the play-offs made them exciting stand-alone matches in their own right, but Leinster's match had added impetus when they found themselves faced with a home tie against the old enemy, Munster. In front of more than 19,000 fans at the RDS Arena, a typically ferocious, high-quality encounter between the bitter rivals ensued. Jonathan Sexton kicked Leinster ahead in a frantic first half before Ronan O'Gara levelled before the break. O'Gara edged the defending champions into the lead after the restart but Sexton's superb exchange of passes set up Rob Kearney for the decisive try.

Sexton added six more points and despite late pressure, Munster were unable to muster a scoring response. This hadn't been a classic Brian O'Driscoll performance, but he had played his part in a convincing 16–6 victory to set up a Grand Final tie with the Ospreys in front of their home crowd in Dublin.

Just as success with Ireland and Leinster in 2009 came in tandem, so, it seemed, did the disappointments and frustrations of the early part of 2010. From a psychological perspective, victory over the Welsh giants in the final would be a major boost for Brian. Lose here, and it would be hard for him to come to a conclusion other than that both Ireland and Leinster had gone backwards in the last 12 months.

As expected, a capacity crowd of just under 20,000 fans gathered at the RDS Arena for what had become Leinster's biggest game of the season. Following the success of the previous few years, the expectations of the fans had risen. A year without a trophy was now a bad year as far as they were concerned – a sentiment shared by most of the Leinster players. This was, of course, Michael Cheika's last game as coach, and Brian was eager to win this match as a tribute to all his hard work during his five years in charge. On paper, this looked like being a mouth-watering contest. Both sides had won the Celtic/Magners League on two previous occasions, and the Ospreys side featured many of Welsh rugby's biggest names, along with Brian's Ireland colleague Tommy Bowe.

There was to be no fairytale ending to Michael's tenure as coach. Bowe raced over for the Ospreys' first try in the 19th minute, with Dan Biggar converting to make it 7–0. Jonathan Sexton kicked a penalty but Lee Byrne added the second try before half-time, Biggar again adding the two points to increase his side's lead. Sexton was successful with three of his four second-half penalty attempts, with Biggar kicking a penalty for Ospreys, to give them a 17–12 victory and the Magners League title.

Brian had failed to make his presence felt and offer a major contribution to the game. This time last year, he had just won the Heineken Cup with Leinster and had guided Ireland to Grand Slam glory. Now, both were trophy-less, and he found it hard to take any positives from the events of recent months. Certainly, it had felt like a harder season in many ways. A trip to Paris in the Six Nations was always going to be a tall order, as was facing Toulouse on their territory in the Heineken Cup. Even so, both Ireland and Leinster had achieved what they did in 2009 on merit, and he wasn't willing to use tough away trips as an excuse. On a personal level, he had a few 'off' games, but most discerning rugby fans still acknowledged him as the greatest number 13 in the world. Rugby is a team game and Brian knew that, as a team player, there was work to be done with both the Leinster and Ireland squads if he was to fulfil his ambitions in the final few years of his playing career.

Chapter 18

A FRESH
START

Brian's life was going through a period of huge change at the start of the summer of 2010. Michael Cheika had left Leinster and Joe Schmidt had come in as coach. At 44, Joe was regarded as one of the brightest coaching talents around, and his signing was perceived as a coup, with his former Auckland Blues prodigy Isa Nacewa paying a glowing tribute to his old mentor upon hearing of his appointment at Leinster. His philosophy was expected to be more defensive in approach than Michael's had been, but Brian knew that this was a man worth listening to, and perhaps a fresh approach was needed after the disappointing season they'd just been through.

Whatever the future held for Brian at Leinster, they

would have to face it without stalwarts Malcolm O'Kelly and Girvan Dempsey, who had announced their retirement from the game. These men had both been fine servants for club and country and these weren't going to be easy boots to fill.

Brian was also now just weeks away from the most important day of his life when he was to marry Amy. Their relationship had been rock solid through what had, in many respects been a challenging few years, but they only grew stronger together as a result and neither was in any doubt that they wanted to be with the other for the rest of the lives.

With Ireland, it was time to put the disappointment of the Six Nations campaign behind them as they embarked on a short but gruelling summer tour of New Zealand and Australia. In a sense, expectations from the fans were lower than they would have been had Ireland done better in the Six Nations, but they were still expected to put up a respectable fight out there. As a country, Ireland was going through a deep recession – there was a lot of doom and gloom around and it didn't look as though things were going to improve anytime soon. The Irish rugby team was one of the few things that could still bring people together and give the nation something to celebrate. For this reason, Brian was very much aware that if he was to lead Ireland to a turnaround in fortunes on the pitch in the months ahead, he could bring some joy and light relief into the lives of millions of ordinary people who were going through a difficult time.

The squad flew out to New Zealand knowing that few people expected them to finally win their first match against the All Blacks in 105 years on this occasion, but they did expect to use the Test as an opportunity to put right some of the wrongs of the Six Nations campaign. However, there were a number of setbacks they had to come to terms with. Paul O'Connell would be missing the entire tour through injury, as would Rory Best. A number of the squad had little or no experience at international level and inevitably the tour would be a useful learning curve for them.

Even so, what followed when the referee blew his whistle at Yarrow Stadium, New Plymouth, was one of the most humiliating and embarrassing episodes in Irish rugby history. The All Blacks simply overran Ireland in a completely one-sided first half. Having gifted Conrad Smith an early try, the Irish had number eight Jamie Heaslip sent off for kneeing at a ruck. Kieran Read, Ben Franks and Jimmy Cowan (2) got tries with Dan Tuohy replying for a 38–7 half-time scoreline. After the interval Smith, Sam Whitelock (2) and Neemia Tialata added to the All Blacks' tally. The try was Brian's 40th for Ireland but it was scant consolation as they went down to a 66–28 defeat – a record against the All Blacks.

In truth, the first half had been an absolute horror show, as Ireland gave away a lot of soft tries and missed tackles.

The players managed to keep the ball slightly better in the second half, but even then they didn't look like a side that could seriously compete against the mighty All Blacks. It was going to be a long road back to the top.

A second-string Ireland XV took to the field in the match against New Zealand Maori, but it still contained plenty of big names such as Geordan Murphy, who captained, along with Jonathan Sexton, Shane Horgan and Paddy Wallace, so it nevertheless came as a disappointment to the squad when they lost the game 31–28, but they did deserve some credit for fighting back to lead after being 15–0 down.

Brian knew that he had to look at the final match of the tour against Australia at Suncorp Stadium, Brisbane in its correct context. There was no point in comparing this to the 20–20 draw at Croke Park the previous autumn. The make-up of this current Ireland side was quite different and the priority had to be to improve on the enormous defensive frailties that had been so prominent in the Test against the All Blacks.

Two Jonathan Sexton penalties to one by Quade Cooper gave Ireland the lead but Luke Burgess scored an 18th-minute try. Johno kicked two more penalties and Cooper one before fly-half Cooper gave Australia a 16–15 half-time lead with a wonderful try shortly before the break. Matt Giteau was successful with two second-half penalties to condemn the Irish to a 22–15 defeat.

Ireland had defended fairly well but had made too many errors when attacking, which Brian found frustrating. He had gone through a far better game by his own high standards but admitted in his post-match comments that the seven-point winning margin probably flattered them. He said that although tours were ultimately judged by results, they had succeeded in putting a bit of pride back in their defensive performance after the debacle against New Zealand, and it had been a worthwhile learning experience for the less experienced players.

Most of the squad could now look forward to four or five weeks holiday before getting back down to work, but when Brian arrived home he would be just days away from the most important day of his life. Fortunately, none of the Australian players gave him a black eye as a memento for the occasion, albeit one that would spoil the wedding photos.

When they were making preparations for their big day, Brian and Amy were adamant that they wanted this to be a fun occasion for their families and friends. This wasn't going to be some big showbiz wedding. They were both essentially level-headed, down-to-earth people, and the guest list only contained 250 people, all of whom were known to them.

The day's proceedings were to begin at mid-afternoonn with the ceremony itself – a traditional Roman Catholic Mass at the relatively small yet beautiful St Joseph's Church in Aughavas, County Leitrim. Brian was especially pleased that Father Vincent Twomey, uncle of Barry, was going to be the celebrant. Brian still thought about Barry every day and the fact that he wasn't there brought a tinge of sadness to what was otherwise a perfect day.

The village of Mohill was the closest urban centre, and locals marked the route with banners wishing the couple well. Outside the church, Gardai estimated that somewhere between 500 and 1,000 locals had gathered hours in advance to wish the couple well, braving some heavy downpours. Brian's rugby friends Shane Horgan, Gordon D'Arcy, Denis Hickie, Luke Fitzgerald, Donncha O'Callaghan, Paul O'Connell and Victor Costello all arrived in good time for the ceremony. Ronan O'Gara and his wife were unable to attend as she had given birth just a couple of days earlier. Other notable figures on the guest list included actress Victoria Smurfit, concert promoter Denis Desmond, actor Chris O'Dowd, famous for his role in *The IT Crowd*, and Pauline McGlynn, best known for playing tea-loving Mrs Doyle in *Father Ted*.

Brian arrived some 20 minutes early, wearing a dark Louis Copeland suit, grey waistcoat and champagne coloured tie. Amy arrived a fashionable 20 minutes late in a white Bentley with a Garda escort. When she got out of the car, the bride gave a simple thumbs up to the crowd, which provoked applause and cheers. She was wearing an off-white, strapless dress with a half veil by designer Stephanie Allin, and posed for photos before entering the church clutching a pink bouquet whilst surrounded by four bridesmaids.

The ceremony lasted just over an hour, with the couple gathering in the church porch at their way out to share a kiss. They mingled among guests in the courtyard before leaving amid a confetti shower in the Bentley, glass of champagne in their hands, to a round of applause.

Later that day, guests enjoyed a champagne reception on the lawn of Lough Rynn Castle, followed by a six course meal with the Camembert Quartet providing the entertainment. They partied well into the night, and at around 2am, the rugby lads decided it would be a good idea to perform the Hora. As the custom dictates, Brian and Amy were hoisted onto two chairs. Brian was having the time of his life, but his wife was absolutely petrified. Before she knew it, her chair had been lifted up and was being carried around the room by Paul O'Connell of all people. He said, 'Trust me, I've got you, it's OK.' Amy had little choice but to trust him. To her horror, a few moments later she turned her head to see Paul walking away from her to the bar to get a drink. Somebody else had taken over, and she wasn't quite sure who he was. It was all good fun, and everyone there agreed this had been a wedding party to remember.

The day after the wedding, a barbecue was held for close family and friends, with The Coronas and The

Bogus Brothers performing. This had been a truly magical couple of days for Brian and Amy. They had committed the rest of their lives to each other, and had given their friends and families a celebration they'd never forget. In fact, Amy had been enjoying the party so much that by the Sunday she had completely lost her voice. Brian took a great deal of comfort in knowing that whatever ups and downs the future held, he and Amy would be facing it together.

Chapter 19

A NEW ERA BEGINS

At the start of the 2010/11 season, Brian had a lot to look forward to. Joe Schmidt had begun to make his presence felt at Leinster. Ireland would soon be playing in the new Aviva Stadium, and the Rugby World Cup was now little over a year away, and inevitably Declan Kidney and Brian were planning ahead with that in mind. Brian knew this was very likely to be his last chance to lift the Webb Ellis Trophy, and preparations had to begin now to give him and the rest of the Ireland squad the best possible chance of lifting it.

Brian's first taste of the new Aviva Stadium arrived with Leinster rather than Ireland. There was a degree of flexibility over its use, meaning that Leinster could use it if demand for tickets was greater than the number of seats available at the RDS, and provided the stadium wasn't booked for another purpose. Therefore, Brian's first taste of the fabulous new ground came in early October when he faced Munster in front of more than 50,000 spectators – easily a record for the Magners League.

Leinster went into the game under some pressure after a poor start to the season that had seen them lose three of their first four matches, mainly due to teething problems due to Joe coming in and other changes that had taken place at the club with old faces leaving and new ones coming in.

The sides were level at 3–3 at half-time with Isa Nacewa cancelling out a Ronan O'Gara penalty. Two O'Gara penalties nudged Munster 9–6 ahead but the game came to life in the 70th minute. With time running out, the impressive O'Brien burst past Paul Warwick and threw a backhanded pass out of the tackle for the supporting Brian to run in from the right and score a magnificent, match-winning try. Nacewa added the extras to give Leinster a 13–9 victory. Leinster had now won five in a row over Munster, the first time they had done so since the 1930s. This was exactly how Brian wanted to begin his career in this awesome new stadium.

A month later, the serious business with Ireland got underway as they began their Autumn Internationals campaign with a Test against South Africa. Ireland were chasing a fourth consecutive win over the world champions, who had lost their last three matches. Some of the omens were good – the Boks were missing a dozen first choice players, including the dreaded Schalk Burger, but this was still a very powerful side. Both teams had gone through a tough period and they were out to prove a point. Brian had recovered from a hamstring injury and would be partnered at centre with Gordon D'Arcy.

The one element of sadness was that only around 35,000 spectators were at the Aviva Stadium for this game, due to a backlash by Ireland supporters over the IRFU's controversial ticketing strategy. Initially, the IRFU announced that tickets to the November Tests would only be sold as packages for all four matches. Later, it announced that the tickets would instead be split into two packages, with the South Africa Test bundled with the following week's match with Samoa for a minimum of €150, and the New Zealand and Argentina Tests bundled for a minimum of €190. Single-game tickets were to be available only for the Samoa and Argentina Tests. On 1 November, the IRFU backed away from this plan amid heavy criticism from member clubs that had problems selling the packages in such a difficult economic climate, but for the game against the Boks, the damage had been done.

A penalty from Morne Steyn – who later saw his successful run of Test kicks end at 41 – and converted Juan Smith try gave the Boks a 10–0 lead. Three Jonny Sexton penalties and two further Steyn efforts made it

16–9. Gio Aplon's score sent the Boks clear, but Ireland weren't quite finished yet. They turned to Ronan O'Gara, who came on for Sexton for his 100th Ireland cap, and he wound back the clock to 2009 with a precise chip as he and Tommy Bowe produced a repeat of Ireland's Grand Slam-winning try in Cardiff. Ronan converted and the crowd nearly lifted the new roof clean off its bearings when Kearney crossed out wide to finish off a sustained multi-phased attack sparked by a Jamie Heaslip breakout. Ronan had the chance to level the scores from wide out but his conversion attempt hit the post, and from then on South Africa held on for victory.

The match had essentially been lost because of the slow Ireland start, but Brian was keen to take some positives from the game. The conditions weren't great, and the greasy ball made it difficult to play the sort of game they wanted to early on, but he knew that in the last quarter especially, this had been a massive improvement on where they were in the early summer.

With all due respect to their opponents, Ireland were expected to win their next Test against Samoa by some distance. Once again the Aviva Stadium was half empty as Brian led his team out onto the pitch. Jamie Heaslip's 18th-minute try helped Ireland lead 10–0 but Leicester star Alesana Tuilagi replied for the visitors with the score of the match.

Ireland's 13–7 half-time lead was cut to three points as

Samoa dominated. But Peter Stringer's quick penalty enabled Ronan to score a late try which came as a massive relief to Brian and to the Ireland fans.

Debutant Devin Toner deserved some credit for helping the Irish line-out operate more effectively, but their scrummaging had been an absolute mess for most of the match and this was hardly the sort of message they wanted to be sending out to New Zealand with a match against them just a week away. This had been a grinding, tough victory, and was far from pretty. Still, at least Ireland had ended their run of four straight Test defeats.

A lot of work was done in training in the week's build-up to the Test against the All Blacks, and when Brian led his team out, he did so in front of more than 46,000 supporters – not a sell-out, but a vastly bigger crowd than had witnessed the first two Tests, giving it an atmosphere worthy of the occasion. Declan had made 11 changes from the match against Samoa, effectively returning to his strongest side. The All Blacks performed their first ever Haka at the Aviva Stadium, and it was down to business.

New Zealand led 19–13 at half-time thanks to an Anthony Boric try and 14 points from the boot of Dan Carter. Stephen Ferris scored Ireland's first-half try and Jonathan Sexton kicked eight points but, the Kiwis pulled away after the break. Read charged over for a try on 45 minutes with Carter adding the conversion, and three minutes later replacement second row Whitelock crossed the line with his first touch of the ball for his side's third try.

The Irish defence was struggling to cope with the All Blacks' pace, but with 56 minutes gone they regrouped when Rob Kearney and Jamie Heaslip made ground and when the ball ran loose Brian picked it up and managed to roll over and apply pressure on the ball despite the attention of two All Black tacklers, a consequence of his quick-thinking and years of experience. Sexton's conversion rebounded tantalisingly off the upright.

The final period of the match was an entertaining and open encounter played at a frantic pace, with Ireland proving, physicality, to be a match for their opponents. Keith Earls almost scored his side's third try in the 74th minute but the television match official judged that the ball had touched the goal-line as he grounded. Read got his second try for the All Blacks in the final minute of the match, although Carter was unable to add the conversion.

Ireland had lost 18–38, but this had been a proud display and Brian was keen to focus on the positives, of which there had been plenty. Brian believed Ireland had played a great game for 67 or 68 minutes in perfect conditions, but the All Blacks had pounced during their brief periods of weakness. This was much more like the sort of rugby Ireland would need to play if they were to win the Six Nations and pose a serious threat in the World Cup.

The final match of the series saw Ireland pitted against Argentina. The Pumas were interesting opponents: they didn't see anywhere near as much of them as the southern hemisphere 'big three', but with the World Cup just a year away they were an interesting test of exactly how Ireland's preparations were going. This was a game Ireland were really expected to win, but they had to be on top of their game and certainly couldn't take anything for granted.

Declan made five changes from the match against the All Blacks, which gave some fringe players the chance to get some valuable experience against worthy opponents. This game saw Brian come face to face with his old Leinster colleague Felipe Contepomi, and although he was now in the autumn of his career, this was a man who was still regarded as one of the greatest kickers in world rugby.

In the event, this was a convincing Ireland victory. They led 19–3 at half-time with Stephen Ferris scoring a 20th-minute try and Jonathan Sexton (who was effectively Contepomi's replacement at Leinster) kicking four penalties and a conversion. Sexton landed another penalty after the interval and Ronan O'Gara converted Gordon D'Arcy's injury-time try. Contepomi had a poor game by his standards kicked one penalty in the first half and two after the break but missed with three other attempts. Meanwhile, Brian was substituted on 68 minutes after taking a blow to the jaw, which would keep him off Leinster duty for nearly three weeks.

Ireland had won 29–9, and this had been a positive end to an autumn international campaign that had started poorly but had got better in the final two games. Crucially, they had matches the Pumas' aggression, however, Declan knew at the end of the series that there were a number of areas that needed to be looked at in the lead-up to the Six Nations campaign. They had let themselves down badly in the first 10 minutes of the second half against New Zealand in what had otherwise been a decent performance, and against Argentina they allowed their opponents to keep the ball too well. Ireland were far from the finished product, but they were in far, far better shape than they had been a few months earlier.

In the intervening period between the end of the autumn internationals and the start of the Six Nations, Brian played in a memorable Heineken Cup pool game for Leinster against Joe Schmidt's old side Clermont Auvergne at the Aviva Stadium in front of more than 44,000 spectators. The previous week, Brian had missed the reverse fixture which resulted in a 20–13 defeat because of the jaw injury he sustained against Argentina, but on this occasion he was very much ready for the battle. Cian Healy drove over for the opening try after early Leinster pressure and the hosts led 10–3 at half-time. Leinster piled on the pressure after the restart and were duly rewarded with tries from Healy and Sean O'Brien, both converted by Jonathan Sexton. Clermont finally broke through the defence after 69 minutes with a Napolioni Nalaga try, but Leinster had done enough, and had completed a 24–8 victory. In the end, their away defeat to Clermont was the only loss of the pool stage and they finished top to progress to the knock-out stage in the spring.

At the start of 2011, Brian wasn't underestimating the importance of the year that lay ahead. He was just a few weeks away from his 32nd birthday, and was inevitably approaching the final few years of his playing career. Although he was still playing to his best and felt in great shape for the time being, he could not be certain when his last Six Nations campaign would arrive, and it seemed likely that the Rugby World Cup at the end of the year would be his last chance for him to lift the game's biggest prize with his country. He also felt that there was unfinished business with Leinster, and with good progress being made in the Heineken Cup and Magners League, he knew he had to make the most of his remaining chances to pick up silverware. With the number of years left in his playing career running out, the need to win gathered an added urgency.

The year's first big challenge, was, as always, the Six Nations campaign. The first match away at Italy was a chance to build on the respectable performances they put in against New Zealand and Argentina a few months earlier. Italy were growing in confidence and ability year on year and none of their opponents could take them for granted. In the event, the match in Rome turned out to be a major step backwards for Irish rugby. They produced an error-ridden first half against the lively Italians as two Mirco Bergamasco penalties helped the home side to a 6–3 interval lead.

A series of thrusts early in the second half was eventually rewarded with a close-range try for Brian once he managed to fend off Martin Castrogiovanni's weak tackle to give his side an 8–6 lead, and Sexton added two more with his conversion. Italy struck back late in the game with Luke McLean's 75th-minute reply to give his side a shock lead. Crucially, Bergamasco missed the conversion to keep Ireland in the game. By this stage, Ronan O'Gara had replaced Sexton and he took his chance with two minutes remaining as his drop-goal helped save Ireland's blushes and put them 13–11 in front. McLean tried to reply in kind with a late long-range effort but it fell into the hands of a mightily relieved Fitzgerald in the final act of the match.

This had been a poor Ireland performance, and Brian had to accept his share of the blame. He had attempted a number of wild passes which had failed to meet their men, and although he had led from the front and scored an important try, this had not been a vintage display from him by any means. In his post-match interview, he was clearly relieved that his side had been let off the hook. He said, 'The longer they stayed in the game, the more threatening they were going to be, as they showed with five minutes to go. We didn't kill them off, I threw a loose ball into touch [to Fergus McFadden] and we missed other chances. You can't cough it up against any side in Test rugby, and Italy nearly made us pay. But it is a great result to come back. With four minutes left we needed a drop-goal and we got one. There are no excuses. It is not as if we haven't been playing a lot of rugby. Thankfully we won, which is probably the only thing we can take out of the game.'

It was clear that there was a huge amount of work to be done by everyone in the squad before their home match against France the following week. Some of the passing and slip-ups against Italy were bordering on the farcical and they simply couldn't afford to do that against the French, who seemed to have carried on where they left off the previous year by winning their opening game against Scotland 34–21.

This was Ireland's first Six Nations game at the Aviva Stadium, and Brian was eager for them to start as they meant to go on. With the absurdities of the IRFU's ticketing policies in the past, a capacity 51,000 crowd gathered to see the contest. They would be disappointed as the Irish paid heavily for indiscipline as five penalties by Morgan Parra and one by his replacement Dimitri Yachvili proved to be the difference. A first Test try by Fergus McFadden and a Tomas O'Leary touchdown helped Ireland to a 15–12 half-time lead. With 54 minutes gone, French winger Maxime Medard raced through for the France's only try with Jamie Heaslip's score setting up an exciting finish. Ireland staged a late rally but it came to nothing. They had lost 22–25 and Brian's men were left to reflect on their error count. Overall, they conceded 16 penalties with nine awarded against the French.

Brian felt frustrated at the way in which Ireland had lost the game. They had scored three tries to France's one, and they had matches their opponents in most areas of the game, but it was their indiscipline that had cost them heavily.

There was now a two week break before their next match against Scotland at Murrayfield, and this gave them a chance to regroup and work on what had gone wrong in the campaign so far. Brian was certain they were moving in the right direction and repeatedly said so in interviews in the intervening period. However, there was still a lot to work on. He was keen to make amends for the match against Scotland the previous year, and Andy Robinson's men were having problems, including the retirement after a horrific injury of the talented winger Thom Evans. In this year's campaign, they had lost both of their opening two matches against France and Wales.

A few days before the game Brian made it clear he wanted to see more variety from his men against

Scotland, saying, 'Much as we want to play a running game, we must also play smart. We've probably been guilty of not kicking the ball as much as we could have, but we're on the right road. If you only play one type of game the opposition do their analysis and you become easy to stop. You must have variety, mix it up and constantly keep defences guessing.' There was no doubt in his mind that it was better to 'win ugly' than 'lose pretty', and that had perhaps been one of their problems in the recent past.

The Irish had dominated Scotland at Murrayfield in recent years, and Brian was keen for this to continue. Ireland scored three tries to none, with Jamie Heaslip and Eoin Reddan going over in the first half. Ronan scored and converted a try after the break to make it 21–9 to Ireland, which earned him the man of the match award, but Scotland fought back. Chris Paterson kicked 12 points while a drop-goal from replacement Dan Parks took Scotland to within three of the visitors, but Ireland held on to win 21–18.

Declan was somewhat frustrated by Ireland's high penalty count, and it was clear this was still something of a problem. They certainly did contest the break down, and there was no need to apologise for that, but some of the penalties they gave away were sloppy, and really they should have won by more. That said, he insisted they still celebrate the victory, which he hoped would bring some joy into the lives of the fans, most of whom were suffering to some degree due to the dire economic situation in Ireland.

They had another fortnight's break to work on their shortcomings before their trip to the Millennium Stadium for what was to be a record-breaking match against Wales, but there would be no happy ending for Ireland. Shortly after kick-off, Brian's Leinster colleague, the scrum-half Eoin Reddan took Lee Byrne's attempted clearance full force in the face, and his participation in the match was over. His replacement, Peter Stringer's impact was instant. He drew several Welsh defenders before off-loading to Tommy Bowe, who in turn sent Brian over the line for a try, his 24th in the Championship, which equalled the all-time record of Ian Smith of Scotland in the Home Nations and Five Nations between 1924 and 1933. Ronan's conversion saw him become the fifth man in rugby history to reach 1,000 Test points.

Ireland led 13–9 at half time, but it wasn't to last, when on 50 minutes Wales caught them napping. Matthew Rees picked out Mike Phillips with a quick throw to send him on his way for a Welsh try. However, the try shouldn't have been allowed, as TV replays showed that Rees had used a different ball – handed to him by a ball-boy, to the one Jonny Sexton had kicked into touch, which is against rugby's Law 19.2. Referee Jonathan Kaplan should really have referred it to the television match official, but chose not to. Nevertheless, the try stood and James Hook converted that score and kicked three out of four penalties as Wales survived a late Irish onslaught to win 19–13.

After the match, Brian was seething at Kaplan's decision not to consult the television official, saying, 'It was clearly an illegitimate try and we feel hard done by. That is what TMOs are for and I am pretty sure you can go to them, even from that far out. We try to play by the rules of the game. I didn't see it myself but when half your team saying it you take their word for it. I tried to relate that to Jonathan Kaplan and the touch judge and they were having none of it and it's really frustrating for such an incident to have a huge bearing on the game. I actually didn't ask Kaplan to use the video official. When I went over to him he was pushing everyone away and I told him I was captain and he said that was fine but he wanted to talk to his touch judge, so I stood there and before anything else could be said he awarded the try. I did mention it to him a few minutes later after I had seen it on the TV and I told him that it was a massive momentum swinger and that it had had a huge bearing on the game, but he just shrugged that off. Games hang in the balance on decisions, everyone is human and wrong calls are made sometimes, but some are unforgivable.'

Declan echoed Brian's sentiments and backed up his captain to the hilt. What should have been a special day for Brian and Irish rugby had been ruined by a shoddy piece of refereeing. Furthermore, this decision ended any prospects they had of winning the Triple Crown or even the Championship itself. Brian knew that in any sport, you had to take the rough with the smooth and that sometimes decisions wouldn't go your way. But for a referee to fail to make use of the TMO on a decision of this magnitude was something he rightly found completely unacceptable, and it was something he found difficult to get over in the days ahead.

As it turned out, Ireland's chances of winning the Championship would have all but disappeared by the end of that weekend anyway, with England's victory over Scotland. Even if Kaplan had made the correct decision and disallowed the Wales try, thereby handing Ireland victory, England, who had won all their matches so far, had too big a points difference thanks largely to a 59–13 victory over Italy in the second week. Even so, it would have been a welcome consolation to win the Triple Crown in front of the Aviva Stadium crowd, but this was now not on the cards and Ireland were essentially playing for pride. Meanwhile defending champions France were now out of the equation having lost to England and, shockingly, had been defeated by Italy at home for the first time ever in week four, losing by a single point.

Although there wasn't a huge amount to play for in the final match against England, there was a lot of pride at stake, and some players were inevitably looking to prove they were worthy of a place in the starting XV with a World Cup around the corner. On the day, this was a vintage Ireland performance, as the side dominated England. Two Jonathan Sexton penalties gave Ireland a 6–0 lead which they nearly extended when Brian also had a try disallowed early on in the half which followed a marvellous passage of play, but Bowe's final pass to Brian was correctly ruled forward. However, they had just been awarded an advantage and made it 9–0. Seven minutes later, Sexton tapped a penalty after England were caught offside, before passing it to Tommy Bowe for Ireland's first try. Toby Flood kicked a penalty for England but Ireland led 17–3 at half-time.

Early in the second half, Brian finished off a sweeping move from his teammates by rounding Louis Deacon and scoring in the corner for his 25th Championship try, overtaking Ian Smith's 78-year-old record. The crowd burst into life singing a chorus of the Fields of Athenry and were only silenced as Sexton added the extras.

England gave themselves a glimmer of hope when replacement hooker Steve Thompson intercepted an Eoin Reddan pass to score from 40 metres, but the normally-reliable Jonny Wilkinson failed to add the extras. Despite increasing periods of possession late on, England couldn't break down the Irish defence and Brian had successfully led his side to a very special 24–8 victory.

After the match, Brian couldn't hide his delight at

what he and his players had achieved after an often-difficult Six Nations campaign. He said, 'We knew we had a performance like that in us but for some reason we had not put it together in our four previous matches. We were very good – we played a smart game, an intense game and they couldn't live with us. To score 24 points was very satisfying and a nice way to end the Six Nations. There were a few things that needed changing and some of the senior players said some powerful things during the week in the run-up to this match. We felt we hadn't set down a marker at the Aviva Stadium and we needed a reason to call it home again. There's no better way to do that than by beating England and it's a nice moment. We are fortunate to have two fantastic fly-halves – Jonathan [Sexton] showed huge character and Ronan O'Gara came on and finished the job – we will savour the moment and a great victory.'

This had been a fantastic international victory – one of the proudest of Brian's career. There were some things that needed looking at on the horizon, such as their lack of consistency from one week to the next, and there was work to be done in training as they continued their build-up to the World Cup. However, as Brian embarked on the traditional end of Six Nations celebration at Kehoe's in Dublin, he knew the Irish team was moving in the right direction after a wobbly period, and with the world's biggest rugby tournament just months away, there was every reason for Irish fans to be optimistic about their team's chances of lifting the Webb Ellis Cup.

Chapter 20

LEINSTER'S
FINEST HOUR

Brian returned from Ireland duty to find Leinster in great shape. They were doing well in the Magners League, and their Heineken Cup quarter-final match against Leicester, their opponents when they won the trophy two years earlier, was now just a few weeks away. After taking a few games to acclimatise to Joe Schmidt's way of doing things, they were now looking like a side that could win some silverware this season.

However, Leinster suffered a setback on Brian's first game back with them after returning from international duty when they faced Munster, who were top of the table. The old enemy won the game when Ronan kicked a penalty over in the final kick of the game to give Munster a 24–23 victory, extending his side's lead at the top of the Magners League table. As irritating as it always was to lose to Munster, the play-off system meant the defeat was not as serious in the grand scheme of things as it would've been a few years earlier.

The following week, just short of 50,000 people packed in to the Aviva Stadium for the Heineken Cup quarter-final match against the Leicester Tigers, and as with the final in 2009, expectations were high. Three Jonathan Sexton penalties put Leinster 9–3 ahead at half-time with Toby Flood replying for the Tigers then Brian carelessly found himself offside. Alesana Tuilagi went close to scoring a Leicester try but the television match official ruled that Sean O'Brien's full-reach tackle had pushed the Leicester wing into touch at the corner flag and it looked the correct decision. Shortly afterwards, Isa Nacewa jinked his way to a superb Leinster score, although they were perhaps a tad fortunate not to have been pulled up for a forward pass by referee Nigel Owens. Sexton made up for missing the conversion by Replacement Rob Hawkins' 77th-minute try for Leicester set up a frantic finish but Leinster held on to complete a 17–10 victory.

Brian was relieved to have got this match out of the way. All the lads knew Leicester were going to try and bully them and they all dealt with that aspect very well. Leicester coach Richard Cockerill said some very ungracious things about Nigel Owens' refereeing, but in truth he could have few causes for complaints.

Leinster's success was, of course, wonderful and Brian couldn't have been happier with the progress the club was making, but on a personal level it did bring its problems. In February, Brian and Amy were honoured and delighted when they received an invitation to the wedding of Prince William and Kate Middleton at Westminster Abbey. Brian had got to know William on the 2005 Lions tour and he was very much looking forward to being part of what would be a very special and memorable day. However, the wedding was to take place on 29 April, the day before Leinster's vital Heineken Cup semi-final match against reigning champions Toulouse.

Brian reluctantly had to pull out, and Amy attended on her husband's behalf. The rugby fraternity was represented by Brian's former Lions colleague, Gareth Thomas, who was now in the autumn of his career and playing rugby league for the Crusaders. However, even he left straight after the ceremony itself because he had to prepare for a Super League match two days later. Brian was especially sad to miss out on this historic occasion, not least because the Queen was to make her first ever trip to the Republic of Ireland just a few weeks later, and most people agreed it would've been a nice gesture to have the country's best-known sports star present at the wedding as part of an increasing spirit of friendship and good will between the two countries.

The match against Toulouse in front of an inevitably-packed Aviva Stadium was always going to be a hard-fought encounter. Florian Fritz scored a fortuitous early try for the French giants, and David Skrela kicked eight points before half-time. One of these penalties came about when Brian was yellow carded on 36 minutes after coming in on the wrong side of a ruck. However, the home side led 16–13 at the interval after three Jonathan Sexton penalties and Jamie Heaslip's try. A Louis Picamoles try on the resumption put Toulouse ahead but two more Sexton penalties helped restore Leinster's lead.

On the hour mark, Sexton gathered a loose ball and took contact before replacement Isaac Boss passed for Brian to slip by Vincent Clerc and Census Johnston for his 30th Heineken Cup try, two short of Clerc's record. Sexton's conversion put nine points between the sides at 29–20 and although they were a try clear, the next 20 minutes or so were going to be a very nervous time indeed to be a Leinster fan. Replacement Bezy landed a penalty from just inside the Leinster half but Sexton completed a fine kicking display by knocking over his sixth penalty in the final minute to complete a 22-point personal haul, helping his side to a 32–23 victory.

This was a massive victory for the entire Leinster squad, a testament to how far they had come in the months since Joe had taken over as coach. They were already in fairly good shape, but he had added some steel to their defence and they were now a very tough side to beat. That said, they were still one match away from lifting the Heineken Cup, and their opponents in the final, Northampton, were going to be incredibly tough to beat, having shown how good they were by thrashing Perpignan 23–7 in their semi-final.

A week later, Leinster, minus Brian, sealed second spot in the Magners League with a 38–3 walloping of Glasgow at the RDS Arena. Munster had topped the table by some distance, but this scarcely mattered under the play-off system, which would see Leinster pitted against third place Ulster the following week in the semi-finals.

Friday the 13th was not an unlucky omen for Brian's men as they outclassed Ulster at the RDS. Fergus McFadden's try and two Jonathan Sexton penalties gave the hosts a deserved 11–0 lead at the break. Ruan Pienaar gave Ulster hope with a superb long-range penalty, but Luke Fitzgerald's late try sealed Leinster's place in the Grand Final in a fortnight's time, where they were to face Munster, who beat the defending champions the Ospreys in their semi-final the following day. However, Brian was one of several players injured, suffering a knee injury in the first half that saw him replaced by David Kearney, which was a major concern with the Heineken Cup final just over a week away.

The week leading up to the Heineken Cup final was an eventful, but very special time for Brian. At the start of the week, his knee injury remained a concern and his participation in the final remained in doubt.

On the Wednesday evening, he attended a State Dinner at Dublin Castle to mark the Queen's visit to the Republic of Ireland, the first by a British monarch since 1911. Brian had met the Queen once before, at a reception at Hillsborough Castle in Northern Ireland shortly after Ireland's Grand Slam win in 2009, but the significance of his second meeting with Her Majesty was huge. This visit marked a major step forward in improving the relationship between Britain and Ireland and moving on from past hostilities. The vast majority of people in the Republic of Ireland welcomed the Queen and Duke of Edinburgh's visit, and Brian felt honoured to be a part of this historic occasion. Also present were Irish President Mary McAleese, British Prime Minister David Cameron, Taoiseach Enda Kenny, Northern Ireland's First Minister, Peter Robinson, and Nobel laureate Seamus Heaney.

Brian listened on as the Queen made a powerful and historically-important speech, saying, 'To all those who have suffered as a consequence of our troubled past I extend my sincere thoughts and deep sympathy. With the benefit of historical hindsight we can all see things which we would wish had been done differently or not at all. But it is also true that no-one who looked to the future over the past centuries could have imagined the strength of the bonds that are now in place between the governments and the people of our two nations, the spirit of partnership that we now enjoy, and the lasting rapport between us. No-one here this evening could doubt that heartfelt desire of our two nations.' Brian knew he was listening to a landmark speech that would be remembered for many years to come, and felt honoured to be present at such a key moment in Irish history.

The following morning, Brian returned to training to see how things went with his knee. Joe Schmidt confirmed after the session that Brian had been at three-quarters pace, but he hoped that on Friday he would be able to stretch out and fully accelerate. It turned out to be true and a day before the match it was confirmed that he would be taking his place alongside Gordon D'Arcy at centre.

The Leinster squad travelled to Cardiff for the match at the Millennium Stadium, one of the greatest venues in world rugby, and a place certainly worthy of a game of this magnitude. It went without saying that the Northampton Saints deserved respect despite only finishing fourth in the Aviva Premiership, and having lost their play-off semi-final against Leicester the previous week. This was a team that included a number of international stars, including Chris Ashton, who was rightly regarded as one of the most exciting young wingers in world rugby. However, Saints would be missing influential England flanker Tom Wood, who had been ruled out with a hairline fracture.

More than 72,000 fans packed the Millennium Stadium for northern hemisphere club rugby's biggest day. Every stand was awash with blue and white flags for Leinster, or black and yellow for Northampton. Brian knew that this would be a career-defining game for him in many respects. Win here, and Leinster would have won two Heineken Cups in three years, and would overtake Munster as Ireland's top province in many people's minds. What followed was a very special game of rugby that no true fan of the game, whoever they supported, would ever forget.

Leinster were a ragged bunch for the first period, overpowered at the scrum, dominated at the breakdown, and flimsy in defence. Northampton got off to a brilliant start with super-charged opening passage of play lasting two minutes and 17 seconds. Centre James Downey cut inside Gordon D'Arcy to launch a Saints attack that went through umpteen phases until a Hartley knock-on brought the first pause in the action.

The Saints pack seemed to have the edge in the first two scrums, confirmation of which came in the third set-to after Sexton's huge clearance kick rolled inches too long, allowing Northampton a scrum back inside the Leinster 22.

Referee Romain Poite called captains Leo Cullen and Dylan Hartley together to lay down the law. After this, Saints drove the scrum, getting the penalty, but Roger Wilson, Paul Diggin and Lee Dickson carried the ball before Calum Clark sent Phil Dowson charging over in the left corner.

Stephen Myler added a fantastic conversion from the touchline, and Northampton had their tails up. Christian Day stripped D'Arcy of the ball, number eight Roger Wilson burst clear from the back of a scrum, but Clark was pinged at the breakdown and Sexton stroked over a superb penalty to make it 7–3.

Saints prop Soane Tonga'uiha and his cohorts splintered the Leinster pack for a second time to earn another penalty after 20 minutes that Myler nudged over from 40m. Leinster probed dangerously and Shane Horgan cut a fine angle through the Saints midfield. Sean O'Brien released Brian and he charged towards the right corner, only to be cut down metres short by Ben Foden.

Saints then dominated Leinster again at the scrum, but by the next set-piece they found themselves a man down after South African prop Brian Mujati was sin-binned for cynically holding back Cian Healy.

Mujati's absence barely made any difference at all to Saints, who extended their lead without him. They sacrificed Clark and brought on prop Tom Mercey, which saw them to push back their opposite numbers even with seven men, earning a third scrum penalty.

Leo Cullen sought clarification from the referee, and he was similarly bemused moments later when Saints won the next scrum against the head deep into Leinster territory. Myler's initial dart was held up, but scrum-half Dickson spun the ball out left and Jon Clarke sent Foden running around Brian's tackle to score. The

Leinster fans' hearts sunk and would have been forgiven for thinking the game was already lost. Myler added the conversion and Saints were 17–3 ahead after 32 minutes.

A high tackle on D'Arcy allowed Sexton to cut the deficit to 11 points, but nothing much seemed to be going their way. They knocked on at the kick-off and Saints finished the half chipping away at the Leinster line, Clarke and Chris Ashton – twice – both held up short. But Saints surged again, and Hartley was adjudged – after consultation with the television match official – to have been driven over for their third try. Myler saw his conversion attempt come back off an upright, but Brian and his teammates, lined up on their own try-line, looked understandably shell-shocked.

In the dressing room at half time, Jonathan Sexton delivered a tub-thumping team talk. He reminded his teammates that comebacks can happen in finals, and he was in no doubt that they could come back. He pointed to Liverpool's comeback from 3–0 down to defeat AC Milan in the 2005 Champions League final as an example of what he meant. He knew, deep down, that the game wasn't dead, and by the time he'd finished speaking, Brian and the rest of the lads shared his belief. Even so, coming back from 22–6 down against a side of Northampton's calibre was a big ask. Leinster replaced Kevin McLaughlin with Shane Jennings at flanker for the second half, and within four minutes they were back in the game.

Brian picked up a loose ball and burst through, Jamie Heaslip and Isa Nacewa were held short, but when the ball was moved swiftly left, Eoin Reddan sent Sexton over for a clever finish. He saw his subsequent conversion bounce over off an upright and with the momentum swinging their way Leinster's threat was all-consuming. After another relentless period of pressure, D'Arcy – with Wilson and Diggin getting boots and arms underneath him, could not ground the ball in the right corner, after a lengthy review process by the video referee.

Saints survived that decision, but by now Leinster's determination seemed unstoppable. After 53 minutes, Sexton battered his way over for his second try after another blue onslaught, and this time there was no missing the conversion as he brought his side to within two points.

By now, the game had been completely turned on its head. Foden dropped a high ball, and Leinster's fired-up forwards took great delight in earning a penalty at the resultant scrum.

Sexton sent it flying between the uprights, and Leinster had transformed a 16-point deficit into a one-point lead within 17 minutes. Immediately the Saints line was under siege once again, and the panicking defence saw Dowson, infringing at a ruck, sent to the sin-bin. Johno put over the resultant penalty, and was converting

Leinster's third try minutes later when Scottish lock Nathan Hines, in his last game before departing for Clermont, crossed the line.

Saints had well and truly been shaken, so sent on four replacements in a bid to stem the blue tide, but one of them, Shane Geraghty, was promptly engulfed by four tacklers and had no option but to concede a penalty. Sexton somehow managed to miss what was a relatively easy kick, but he could be forgiven after his massive contribution to the game.

Foden launched one final dashing counter-attack for Northampton from deep that Ashton carried on, only for Leinster to turn it over. After that, both coaches emptied their benches to give their players a taste of the special atmosphere, but Leinster had done enough, and the Heineken Cup was theirs, winning 33–22.

This had been a truly incredible game, and every single player, without exception, along with Joe Schmidt, the inspirational scrum coach Greg Feek, and the rest of the coaching staff, deserved credit for the way in which they turned the game around in the second half. It was testament to their never-say-die attitude and Brian was delighted to join Wasps, Leicester and, of course, Munster, in that unique band of clubs that had won the Heineken Cup twice. Leinster were no longer the junior partner in their rivalry with Munster. There was still some way to go before they could be named in the same historical context as Toulouse, who had won the competition five times, but they were well on their way, and for now, they were the greatest team in Europe.

In his post-match interview, Brian was quick to heap praise on Johno for his massive contribution to the game, and for his words at half time. He said, 'We had some choice words at half-time and Sexton was phenomenal in the dressing room, he was a man possessed. He said this game would be remembered if we came back and we will remember this for a long time. This was without a shadow of a doubt the best second half I've ever been involved in. I've never known a side to be able to keep up that level of intensity for 40 minutes. It's a pleasure to be a part of this side – we've grown so much over the last couple of years and I think the way we turned that around typified our season.'

After a hard night's partying, the Leinster players paraded the Heineken Cup in front of hundreds of home fans at the RDS Arena the following afternoon. There was a pleasant, family atmosphere, with players mingling freely with supporters, accepting congratulations and signing autographs. The players then allowed themselves one more night's partying in Dublin, followed by a recovery day on the Monday before getting back down to training on the Tuesday in preparation for the Magners League final the following weekend. Brian clearly didn't want to part with the Heineken Cup, he even posted a picture on Twitter of himself appearing to be fast asleep in bed with his arm wrapped around the cup.

The 'rest day' on Monday actually turned out to be a rather busy time for Brian. Late in the afternoon, he was at College Green in Dublin for another very special occasion – a speech by US President Barack Obama. Brian arrived well in advance, as did most of the crowd of around 60,000 people. They made an afternoon of it and were entertained by a host of Irish musicians including Westlife, Jedward, and the Saw Doctors. The compere, GAA commentator Micheál Ó Muircheartaigh introduced a number of sports stars to the crowd including Robbie Keane and Padraig Harrington, but Brian got the biggest cheer when he walked on stage with the Heineken Cup in his hands.

Brian was honoured to meet President Obama in the reception room, and the two men enjoyed a brief conversation about his career. Brian put his sunglasses on and took his place in the crowd, and he listened on as the world's most powerful man delivered an inspirational and sometimes humorous speech about the strong historic links between the two countries and the need for optimism and hope at this difficult time, saying, 'Your best days are still ahead. Remember whatever hardships winter may bring ... spring's just around the corner.'

This had hardly been a typical seven days in the life of a professional rugby player, but to be invited to meet the two best-known heads of state in the world was a measure of the status in which Brian was now held in

Irish society. Even people who had little or no interest in rugby knew who he was and were aware of his achievements, despite the fact he very rarely did anything off the rugby pitch to draw attention to himself. It would be the icing on the cake to bring this special period in his life to a close with victory over Munster in the Magners League Grand Final.

On paper, this looked like being a fascinating contest. Munster had home advantage, and had topped the league in the regular season by a whopping 14 points. However, after Leinster's achievements in the second half against Northampton, they were evidently in great shape. There was talk of perhaps a Heineken Cup hangover for Leinster, but even if this had been an unusual week, the players needed little motivation to get themselves psyched up for a match against their biggest rivals.

A capacity crowd of more than 25,000 people packed in to Thomond Park for the match, but it felt like there were far, far more people there.

Jonathan Sexton completely miscued an early penalty attempt and Munster followed this with a sustained period of pressure. Their dominance paid off in the 12th minute when scrum-half Conor Murray fed Lifeimi Mafi, whose goose step bemused the Leinster defence, and Doug Howlett crossed for the opening try. Ronan O'Gara added the extra two points with an impressively struck conversion from the touchline against the wind.

With 24 minutes gone, Brian looked to be in a bad way when he was receiving treatment on the pitch, but he lept up from being treated to tackle Keith Earls. This was extraordinary dedication from Brian, which brought a reaction of amusement, astonishment and admiration from the crowd.

Johno kicked his first successful penalty of the game in the 29th minute, and a first half dominated by turnovers ended with Munster enjoying a four-point advantage.

Leinster took control of possession at the start of the second half but the Munster defence held out stubbornly. The pressure eventually told when Donncha O'Callaghan was sin-binned for not rolling away in front of the posts and Sexton knocked over the resulting penalty, and he added another midway through the half to nudge his side ahead for the first time.

Munster got their act together and Luke Fitzgerald made a vital tackle on Howlett as the Kiwi winger made for the line. In the 66th minute, O'Gara found Earls with a perfectly executed cross-field kick and the winger danced past Isa Nacewa and shrugged off a challenge from Shane Horgan before stretching to put the ball beyond the try line.

However, the game was kept alive when Ronan was unable to add the conversion and was also off-target with a penalty effort soon afterwards. Munster seemed increasingly in control and Howlett went on a breathtaking run through the Leinster defence but was unable to find a team-mate with the crucial pass and the chance was lost.

Time was running out for Leinster to pull something out of the hat, and aother great comeback was looking increasingly unlikely. With one minute remaining, Munster were awarded a penalty try after Leinster infringed at the scrum, and Ronan added the extras. Replacement Kevin McLaughlin went close to scoring a consolation try for Leinster but the television match official ruled that he had not grounded the ball over the line. Nathan Hines suffered a similar fate as the video ref adjudged that he had been put into touch before crossing the line. Referee Nigel Owens then blew the final whistle, and Leinster had lost 19–9.

Afterwards, Joe Schmidt admitted that fatigue may have been a factor in the defeat, and coming a week after the Heineken Cup final, their energy levels may not have been as high as those of Munster. He also said he felt Munster needed it more than Leinster wanted it. That distinction was important, as Munster would otherwise have gone the season without a trophy. However, it was naturally disappointing to lose to their biggest rivals, and to miss out in the Magners League final for the second year in succession.

Perhaps the most fitting comments came from Munster captain Paul O'Connell, who said that the game was a very good thing for Irish rugby, 'Both sides have a lot of leadership, and no little skill, people talk about this being a good era for Ireland.' Indeed, this had been a good year for the Irish provinces. Aside from Leinster winning the Heineken Cup and Munster the Magners League, in the regular season table, Munster, Leinster and Ulster had finished first, second and third respectively, and that could only bode well for the future. The quality and intensity of the Grand Final suggested that the Welsh and Scottish sides had a lot of work to do before they could match either side, and the previous year's winners, the Ospreys, had declined significantly.

If Brian's career had, for whatever reason ended after the 2008 Six Nations, he would have gone down in history with his reputation as one of world rugby's greatest ever outside centres secure, but he would also have been remembered as one of the unluckiest players in history, with very little silverware to match his ability. However, in the latter years of his career, he has finally been rewarded with the trophies a player, and leader of his calibre deserves. For all the ups and downs of the last three years, the reality was that he had led Ireland to their first Grand Slam in 61 years, and had won a Magners League title and two Heineken Cups in three years with Leinster.

Chapter 21

THE LAST
CHANCE SALOON

Brian was now 32 years old, and inevitably in the autumn of his playing career. The life of a modern-day centre is a punishing one. The daily ritual of strict dieting and specific, often scientifically designed training becomes more difficult with age, while the inevitable lingering injuries of battle begin to take their toll. If he was fortunate, Brian had one World Cup, three Six Nations campaigns and possibly a Lions tour left in him before he was forced to call it a day.

Few would deny that he had lost some of the blistering pace that defined him as a younger player, but he compensated for this with his excellent rugby brain and sense of judgement on the pitch. The leadership he offered was also invaluable, and there was every reason to believe he still had a great deal left in the tank for both club and country.

The summer of 2011 was a short one, as, starting in early August, Ireland faced a series of warm-up matches for the World Cup which followed in the autumn. Brian was ruled out of the opening two matches away at Scotland and France with a neck and shoulder injury, but even so he didn't underestimate the importance of these in getting the squad both physically and mentally prepared for the World Cup. They had gone through an occasionally promising but terribly inconsistent Six Nations campaign, and these matches were an opportunity to iron out the creases.

It certainly felt strange travelling to Murrayfield to play against Scotland in the middle of summer, but coach Declan Kidney and stand-in captain Leo Cullen both knew the importance of this match.

Ireland were the better side for much of the game and were 6–3 in front with two minutes remaining, but with the clock ticking down, Scotland centre Joe Ansbro found himself on the wing and raced on to score from Nick De Luc's fine pass. Ruaridh Jackson added the conversion to give the home side a 10–6 victory. In the post-match interview, Declan focused on the positives. It had been a strong defensive performance but the attack had struggled to hold on to the ball. However, their attitude had been encouraging throughout the 80 minutes, and it was good to see Jerry Flannery and Rob Kearney return from injury.

Next up came back-to-back matches against France, the first one being away in Paris, where Ireland were lethargic for most of the first half. They failed to muster any kind of attacking threat and continually gave away possession, but a successful penalty attempt from Ronan at the end of the first half saw them go into the break 13–3 behind. Ireland were a transformed team after the restart – they had a new-found urgency in their play and were stronger in the tackle. The key factor was the introduction of Paul O'Connell, and the urgency resulted in a series of Irish pressures. Ronan managed to kick three before missing a fourth, leaving his side just a point adrift. France regained control, however, thanks to two Yachvili penalties, and although the Irish pressed in the final minutes they squandered a five-metre scrum and a line-out close to the French line, and they lost the match 19–12.

Despite the defeat, this had been a spirited fight-back and there was genuine cause for optimism. At midweek, it was confirmed that Brian would be back for the return fixture in Dublin the following weekend. Gordon D'Arcy would also return after recovering from ankle surgery, but with Rob Kearney ruled out for a week with a groin strain, Felix Jones would be making his first start at full-back. Andrew Trimble, who had impressed over the last two weekends, retained his place on the right wing while Keith Earls took the number 11 jersey. With ten changes from the previous week, this was fairly close to Ireland's strongest possible starting XV, and there could be no excuses this time around.

Days before France's return visit, a select XV took on Connaught in Donnybrook. Leo Cullen and Geordan Murphy were among the try scorers as they recorded a 38–3 victory. A number of players put in impressive displays and it gave Declan plenty to think about.

In the game against France Ireland attacked relentlessly early on and a Jonathan Sexton penalty opened the scoring after two minutes. They continued to pile on the pressure, and Cian Healey earned his first international try after 20 appearances when he blew away the French scrum-half, Morgan Parra. Sexton put the extras wide, but Ireland thoroughly deserved their 8–0 lead after 11 minutes.

However, Ireland's strong opening wasn't to last, and France turned the game around in the space of five minutes when Parra opened his account with a straightforward penalty on 26 minutes, and François Trinh-Duc punished a poor clearance by Tomas O'Leary to kick a successful drop goal from just inside the Irish half. Ireland's discipline collapsed and Aurélien Rougerie cut through the midfield with ease before passing to Cedric Heymans, who claimed the try and put his side into the lead for the first time. Parra added penalties either side of half-time, and the visitors added a second try when O'Leary's suicidal attempted pass to Sexton was intercepted by Trinh-Duc, who touched down unopposed. Sexton and Sean O'Brien got consolation tries for Ireland late on, but in all honesty the 26–22 scoreline flattered them.

This was an extremely disappointing return for Brian, and with only one match left before the World Cup, there was a very real possibility they would travel to New Zealand without a win under their belts. During the match, Brian suffered a 'stinger' to his shoulder, and although he was able to run around in training, the decision was taken to rest him for the final warm-up game against England at the Aviva Stadium. This was frustrating for Brian as his own personal preparations for the World Cup were important to him, but it wasn't worth risking himself in a contact situation with far bigger battles ahead.

A win against England would come as a massive morale boost after what had been an indifferent period for the side, especially when compared to the high standards they set themselves these days, but it wasn't to be. An early Manu Tuilagi try and two Jonny Wilkinson penalties helped the visitors dominate the first half, but three penalties from Ronan kept Ireland in touch at the interval. Heavy rain made conditions tricky in the second half, but England dominated and a Delon Armitage try saw them extend their lead and win 20–9. There was no getting away from the fact that this was a desperately disappointing performance at the end of what had been an underwhelming series for Ireland.

Declan was normally a man who looked for the positives in any situation, but even he couldn't hide the fact that this was a worrying performance so close to the World Cup.

This World Cup meant a huge amount to Brian. He was Ireland's most-capped player, as well as the nation's most prolific try-scorer, and had captained his country more than twice as many times as his nearest rival. He held the record for the number of tries scored in the Six Nations. As Ireland captain, he had guided his men to a Six Nations Grand Slam, along with the Triple Crown on no fewer than four occasions. The previous year, he had been voted 'Player of the Decade' by readers of *Rugby World* magazine. Yet he still had a number of unfulfilled ambitions. He hadn't achieved as much as he'd liked with Ireland or experienced real success outside the relative comfort zones of Northern Hemisphere rugby. This World Cup would inevitably be his last chance to lead his country to the game's biggest prize. He headed off to New Zealand determined to make the most of this opportunity, despite the disruptions and disappointments of the build-up. Although a humble and unassuming man to meet, Brian had great confidence in his own ability, and believed Ireland were capable of winning the World Cup.

During an interview with *Rugby World* shortly before the World Cup, he gave an insight into his mind-set and attitude towards self-improvement. He said, 'I always try to improve – you should work on your strengths as much as your weaknesses. You're renowned for some good things – why not make them truly outstanding? Keep chipping away at the thing you need to improve but if a player has great feet, brilliant defence or incredible composure, he should look to enhance those skills.' Brian's ethos is a simple one – play to your strengths and work to become brilliant at them, but also never give up when it comes to ironing out your weaknesses.

In the pool stages, Ireland would face USA, Australia, Russia and Italy, and with only the top two finishers making it through to the quarter-finals, there was no room for complacency. With all due respect, they would expect to beat the USA and Russia comfortably, even on a very bad day. However, a win against Australia or Italy would almost certainly be required if they were to progress to the knock-out stages, which meant they couldn't afford a repeat of the erratic performances in the warm-up matches.

Memories of previous trips to New Zealand didn't exactly fill Brian with feelings of undiluted joy, but as the squad arrived and prepared for the opening match against the USA, his primary concern was for his shoulder, which still hadn't fully recovered. He took part in training sessions from the time they arrived in New Zealand, but was careful not to do too much contact as a precaution. As the countdown to the opening game gathered pace, it became clear he could expect to play a full part in the match.

There was no denying that the match against the USA was something of a gentle start to the tournament, but as Brian and the team took to the pitch at Stadium Taranaki in New Plymouth, he knew this was an opportunity to give both himself and the team a morale boost as they prepared for bigger challenges to come. The USA were coached by Eddie O'Sullivan, and although his time at Ireland had ended on a sour note, his influence had been pivotal in transforming them into a world-class side who could compete for trophies in the professional era. Ireland went into the game knowing that Eddie would have got his team well prepared, and although they might not be the most gifted side in the world, they could be sure there would be no shortage of passion and commitment from their opponents.

Once again, this was far from an impressive performance. The first half was littered with handling errors but they plundered a Tommy Bowe try shortly before half-time. After the break, James Paterson got the Americans off the mark with a penalty before hooker Rory Best touched down, and shortly afterwards Brian passed back inside to give Tommy his second try to help Ireland to a 22–10 victory.

The wet conditions made ball handling tricky, but the sheer number of Irish mistakes was a very real concern for Declan and Brian. They were taken by surprise by a highly committed American defence, but frankly this wasn't good enough and everybody knew they'd have to raise their games in a major way if they were to stand any chance at all of beating Australia in just six days' time. It didn't help that earlier that day the Wallabies had thrashed Italy 32–6. There was little cause for optimism, and a huge amount needed to be worked on in training during the week.

In the days leading up that match, the squad focused on key areas, especially defence, maintaining possession, keeping discipline at the breakdown, and ball control. It was in basic areas like these that they had let themselves down in recent matches. Day by day, they worked to put these things right, and as Brian prepared to lead his team onto the field at Eden Park the following Saturday, they were all in a very different frame of mind to the previous week. The day before the match, there was a poignant moment when Jerry Flannery, who was forced to withdraw from the squad after the USA game with a troublesome calf injury, handed out the team jerseys. Jerry was to turn 33 the following month, and sadly any ambitions he had of being part of a World Cup winning side were now over, but Brian was certainly glad to have him around and was humbled to receive the jersey from him.

Brian took to the field to the sound of more than 58,000 spectators cheering him on. While many in the ground had made the relatively short flight across from Australia, there was a significant Irish contingent. He and all the boys knew they owed it to them to put in a strong performance. Ireland was going through an extremely difficult time economically and many of those fans had made considerable sacrifices to support their team. What followed was a complete and utter transformation in the team's performance.

Ireland produced an encouraging first-half display, but Australia nudged ahead with a James O'Connor penalty following a collapsed Irish scrum. Jonny Sexton sent his first penalty attempt wide but on 16 minutes he levelled at 3–3. This lifted the team's mood and a good period followed as the fired-up pack made inroads, and Jonny soon put his side 6–3 in front with a well-judged drop goal. O'Connor kicked Australia back on terms at 6–6 and both kickers missed chances before the half-time interval.

It was worth remembering that the Wallabies had gone into the break at 6–6 the previous week against Italy, but had gone on to score four tries in the first 17 minutes of the second half, so a backlash was more than possible when play resumed. However, Ireland were determined to put in a gutsy effort that reflected Declan's pragmatic approach to the game. Nine minutes after play resumed, Jonny restored Ireland's lead with a penalty. He struck the post with a later attempt, but then Ronan came on for the injured Gordon D'Arcy, and he assumed kicking duties for the remainder of the game, slotting over two further penalties to help his country to a 15–6 victory.

This had been a breathtaking performance, and Ireland had created the biggest shock of the tournament so far. Declan's coaching during the week had paid off, while Brian had once again demonstrated why he was the greatest on-field leader in world rugby.

In the post-match press conference, Declan was quick to bring his team, and indeed the wider Irish support base, back down to earth. He admitted that it was 'quite nice' to get a win over Australia, but added that they were still a long way from qualifying from their pool, and it would be 'meaningless' if they did not go on to progress. When Brian spoke, he was humble, and said that first and foremost, they 'owed' themselves a big performance, but they also owed the Irish public one as well. They had been made to sit through more than their fair share of poor displays in recent months, and this performance had gone a long way towards putting things right. Brian also echoed Declan's sentiments about not getting too carried away with this win. Their job was far from over and it was important to keep their feet on the ground.

In the next match they faced Russia, who, although by far the weakest team in the group, had managed to score 17 points against Italy. Declan decided to rest Brian as part of 10 changes he made from the victory over Australia. Brian wasn't really suffering with injury, but at the age of 32 Declan thought it best to save him for the bigger battles that lay ahead. Russia were no match for Ireland under Leo Cullen's captaincy. They scored a total of nine tries on their way to a 62–12 victory, leading them to the top of Pool C with one game to play.

Ireland had plenty of experience against their final pool opponents, Italy, and Brian knew what to expect as he returned to captain the side. During the past decade, they had grown in stature, year on year, and, on their day, were capable of beating any of the Six Nations sides. A side that included the likes of Martin Castrogiovanni and Mirco Bergamasco could not be taken for granted. Indeed, Geordan Murphy knew Castrogiovanni very well from their time together at the Leicester Tigers, where they went into business together running an Italian restaurant in Harborough. Italy had recovered from the second-half disaster in their opening match against Australia to record convincing wins against Russia and the USA. With Australia holding such a strong points difference, both sides needed a win in this game to progress to the quarter-finals.

The first half at Otago Stadium, Dunedin was a fairly even contest, but three penalty kicks from Ronan put Ireland 9–6 in front at the interval. Not for the first time in his career, Brian's side fell victim to a highly dubious decision by referee Jonathan Kaplan, who disallowed a Tommy Bowe try on the half-hour mark following an alleged 'forward pass' by Sean O'Brien, which replays showed to be absolutely fine. However, it was in the second half when the game really came to life.

Three minutes after the restart, Ronan kicked his fourth penalty of the match, and shortly afterwards, his audacious drop-goal attempt went wide of the posts as Ireland tried to make their territorial dominance count. Then, on 47 minutes, Brian scored the first try of the game when he ran in under the posts after anticipating and accepting a deft inside pass from Tommy, who had broken through the Italian defence.

Brian had reminded everyone of why he was still the greatest outside centre in world rugby. His judgement was spot-on as he outwitted his opponents. Ronan added the extras and later in the half Keith Earls, who was celebrating his 24th birthday, scored two tries to help Ireland to a convincing 36–6 victory.

The win meant that Ireland had gone through their four pool games undefeated, and now faced a nail-biting quarter-final encounter against Wales. In the post-match interview, Brian paid a warm tribute to the passion displayed by the Irish fans. He was fully aware of the sacrifices they had made to support the team at a time when money was tight. With a capacity of around 30,000, this was one of the smaller stadiums, but it was like a sea of green and the noise generated had been incredible. Brian also thanked the ex-pats living in New Zealand, as well as local people who had got behind the side.

The quarter-final match against Wales was undoubtedly one of the biggest matches of Brian's career.

He had come up against Wales sides of varying strength throughout his long career, but never before had he faced them in a match of this magnitude. This was far bigger than any Six Nations game. Indeed, from a purely selfish point of view, it was far bigger than any World Cup match he had played before. There would be no 'try again in four years' for Brian. Lose this match, and never again would he have the chance to captain a World Cup winning side.

Wales's path to the quarter-final had been a relatively untroubled one. They were unfortunate to lose their opening Pool D match against South Africa by a single point, but made it through to the last eight comfortably and had played some impressive rugby along the way. This was a team that had gone through gruelling training camps in Poland before the tournament, and were now a very different prospect from the mediocre outfit that had narrowly beaten Ireland during the Six Nations earlier in the year. Brian knew that the Irish boys would have to produce a performance similar to the one against Australia if they were to keep their dreams of lifting the Webb Ellis Cup alive.

Brian led his team onto the pitch at the compact Westpac Stadium in Wellington knowing that this was arguably the biggest game of his career to date. Mess up today, and never again would he play in a World Cup match.

Unfortunately, Ireland got off to the worst possible

start as their opponents patiently built a multi-phase attack in which Jamie Roberts took a high ball going forward before Leigh Halfpenny put Shane Williams over in the right corner, which was soon confirmed as a try by the video referee. Rhys Priestland added the conversion to put the Welsh 7–0 in front.

Ireland failed to build pressure on the back of Welsh indiscipline, and instead of kicking for goal, the Irish settled for a series of attacking line-outs, which with the benefit of hindsight was a rare poor captaincy decision by Brian. Roberts eventually put Wales on the front foot, but Brian intercepted his pass to Mike Phillips to launch Ireland's best attack of the opening half. Gordon D'Arcy timed a brilliant dummy run, but Williams somehow managed to hold Sean O'Brien off the floor as the flanker crossed the line to deny the Irish a first try.

A penalty kick from Ronan finally put Ireland on the scoreboard, but Halfpenny's long-range penalty restored Wales's seven-point advantage at the interval. Declan's half-time team talk had quite an impact on Ireland early in the second half as Stephen Ferris and Tommy Bowe combined to give Keith Earls the time and space to score in the corner, and Ronan added the extras to level the match at 10–10.

However, the scores remained level for just five minutes as Mike Phillips stole away on the blindside on the back of Alun Wyn Jones's powerful drive. Priestland failed with the conversion and also saw a penalty rebound off the post, but Wales went further ahead when centre Jonathan Davies fended off Cian Healey and burst clear to score. This time, Priestland added the conversion to put the Wales 12 points ahead with 15 minutes remaining. Brian's dreams of leading his country to World Cup glory were disappearing forever.

Ireland didn't go down without a fight. Replacement scrum-half Eoin Reddan conjured a superb pass to Sean O'Brien, but the Irish flanker was halted three metres short and knocked on before Healey was penalised at the scrum, allowing Wales to clear. Ireland kept battling and threw all they had left at Wales, but they couldn't break down the defence and ended succumbed to a 22–10 defeat.

For all Brian's ability, he was unable to come up with any answers for unlocking the Welsh defence, who had been coached to perfection by rugby league great Shaun Edwards. As he left the pitch, he knew that was the end – he would not go down in history as the man who led Ireland to World Cup glory. Speaking to the media shortly afterwards, he admitted he had been wrong in choosing line-outs over penalty kicks in the first half, and admitted he was bitterly disappointed both for himself and for the team.

Brian has always kept life's ups and downs firmly in perspective, and has never been one for hyperbole, but he admitted that losing this game after such a promising start to the tournament was tough, and having to accept that he would never lead his country to World Cup glory was a bitter pill to swallow.

Chapter 22

KINGS OF
EUROPE

There was little point in Brian dwelling on where things had gone wrong in New Zealand. As he arrived home, the 2011/12 season was well underway, and he had plenty he wanted to achieve with both Leinster and Ireland in the months ahead. His club had won two Heineken Cups in three seasons, and he felt that under Joe Schmidt's guidance and Leo Cullen's captaincy, there was no reason why they couldn't go on and win it again. At Ireland level, for all the great individual performances and Triple Crowns, the reality was that they had won the Six Nations (and its predecessor, the Five Nations) just once in the last 27 years. The Grand Slam was now nearly three years ago, and felt like a distant memory. For a man of Brian's ambition, and for a team of this ability, this wasn't good enough.

Shortly after landing home, Brian gave an interview with the *Evening Herald* in which he mapped out his plans for the future. He intended playing two more seasons for both Ireland and Leinster, but would bow out after the 2013 Lions tour in Australia. Brian had battled through the World Cup with a shoulder problem that wasn't regarded as a major cause for concern at the time. In fact, he had been suffering from it on and off since the Six Nations in the spring. Three weeks after arriving home from New Zealand, Brian was due to line up for Leinster as they faced arch rivals Munster in the RaboDirect PRO12, but when he didn't play any part, rumours began to circulate that his shoulder problem was more serious than previously thought. After the weekend, it was confirmed that he would undergo surgery for a trapped nerve in his shoulder the following week and would be ruled out for up to six months.

The news came as a bitter blow to Brian. He was shortly to turn 33 and he was running out of chances to win major silverware with Ireland. Indeed, after such a long lay-off at his age, he could be far from certain of returning to international rugby ever again. He was also extremely disappointed to be ruled out of Leinster's bid to retain the Heineken Cup, although there was a possibility he could return for the latter stages if his recovery went to schedule. Realistically, this surgery needed to be carried out not only to prolong his rugby career, but to give him a good quality of life. It was causing him problems not just in his shoulder, but also in his neck, and intermittently he was suffering from pins and needles. He was the first to admit that in recent games, he had needed several minutes to recover after instances of heavy contact, and he felt he wouldn't be doing himself or his teammates justice if he carried on like this for too long.

During Brian's lengthy recuperation, Leinster ended Heineken Cup Pool 3 unbeaten as they completed convincing victories over Glasgow Warriors, Bath, and Montpellier, with the only slight slip-up coming in the shape of a 16–16 draw away at the French outfit. The Six Nations was a far less happy experience, as Ireland, captained in Brian's absence by Paul O'Connell, completed victories over Italy and Scotland, but suffered a narrow defeat against Wales on the opening weekend and later on a substantial loss against England. Their match away at France in week two was postponed due to a waterlogged pitch, but was rescheduled for the rest weekend between weeks three and four, and two Tommy Bowe tries helped Ireland to a 17–17 draw. Ireland ended the championship third in the table, well behind Grand Slam winners Wales and a strong England side. However, they could take some consolation from the fact they topped the 'tries scored' column with 13, three more than Wales, but they had conceded significantly more points than the top two finishers.

Brian's recovery was going well, and by the middle of March he was ready to return to action for Leinster. In his absence, they had gone on a 20-match unbeaten run, and sat comfortably at the top of the RaboDirect PRO12 table. His comeback match saw them take on the Ospreys at the RDS Arena. A crowd of more than 18,000 gave Brian a rapturous reception as he took to the field for the first time since the World Cup, but it was to be a disappointing evening for his team. Brian beat two defenders in his first attacking move of the game, but soon began to fade, and Leinster lost the game due to a hugely controversial Ospreys try by Richard Hibbard in the 77th minute, which the television match official appeared to get wrong, earning the visitors victory by a single point.

Things went much better for Brian a fortnight later when he took to the field for Leinster for their Heineken Cup quarter-final against the Cardiff Blues in front of a crowd of more than 50,000 people at the Aviva Stadium. Brian looked razor-sharp throughout the match and played a major part in the 34–3 victory, setting up a Rob Kearney try on the half-hour mark before adding one himself four minutes later.

Things were much tougher in their semi-final encounter away at big-spending French outfit Clermont Auvergne. Cian Healey's try moments after half-time proved decisive, while Jonathan Sexton kicked 11 points and Man of the Match Rob Kearney slotted a terrific drop goal. However, Leinster's defence was put to the test in the final five minutes as they withstood a barrage of Clermont attacks. Wesley Fofana thought he had won it for the hosts with more than 78 minutes gone but TV replays showed the lightning-fast centre had dropped the ball over the try line. Even after Leinster won the resulting scrum five metres from their own line, Clermont somehow earned another shot at glory as the clock ticked towards 80 minutes. But with three points for a penalty not enough to win it for Clermont, their final surge to the try line ended in disappointment as they infringed at the ruck and Brian breathed a huge sigh of relief as his side hung on to win the match 19–15 and book their place in the final for the second year in a row, where they would face Ulster, who had won a close encounter against Edinburgh the previous day.

Joe Schmidt and Leo Cullen were taking Leinster from strength to strength. They ended the regular season top of the PRO12, having lost just three games all season. Unfortunately, Brian suffered a minor setback just days before he was due to play in their PRO12 semi-final encounter against the Glasgow Warriors, when he twisted his knee in training. He had to undergo keyhole surgery to trim his cartilage, but there was little danger that he wouldn't be fit to take part in the Heineken Cup final the following weekend. Leinster completed a narrow 19–15 victory over the Glasgow Warriors without Brian and Rob Kearney, and played the final 60 minutes of the match without the injured Gordon D'Arcy. This victory, just a week before the Heineken Cup final, was a tribute to the squad depth and strong team spirit that had been developed during the last few years.

In the week leading up to the Heineken Cup final at Twickenham, all the signs were promising. Brian was a tad frustrated at having to spend so much time sitting at home and resting. He had never been a great watcher of rugby from the sidelines, and hated not being involved, but he felt good as the days ticked down. Gordon D'Arcy had to have stitches in a head wound sustained against Glasgow, but it soon became clear he'd be fit for the final. Meanwhile, Rob Kearney's back problem was responding well to treatment, and he would be raring to go come the following Saturday.

This was to be a Heineken Cup final like no other. It was to be played in front of a crowd of more than 81,000, larger than any previous final of this competition. Leinster were going for their third win in four years. There was now a sad inevitability that Brian would be forced to end his international career with a trophy cabinet somewhat emptier than a player of his stature would merit, but with Leinster, a win here would cement his status as an integral part of a truly great club side.

The roar from the Twickenham crowd as Leo Cullen led Leinster onto the pitch created an atmosphere comparable to a major home game at the Aviva Stadium rather than an away trip to the home of English rugby. Ulster, who became the first Irish province to win the trophy 13 years earlier, started the stronger side, as centre Darren Cave jinked through a hole in midfield, John Afoa and Stephen Ferris carried strongly, and Ruan Pienaar calmly kicked the first penalty after seven minutes.

This seemed to wake Leinster up, and they began to launch their off-loading game. Their first try arrived in the 13th minute after they won a turnover on the Ulster 22. Referee Nigel Owens had already signalled a penalty but the powerful Sean O'Brien sensed an opening and slipped through Tom Court's tackle from close range, and after a lengthy consultation with the television match official to determine downward pressure on the ball, a try was awarded.

Ulster was expected to play a territorial kicking game but instead seemed to want to match Leinster's off-loading, and on occasions it came close to paying off. Soon, Leinster broke into Ulster territory again, when Eoin Reddan appeared unsure whether he had the pace to get to the line and was held short in the right corner, before Brian's offload almost put Isa Nacewa over on the left corner.

Brian showed his genius after 31 minutes when a

delicious offload out the back of his hand to the charging O'Brien led to Leinster's second try. Sean weaved around one tackler before being stopped a metre short, but prop Cian Healey twisted out over Andrew Trimble's tackle to score, and Jonny Sexton added the extras.

Leinster were 14–3 ahead with nearly 50 minutes still to play, and things looked ominous for Ulster, but they did have a half-chance shortly before half-time, only for the inexperienced fly-half Paddy Jackson to fluff a drop-goal attempt inside the Leinster 22. However, a Pienaar penalty brought a degree of competitiveness to the scoreline at the interval.

The Ulster surge was short-lived as Leinster turned up the heat early in the second half. A thumping tackle by Nacewa on Cave was a statement of intent, and they were ruthless in exploiting Jackson's naivety. The youngster kicked out on the full from just in front of his own 22 to hand Leinster an attacking platform. This was to be his last move before being replaced by Ian Humphreys.

Leinster built up a head of steam from the line-out and when Trimble dived in to bring down the maul rumbling to the Ulster line, the referee had no hesitation in awarding the penalty try. Jonny's conversion gave Leinster a 15 point cushion, which remained intact as he and Pienaar exchanged penalties in quick succession.

With 24 minutes remaining, Leinster had a 24–9 lead, and Ulster soon turned down an easy three points in favour of a scrum. It looked a dubious decision, even more so when Wannenburg's speculative blind pass behind him went forward. Humphreys then went solo with numbers outside him as another chance went begging. To their credit, Ulster kept plugging away, and their persistence paid off as Paddy Wallace worked some room and popped up a pass for lock Dan Tuohy to dive over in the left corner. Pienaar missed his first kick of the day with the conversion which kept it a 10-point game, and a Leinster penalty soon saw that extended by three. Jonny added another to seal victory with six minutes left after Terblance was sin-binned for a tip tackle on Leinster replacement hooker Sean Cronin.

There was still time for some icing on the Leinster cake, and this came when replacement prop Heinke van der Merwe went over for the side's fourth try. This equalled Brieve's record of four tries, and their 19-point winning margin in the 1997 final. Fergus McFadden missed the conversion, but there was more to come when Cronin sprinted the length of the field to score, breaking all sorts of records and helping his side to an astonishing 42–14 victory.

This had truly been one of the most special days of Brian's career. Any kind of win in this game would have confirmed this squad's status as one of the greatest club sides of all time, but the sheer magnitude of this victory was a tribute to all the hard work and dedication of everybody connected with the squad. It was a shame in some ways that Brian had missed so much of the domestic season, and hadn't played any part in Leinster's pool stage victories, but when it mattered, he had delivered.

Nobody deserved this success more than Brian. He had stayed loyal to Leinster throughout the 13 years of his professional playing career. It was becoming increasingly fashionable for leading players to accept big-money moves to wealthy French clubs (or in some cases English ones), but Brian had always remained true to his roots. After many years of frustrations and internal difficulties, he had become an integral part of one of the greatest club sides in rugby history.

Brian and the boys couldn't allow themselves to get too carried away with this victory, as the following weekend they had to be fit and ready for the PRO12 final at the RDS Arena. This time last season, they had lost the final of the same competition to Munster a week after winning the Heineken Cup, and this time Brian knew it was important to keep their feet on the ground as they prepared to face Welsh outfit the Ospreys.

Leinster had home advantage, but the Ospreys' regular season had been almost as impressive as theirs, winning 16 matches against Leinster's 18. Two of their five defeats had come against Leinster. Furthermore, the Ospreys had hammered defending champions Munster 45–10 in their semi-final match. This was a massive game for the visitors, not least because it would be the last time the great Shane Williams lined up in their jersey before heading off to Japan for the final stages of his playing career. This was certainly not a game for Brian and the boys to take lightly. Win here, and they would become the first side to win the domestic and European double since Wasps in 2004. Lose, and once again it would look as though they had taken their foot off the gas before the season had ended.

The atmosphere at the RDS was very different to the one generated at Twickenham the previous week. A capacity crowd of 18,500 created a boisterous, intense atmosphere, with every seat and terrace providing a close-up view of the action. The home side got off to a solid start and mounted a series of attacks before Brian showed some great footwork and handed the ball to Sean Cronin, who went through a gap in the Ospreys' defensive line to score the opening try on 26 minutes. Leinster scored again nine minutes later, this time thanks to Isa Nacewa, and the ever-reliable boot of Jonathan Sexton gave the home side a 17–9 advantage at half-time.

A try from Andy Beck brought the Ospreys right back into the game shortly after the restart, but two penalties from Jonny gave Leinster a strong advantage, only for Shane Williams to score his first try of the game in the corner.

Leinster regained their composure and Nacewa grabbed his second try of the game, with Jonny adding the extras, but they had to make do without Nathan White for the latter stages of the game when the tight-head prop was sent to the sin bin. The Ospreys took full advantage as Williams scored his second try of the game. Dan Biggar, who had kicked consistently all day, added the extras to give the Ospreys a dramatic late victory by a single point with the scores at 30–31.

This was a bitter pill for Brian and Leinster to follow, but in truth, they had lacked the intensity of the previous week, and despite their best efforts, they had fallen short of the required standard. It may have come as some consolation that Ospreys players had recently become the dominant force in the Wales national team, and that Shane Williams had brought his time at the region to a close in spectacular fashion.

Once the pain of the defeat had eased, Brian could look back on this season with a sense of pride. His recuperation from surgery kept him on the sidelines for the bulk of it, but he returned to play a pivotal role in what most people agreed was the biggest day in Leinster's history, and had come within a whisker to helping them achieve a European and domestic double. Only a player of Brian O'Driscoll's ability could make this kind of large and immediate impact following such a long absence.

Chapter 23

NIGHTMARES IN NEW ZEALAND

There was little time for Brian to dwell on the events of the last few weeks as he prepared to resume his role as Ireland captain for a summer tour of New Zealand. This was the first time Ireland had embarked on a three-Test tour against the All Blacks, and it marked the beginning of an IRB-backed global calendar that runs through until 2019. In planning the series, it was anticipated that Ireland would face provincial and Maori opposition. However, to allow Ireland to focus on the Tests, the IRFU decided there would be no midweek fixtures. Indeed, Ireland's only preparation before they flew out came in the form of a non-cap encounter against the Barbarians at Kingsholm, Gloucester, which didn't feature any of the Leinster players who had played in the PRO12 final two days earlier. On this occasion, the Ireland XV lost a lively and competitive encounter 29–28 due to a late Felipe Contepomi penalty.

Expectations were modest as Brian headed to New Zealand. Both with and without his leadership, Ireland had been frustratingly inconsistent for the last few years. There would be moments of sheer brilliance, but there were just as many performances littered with elementary mistakes. On this tour, they would have to make do without giants like Paul O'Connell, Stephen Ferris and Tommy Bowe, who had been ruled out through injury, and shortly after arriving in New Zealand, Mike Ross was added to the list of absentees. However, there were some positive vibes as they headed off – Rob Kearney had recently been named European Player of the Year, and had been in sensational form throughout Leinster's Heineken Cup campaign, and Brian was well and truly back following a long absence. This was an important series for him. For obvious reasons, his memories of previous trips to New Zealand were not ones of undiluted happiness, and, knowing this would be his final tour of the country as a player, he wanted to seize this opportunity to put things right.

Brian was keen to make the most of anyone who could help give him an extra edge. Early in his career, he had seen a few sports psychologists about various things, but had been largely unimpressed with what they had to say, and had never built up a long-term relationship with any of them. His biggest gripe was that he didn't think they really worked in a team environment. He thought that in a group of 20 people, most would just say whatever they thought the psychologist wanted to hear. In other words, they would be reluctant to admit they were feeling low, because it could be perceived as a sign of weakness in front of their teammates.

His attitude changed after the 2007 World Cup, when, suffering from a massive lack of confidence, he went to see Enda McNulty, a successful Gaelic footballer for Armagh who was gaining a reputation as a highly-respected sports psychologist. Enda took an impartial approach, and made Brian answer his own questions. He reminded Brian of things he already knew, but made him think of them in a different light. In their sessions, Brian talked a lot about working on his weaknesses in training. Enda taught him to see things differently. He taught Brian to put a greater emphasis on his strengths instead of his weaknesses. He told him to look at what he did well, and to work to make them truly outstanding. Enda saw weaknesses as things to be chipped away at, but the main emphasis was becoming great at your strengths. By this stage, Brian had completely bought into Enda's philosophy. It was also important to remind Brian that 'form' is all in the mind. For this reason, Enda got Brian to jot down a list of his best performances so that he could put together a highlights DVD for him to absorb. They didn't see each other especially often, but Brian found Enda a good person to turn to, and someone who could give him that extra boost as he prepared for the very big occasions, as inches lead to the golden mile.

In fact, Brian didn't like to think of Enda as a 'sports psychologist' at all, but rather as a life coach. He had gone to Enda to organise different areas of his life and he had given him clarity. Brian was now wise enough to go to Enda before a panic or serious problem with confidence had set in. It's quite possible that their relationship could extend well beyond the time when Brian stops playing rugby.

This was a major series for New Zealand. The previous autumn, they had been crowned world champions, but since then their coach, Graham Henry, who was hardly Brian's best friend, had stepped down and been replaced by Steve Hansen. This series was Hansen's first in charge of the side, and would feature a number of new faces.

In an interview a few days before the first Test, Ireland assistant coach Les Kiss tried to build up the match as a clash between Brian and Sonny Bill Williams, who had been included in the All Blacks side after displacing Ma'a Nonu, but Nonu, who had scored two tries in his five appearances against Ireland, paid a warm tribute to Brian, saying: 'O'Driscoll is going great – he always turns out. He's such a great player that I admire. I've been watching him for a long time and he always seems to turn up at the right time, especially for Leinster. The older he gets, the better he gets really.

Brian led his side out for the first Test at a floodlit Eden Park, Auckland, with expectations modest, but he was determined to make the most of this one final chance to leave New Zealand a winning series captain. He tried to block out the intimidating pre-match tradition of the Haka and instead focus on the game ahead. Just five minutes in, Dan Carter, who had missed the World Cup through injury, put the All Blacks 3–0 in front. Jonny Sexton soon levelled things with a good kick, but this was to be his only contribution of the first half.

Unusually for one of Declan Kidney's teams, Ireland were ambitiously moving the ball wide, unafraid to take on the world champions at their own game throughout the opening exchanges. However, Carter, keen to reassert his status as a feared presence in the All Blacks team, kicked two superb long-range penalties to put his side 9–3 ahead. Debutant winger Julian Savea announced his arrival on the international scene with the opening try in the 26th minute, when Sonny Bill Williams off-loaded to Carter, who drew the Irish defence before passing to the youngster. Carter converted for 16–3 and the Irish deficit became 20 just eight minutes later when full-back Israel Dagg passed to Savea who scored his second try, despite the last-gasp efforts of Ireland backs Conor Murray and Rob Kearney.

The All Blacks didn't slack in the second half, as just four minutes after the restart Carter and Dagg were instrumental in another pacey attack which set up Savea for his hat-trick try. Carter's conversion made it 30–3, but Ireland had a fleeting moment of encouragement when Rory Best won possession deep in Irish territory and Jonny kicked forward for winger Fergus McFadden to chase and beat the retreating Richie McCaw to score a consolation try.

It was to be a brief respite for the visitors as the All Blacks piled on the pressure and secured their fourth try of the night from a five-metre scrum in the 57th minute. Kieran Read picked up at the back and fed replacement flanker Adam Thomson to power over with Ireland's defence in disarray. Carter dragged his conversion wide for his only miss of the night. Tired and deflated, Ireland conceded a sixth try late on as a well-timed offload from Carter found replacement Aaron Cruden, who sent a pop pass to centre Conrad Smith, helping him to a try at close-range.

Ireland had lost 42–10, meaning they had been defeated in 25 of their 26 matches against the All Blacks – the exception being a 10–10 draw at Lansdowne Road way back in 1973. In truth, Brian had failed to make his presence felt in this match and at times looked like an old man. Both he and the rest of the side would have to raise their games massively if they were to stand any chance at all of salvaging the series in the second Test the following week.

Ireland welcomed back Gordon D'Arcy, Andrew Trimble and Mike Ross to the side for the second Test at Rugby League Park, Christchurch. A huge amount of work had been done in training to get Ireland physically and mentally prepared for the challenge ahead. There was no midweek game to distract them and few other commitments. Therefore, there were no excuses for another poor performance this time around.

In front of a capacity crowd of 21,000, the Kiwis were rocked when, 10 minutes into the game, Jonny Sexton kicked a penalty into the corner and Ireland successfully claimed Rory Best's line-out delivery. The drive was held up just short but Conor Murray lifted and quickly found the shortest of gaps to touch down. Jonny missed the conversion but soon added a penalty to put his side 10–0 in front. This was a remarkable start by Ireland and a huge contrast with the sloppiness of the previous week. Inevitably, New Zealand gradually turned up the heat and the pressure forced some mistakes from Ireland. An offside call led to Dan Carter's first penalty and he added another after the Irish failed to roll away.

Ireland conceded another soft penalty when Mike Ross was caught coming in from the side and Carter reduced the deficit to 10–9. There were nervous moments shortly before the interval when Carter could have given his side the lead, but he was just short with his long-range penalty attempt.

When play resumed, Ireland were under pressure straight from the kick-off, and after just three minutes New Zealand scrum-half Aaron Smith, who had made his international debut in the Auckland Test, was driven over for his try. Carter added a terrific touchline conversion to make it 16–10, and many would've expected the hosts to pull away from this position.

To Ireland's huge credit, they kept the pressure on. Sexton and Carter exchanged penalties before two more penalties from the Leinster number 10 brought Ireland level with less than 12 minutes remaining.

New Zealand were reduced to 14 men in the 72nd minute when full-back Israel Dagg was sin-binned for a flattening follow-through on his opposite number Rob Kearney. Jonny's penalty attempt, which would have given Ireland the lead, did not have the distance. Ireland looked set to secure a draw, but with the clock past 80 minutes, Carter scrambled over the drop goal following a five-metre scrum in front of the posts to give the home side a 22–19 victory.

For Brian, this was a difficult defeat to accept. Both he and the players he led had been massively better than the previous week, and had been competitive throughout the match, only to lose it right at the death. There could be no coming back from this. For all his achievements in the game, Brian would not be able to list a series win in

New Zealand amongst them. After the match, Brian put things into context, saying, 'We got back on level terms and to concede the way we did was disappointing. Our display was hugely improved from last week and I'm proud of the lads. We let ourselves down in the first Test and we spoke about that, we spoke about the jersey and concentrating on our own game, but the scoreline still says an All Blacks win which is difficult to take considering the effort we put in.'

One of Brian's greatest strengths has always been his ability to remain dignified in defeat and to keep things firmly in perspective. He was never one for excessively emotive comments or exaggeration. Even as a boy, he always kept things in sensible proportions, and as an adult this very much remained the case.

Getting the boys motivated for the final Test in Waikato was always going to be hard work for Declan and Brian. The series was lost, but they owed it to themselves, to their green jerseys, and to their supporters to put in a strong performance. In the intervening week, the All Blacks had received some scathing criticism in their own national media, and as the game kicked off, it became clear they were going to play this game at full throttle, as though they had a point to prove. Ireland saw the return of Paddy Wallace, making it three different inside centres in three matches, while Keith Earls returned, this time at number 11.

New Zealand had to make do without Dan Carter, but

the performance of local favourite Aaron Cruden at fly-half meant he was not missed. The All Blacks were ruthless as they scored four tries in the first 22 minutes, with Cruden playing an instrumental role in three of them before he had to depart injured after 25 minutes. They led 29–0 at half-time, and a further five tries in the second half helped them to a record 60–0 victory, easily beating their previous best, a 59–6 victory in Wellington in 1992.

In his typically understated way, Brian referred to the defeat as 'a bit embarrassing'. He added, 'We started terribly and they came at us. We just made too many errors. We had a lot of tackles to make and that scoreline tells its own story. They were clinical at the breakdown and we were terrible. We knew that we had to start well and we didn't and that's what the All Blacks do – when they get a 15 or 20-point lead they just play their own game and you're running after them for 80 minutes. To be 21 points down before 20 minutes was up, we were going to be chasing the game.'

The reality was that Ireland hadn't recovered from the poor start, and were utterly outclassed at the breakdown – New Zealand won all the collisions. This tour had highlighted everything that had been wrong with Irish rugby during the past few years. At their best, the Irish could give anyone a decent game, even the world champions. After all, they were seconds away from securing a draw in the second Test. Yet a terrible lack of consistency saw them grossly underperform on other occasions, and this simply wasn't good enough if they were to sit at world rugby's top table. Brian was now 33 years old, and inevitably the thoughts of some were turning to a time when he was no longer around. There were even calls in some quarters for him to be phased out of the side over the course of the next year, following poor performances in the first and third Tests, yet there were times in the second where he was close to his brilliant best.

Brian had to come to terms with his disappointment, but he did appreciate what he had in life and what he'd achieved in the game. He would be flying home to Amy, whose career as an actress and novelist was going well. Her first novel, *Hello, Heartbreak*, had been a number one bestseller, while her second, *I Wished for You*, was due out in the coming autumn.

On the acting front, the previous autumn she had starred in a sitcom for Comedy Central (UK and Ireland) called *Threesome*. Three inseparable friends, aged around 30, live together: Amy's character, Alice, her boyfriend Mitch, and their gay best friend Richie. After one particularly big night out, they end up having an unplanned threesome which results in an even more unplanned pregnancy. As a result, they decide to ditch the party lifestyle, go ahead with the pregnancy and raise the baby as a threesome.

There was one rather unfortunate side effect to all this.

The programme debuted while Brian was away on World Cup duty the previous autumn, and an article in a New Zealand paper that read 'Brian O'Driscoll's wife is pregnant, who is the dad?' apparently didn't make it sufficiently clear that it was referring to a TV show. Some of Brian's teammates thought it was really funny and gave him a bit of stick for it, but when he saw the series he loved it and was thrilled by its ongoing success.

The programme was very well received by the critics when it began its original run in October 2011, and a second series was due to air in the coming autumn. Brian was rightly very proud of all Amy's achievements and she continued to bring a sense of stability, happiness and perspective to his life. She remained a level-headed, down-to-earth and totally unpretentious lady who understood how her husband's mind worked and what he wanted to achieve both in rugby and in life. They had been married for two years now, and by the autumn, they had announced to the world that Amy was expecting their first child – for real this time!

Chapter 24

A SEASON
OF CONTRASTS

The 2012/13 season got off to a wobbly start at Leinster. Brian was one of 11 internationals missing from the side as they lost 45–20 away to the Scarlets. The depleted squad were more impressive in their next match, as 18 points from the boot of Ian Madigan helped them to a home win against the Newport Gwent Dragons, but it was apparent they were a long way from their form the previous season.

Brian returned to action for the next match away at Benetton Treviso, where he played a pivotal role in securing their 18–19 victory against the rapidly improving Italian outfit. The home side dominated the first-half scoring, but a penalty from Jonny Sexton shortly before the interval cut their lead to 8–3. Four minutes after the restart, Brian ran from midfield to cross the line unopposed. Treviso looked to have snatched a dramatic win as replacement scrum-half Fabio Semenzato scored three minutes before the end, but there was still time for a superb match-winning drop goal from Jonny.

Without Brian, they secured a comfortable win against the Edinburgh Warriors, but the following week suffered a humiliating 34–6 away defeat at Connaught, where Dan Parks made his presence felt on his debut. Brian was back for the big home match against arch rivals Munster. Some clever running from Fergus McFadden and Richard Strauss helped Brian to score in the left corner. He left the field early but played a commanding role in the 30–21 victory for his side.

This boost was important as they were now just days away from the start of their Heineken Cup match at home to the Exeter Chiefs – a formidable side who were always going to be tough to break down. Leinster showed flashes of brilliance but despite getting in the 22 four times in the first half, they got nothing from it. However, three penalties from Jonny gave them a 9–6 victory in what was ultimately a nervy display. Both the players and the fans at the RDS Arena were visibly relieved to have started the campaign with a win, albeit an unconvincing one.

The following week, Leinster travelled to the Parc Y Scarlets for the second time in as many months for their second Pool 5 match, knowing they'd need to raise their game both on the previous week's match and on their last visit to West Wales. A few days before the match, Brian admitted during an interview with the *Daily Telegraph* that he was 'excited' at reports linking him with a possible big-money move to Australian side New South Waratahs before the end of his career, where he would link up with ex-Leinster coach Michael Cheika. Brian tempered his enthusiasm by adding that 'time might have passed on that front' but added that he was 'definitely a never say never sort of person'. He said, 'You look at the individuals and you look at the calibre of sides and the quality of Super Rugby and the intensity of it, obviously it is a hugely high standard.' In response, Cheika made it clear that he would not approach Brian mid-season but said it was 'no secret' that Brian was one of a number of players in the PRO12 who would love to play club rugby Down Under. However, it was also possible that Brian was using this as a means of strengthening his negotiating hand with Leinster when his contract came up for renewal at the end of the season. It seemed unlikely to many that with Amy doing so well with her career and a baby on the way that he would seek to up roots at this time.

In the game against the Scarlets, Brian couldn't get on the scoresheet, but he played his part as Isa Nacewa's try and 15 points from Jonny's boot helped them to a 13–20 victory. These were two big wins in two weeks, and they appeared to have put their early season wobbles behind them.

There were now only a few weeks left before Brian was due to skipper Ireland in the Autumn Internationals, where they would face tough encounters against South Africa, Fiji and Argentina. Brian was keen to get himself as match-sharp as possible before then, and was committed to turning out for Leinster as they returned to PRO12 action. Leinster won their next match at home to a woeful Cardiff Blues side 59–22, but the victory came at a cost as Brian was forced off with an ankle injury.

The incident happened in the 18th minute, when he played a key role in helping Jamie Heaslip gain Leinster's third try. Brian had injured his ankle in the move, and attempted to play on but was forced to depart in the 23rd minute. Joe Schmidt was initially keen to emphasise that Brian's departure was precautionary and said that his ankle sprain was 'not serious', but three days later, after further tests had been carried out, it was revealed that he needed an operation and would be out for up to three months.

This was a bitter blow for Brian. At the age of 33, a year was a long time and he certainly could not guarantee that he would be fit and ready to line up for Ireland the next time they were due to take on Southern Hemisphere giants in the autumn of 2013. He was also frustrated not to be playing his part in Leinster's Heineken Cup campaign, where they would face back-to-back matches against Clermont Auvergne in the run-up to Christmas.

Ireland would have to cope without Brian, Rob Kearney and Sean O'Brien for the three upcoming Tests, so Jamie Heaslip was always going to have his work cut out as he captained the side for the series, which was to be played in Ireland. In the first match against South Africa, Ireland went from 12–3 in front at half-time to 12–16 losers. The visitors had been a different side in the second half – they had played their mauling game and managed to smother Ireland, but even so, there could be no excuses for a collapse of this magnitude. The reality was that Ireland had now lost five matches in a row – their worst run for 15 years.

Next up came an unofficial match against Fiji at Thormond Park, where Ireland fielded a much-changed, but still strong side, and scored eight tries, including three from Craig Gilroy, as they ended the match 53–0 winners. In the final match of the series against Argentina, Ireland produced a brilliant seven-try display to hammer the visitors and guarantee a crucial top eight ranking ahead of the 2015 World Cup draw. The superb Gilroy, Jonny Sexton, Richard Strauss and Simon Zebo notched up first-half tries for the home side as they led 24–9 at half-time. Jonny's second try was followed by two more Tommy Bowe touchdowns to give them a convincing 46–24 victory.

What was clear from this series was that Ireland were,

in many ways, starting to prepare for life without Brian. Younger men like Keith Earls and Darren Cave had worn his number 13 jersey with distinction. Cave, in particular, had made rapid progress in the last few years and was certainly one to watch for the future. From now on, Brian couldn't take the captaincy or indeed his place in the side for granted. He was slower than he once was, but his judgement was still very good and his leadership skills were among the best in world rugby.

In early December, and with Brian still out injured, Leinster lost their first Heineken Cup match in 17 when they were beaten 15–12 in a chess-like match away at Clermont. The following week at the Aviva, the French giants once again won 21–28, putting Leinster's hopes of making it through Pool 5 under serious threat. Nothing had gone seriously wrong in either of these matches, but this really was a clash of two of giants of European rugby, and without Brian they had fallen slightly short on these occasions.

Attentions returned to the PRO12 during the period either side of Christmas, and it was important, from both a psychological and mathematical perspective, that Leinster put the bruising encounters of the last few weeks behind them. Brian returned to light training around this time, but it would be a few weeks before he was match-fit. The match away at Ulster a few days before Christmas was always likely to be a tough encounter. Ulster had been unbeaten in the PRO12 all season, and had lost just one match in the Heineken Cup when Northampton Saints beat them by a single point. Leinster put up a decent fight as Fergus McFadden raced in on the left wing and Ian Madigan kicked four penalties, but the home side clinched a 27–19 victory when Andrew Trimble got over following Ruan Pienaar's crossfield kick.

In the period between Christmas and New Year, an Ian Madigan try helped them to a convincing 17–0 victory over Connacht at the RDS to end 2012 on a high. Brian's recovery was going well and he was set to play in their first match of 2013 away at a struggling Edinburgh. In front of fewer than 4,000 fans at Murrayfield, Leinster took a while to get going, but eventually won 16–31, securing them a bonus point. This was a low-key return for Brian, which was probably what he needed, and he was only really at the centre of the action when he was the victim of a high tackle by Allan Jacobsen.

The following week, it was back to Heineken Cup action at home to the Scarlets, in what was a must-win game if they were to have any chance at all of qualifying for the knockout stages. Leinster ran in five tries as they came out 33–14 winners, but the win was overshadowed when Brian, who came on as a replacement in the 61st minute, sustained an injury on his 'good' ankle that threatened his Six Nations campaign. After the match, Brian assured Joe Schmidt it was fine, but he said the same thing when he injured his other ankle earlier in the season.

During the course of the week, it became clear that Brian's injury wasn't as bad as first feared and he would be fit to play in their final pool game away to Exeter Chiefs, but it was at this time, with his 34th birthday just a few days away, that he received the news that Declan Kidney had replaced him with Jamie Heaslip as Ireland captain. The decision wasn't a massive surprise. Jamie had led Ireland through the Autumn Internationals and was widely regarded to have done a good job. He was five years Brian's junior, and Declan took the view that with Brian inevitably coming towards the end of his playing career, reappointing him as captain would be a step backwards. For Brian, he was understandably disappointed to have his ten year reign as captain brought to an end, but in interviews he was pragmatic and admitted that the upcoming Six Nations campaign might be his last. Nevertheless, he was committed to the cause as he returned to the rank and file, and there was never any suggestion that he would be anything other than a reliable team player and a source of support and encouragement for the younger players.

There was barely time for Brian to dwell on this news. Amy was now heavily pregnant and he was busy getting things ready at home for the arrival, and soon had to head to Exeter for a must-win game. The Chiefs had been through an up-and-down campaign. They had lost three of their games, but these had come away at Leinster, and both matches against Clermont, none of which had exactly been poor performances. They deserved respect and Brian went into the match knowing Leinster would have to be at their best if they were to come away with the win, which might, just, keep their campaign alive by earning them a best-placed runners-up spot with the help of a bonus point.

Leinster got off to the perfect start after just three minutes when Jonny Sexton's penalty to the corner gave Gordon D'Arcy the chance to step inside his man and score. Despite having England flanker Tom Johnson stretchered off with a knee injury after 14 minutes, Exeter remained competitive, and, like Leinster, rejected the chance to kick at goal, and were handsomely rewarded with a try from Neil Clark.

Leinster were back in front 11 minutes later as superb handling from Brian and Jonny sent Rob Kearney over in the corner. Jonny missed the conversion and Exeter hit back to take a five-point lead at the interval, with another line-out drive earning them a penalty try, and Gareth Steenson added the conversion and a late penalty. This looked like being the end of Leinster's Heineken Cup defence, and Brian knew he would have to produce a vintage performance in the second half if they were to stand any chance at all of progressing. They weren't going to go out without a fight. Four minutes into the second half, Brian finished off a fantastic multi-phased try in which he, Luke Fitzgerald and Leo Cullen all featured twice. Jonny added the extras, and eight minutes later, Jamie Heaslip powered over from the base of a five-metre scrum. Jonny once again converted, and although the two sides exchanged penalty kicks before the end, Leinster came through 20–29 winners, earning them a bonus point.

They now had an anxious wait until the following day as their place in the competition hung by a thread. Assuming Saracens beat a winless Edinburgh, the old enemy Munster would need four tries to claim Leinster's place in the quarter-finals. Unsurprisingly, Saracens won their game 40–7. Meanwhile, Munster put in a superb display as two tries by Simon Zebo and one each from Conor Murray and Mike Sherry gave them the four tries they needed. Leinster's incredible run in the Heineken Cup was over. They had become the first champions to exit at such an early stage since Wasps in 2008, and would have to settle for a place in the Amlin Challenge Cup, which was very much a consolation prize.

The time had come for Brian to join up with Ireland and prepare for what could well be his final Six Nations campaign. For a player of his stature and talent, four Triple Crowns, and one Championship (albeit a Grand Slam) was not enough, and overall, the team had underachieved during his years with them. A side that contained the likes of him, Ronan O'Gara, Geordan Murphy and Gordon D'Arcy should really have won the tournament more often. Now, the baton was gradually being handed on to a new generation, but Brian wasn't quite finished yet. There had been some unbelievably bad luck both for him and the squad as a whole over the years, but he was determined to make the most of this chance to put things right.

For Ireland, for coach Declan Kidney, and for new captain Jamie Heaslip, it was time to step up to the mark. The provinces Leinster, Munster, Ulster and Connacht had all enjoyed success in recent years against club sides from across Europe. When the cream from those sides joined up to represent Ireland, there was no excuse for them not to replicate this success at international level.

The first match saw Ireland travel to holders Wales. This was an unusual, unsettling time for the Welsh side. Grand Slam winning coach Warren Gatland had been largely absent from the setup for much of the last 12 months. Shortly after their Six Nations triumph, it was announced that Gatland would become Head Coach for the Lions tour of Australia in the summer of 2013, meaning he would be absent from the first part of Wales's Autumn Internationals and the whole of the 2013 Six Nations. Weeks later, Gatland broke both his heels falling from a ladder while spending time with his family in New Zealand, which left him unable to lead Wales in their summer tour of Australia. In Gatland's absence, attack coach Rob Howley was promoted to Head Coach, and his track record with the reigning Grand Slam champions had been a poor one to date.

They had lost all three matches in Australia, and had been defeated in both the Autumn Internationals he took charge of against Argentina and Samoa. However, when Gatland had returned for the final two matches, they lost heavily to New Zealand but had come within a whisker of beating Australia.

It was hard to gauge what kind of side Howley would bring to the Six Nations. The reality was that Wales hadn't won a match since the day they won the Grand Slam. There were huge question marks about his own judgement and abilities as a coach, and there was a degree of uncertainty as to whether Gatland would ever return, which unsettled the squad. Brian had got used to Gatland's snide digs at Ireland in the build-up to matches against Wales in recent years, which were a consequence of personal bitterness he felt at the way the IRFU had disposed of his services more than a decade earlier, but with him off the scene, things felt quite different. The personnel of the Wales playing squad hadn't changed much in the last 12 months, but their confidence had been knocked by recent humiliating defeats, and they no longer had the coach who had guided them to glory the previous year.

In the first match of the tournament on a Saturday lunchtime, Jamie led the side out in front of a packed Millennium Stadium. Ireland got off to a perfect start, when on the 10- minute mark Brian jinked inside Alex Cuthbert before delivering a sumptuous pass to Simon

437

Zebo, who scored the opening try. This was a classic Brian O'Driscoll manoeuvre, and he had silenced those who said he could no longer perform at this level in spectacular style. A try from Cian Healey helped them go 0–17 in front after just 23 minutes, and only a penalty kick from Leigh Halfpenny dented the lead at the interval. Ireland had completely dominated the first half and Brian's display had been a major factor in their success.

Three minutes after the resumption, Wales fly-half Dan Biggar missed a couple of tackles and Rob Kearney was held up on the line before Brian extended his Six Nations try count to 26, his 46th overall for Ireland. Jonny Sexton's conversion made it 30–3. From then on, Wales produced an astonishing fight-back as tries from Cuthbert and Halfpenny brought them right back into the match, and when Craig Mitchell's try on 75 minutes helped them to 22–30, an unlikely comeback seemed possible, but Ireland's defence held on for the win.

Brian, who was named Man of the Match, had silenced his critics in the best way possible. Those who were writing his international rugby obituary had been extremely premature. He may no longer have been captain, and his pace wasn't what it once was, but this had been a vintage performance, up there with the very best of his career.

There were areas for Ireland to work on as they prepared for their next match at home to England the following week. Despite dominating the first half against Wales, in the final half hour their concentration and intensity had dropped somewhat, and they couldn't risk a repeat of this in future matches.

Brian's mind wasn't entirely on the following Sunday's game against England as he returned to Dublin. Amy was due to give birth any day, and, although he tried to continue his preparations for the game as normally as possible, he was on standby in case she went into labour. They had chosen not to find out the gender of the baby beforehand, so there would be an element of surprise about it. On the Saturday evening, a heavily pregnant Amy attended the Irish Film and Television Awards with her mother, Sandra, while Brian remained at the Shelbourne Hotel with the Irish squad. She had previously joked that her worst nightmare would be to go into labour during the ceremony, but on the night, she added, 'If I was to go into labour tomorrow – it wouldn't come straight on. So there wouldn't be a problem with him [Brian] missing the match.'

Overnight, Amy was taken to the private wing of the National Maternity Hospital where she gave birth to a baby girl by caesarean section just before 10.30 am on the Sunday morning. Brian was at her side, and he was obviously delighted that baby Sadie had arrived safely and healthily. Becoming a parent is one of life's most amazing gifts, and Brian was naturally thrilled. His life had truly changed forever. When making future decisions, whether about his business interests or his rugby career, he would now not only have to think about Amy, but take into account what is in the best interests of his daughter.

Amy's timing could have been worse, but being up all night was hardly the best preparation Brian could have had for the match against England that afternoon. Within an hour or so of Sadie being born, Brian rejoined his teammates and prepared for the battle ahead. Despite the lack of sleep, there was a certain spring in Brian's step as he took to the field at the Aviva Stadium that afternoon.

Brian played his part in the match, his best move coming early on when he put in a brilliant pass to set Keith Earls clear, only for Mike McCarthy to knock-on and toss away the momentum. On a wet and miserable day, it was seldom a pretty game, and two penalties from Owen Farrell against one from Ronan made it 3–6 at the interval. When James Haskell was sin-binned with a quarter of the game left, Ronan's second penalty saw Ireland level at 6–6. The hosts looked set to take control, but with skipper Chris Robshaw leading from the front, the 14 men instead first stood firm and re-established their lead with two more kicks from Farrell gave them a 6–12 victory.

It was the first try-less game between the sides since 1984, and neither side really looked like scoring one for most of the game. It was also the lowest-scoring game in the 13 years the Six Nations had been contested in its current form. It wasn't easy playing in these sorts of conditions, with sheet rain sweeping across the pitch for much of the game, but the reality was that Ireland made far more mistakes with the ball in hand and seldom showed the fluency that they produced against Wales.

There was now a two-week break before their next match away to Scotland, and it gave Brian a bit of breathing space to take stock and adjust to life as a new father. The following Friday, Amy and baby Sadie were discharged from hospital, and doting dad Brian did the honours as he carried his daughter to the car in her baby car-seat.

As he regrouped with the Ireland squad, there was still everything to play for. Only England had won both of their opening matches, so there was every reason to believe that Ireland could still win the title. Once again, they would have to wait until the Sunday to play their match, and the previous day, both England and Wales won their matches, which didn't help their cause.

Ireland largely dominated the first half, with debutant inside centre Luke Marshall being especially impressive. However, they blew several scoring chances, not least when Keith Earls decided to go on the outside when he had Brian inside him and was bundled into touch by Sean Maitland. Another debutant, fly-half Paddy Jackson, kicked a penalty on 35 minutes to put Ireland 0–3 in front at half time. Scotland had been leaking penalties at the scrum and breakdown, and Ireland should really have got more points on the board.

Ireland continued to apply the pressure early in the second half, and were duly rewarded when Craig Gilroy touched down on 43 minutes, but Jackson failed with his conversion attempt. Two penalties from Greig Laidlaw reduced Scotland's deficit to two points, while Jackson missed two further penalty chances to increase Ireland's concern. Laidlaw gave Scotland the lead with another three-pointer after Ireland collapsed a maul, and although Ronan O'Gara replaced Jackson on 66 minutes, the veteran was unable to make his presence felt as the home side seemed content to kick for territory. When Marshall knocked-on, Laidlaw kicked another penalty to give Scotland a 12–8 victory.

Frankly, this performance had not been good enough. Ireland had been undisciplined on too many occasions and this had cost them not only the match, but any remaining hopes of winning the Championship. For Brian, the reality was that he was surrounded by men largely younger than himself, in some cases by more than a decade, and his final chance at winning another Six Nations title may have just passed him by.

Serious questions were now being asked about Declan Kidney, whose contract expired at the end of the tournament. It was clear that as individuals, these players were among the best in the Northern Hemisphere. Their achievements at club level more than backed this up, yet as a unit at Ireland, they were often poorly disciplined and made far too many basic errors. The calls for a new coach with fresh ideas were becoming increasingly loud. His methods had always been more about pragmatic than progressive rugby, and while fans were willing to put up with this when the side was winning, it was often hard to watch when things weren't going so well.

There was now another two-week break before their next match at home to France. This was hardly a vintage French side. They had lost all three matches so far to Italy, Wales and England. This was a match, in front of a packed crowd at the Aviva, that Ireland would be expected to win. The Six Nations title may have been out of reach, but there was still self-respect, jobs, and places in the side to play for. Brian had been around long enough to know that there was no excuse for giving anything less than your absolute best, and this was something he was keen to emphasise to younger members of the squad. He was also very much aware that this could be his last ever Six Nations game on home soil, as were the crowd, who gave him a huge and very moving ovation as he took to the field.

Ireland got off to a positive start and after 10 minutes, captain Jamie Heaslip touched down after a couple of devastating driving mauls. Paddy Jackson, who had been so wasteful against Scotland, was a different man on this occasion and helped put Ireland 13–3 in front at half-time. Ireland tired badly as the second half wore on. Louis Picamoles scored a try for France with six minutes remaining and Frederic Michalak landed the crucial conversion to bring the final score to 13–13, the second time the battle between these two teams had ended in a draw in as many years.

While the billowing wind and heavy rain made free-flowing rugby unlikely, Ireland had once again made too many mistakes, especially in the second half, and they had failed to beat what was, truth be told, an insipid French team. Declan Kidney's post-match comments that they did a lot of good things and that they were getting stronger in each game didn't sound particularly credible, although he conceded that it was 'frustrating we did not manage to close out the deal'.

Brian always considered it a privilege to pull on a green jersey and represent Ireland, but even he could be forgiven for failing to be motivated for the final match of the tournament away to Italy. France were yet to win a game, but if they beat Scotland, and Ireland lost to Italy, depending on points difference, it was possible the Irish could still end up with the wooden spoon. Italy had never beaten Ireland in the Six Nations, but this didn't seem to count for much now. This was a side who deserved respect – they had beaten France in the first round of fixtures, and although they had gone off the boil in recent weeks, they were more than capable of beating Ireland if the Irish made similar errors to those in the last three matches.

Paddy Jackson drilled over an early penalty to settle his, and Ireland's nerves, but Italy's captain Sergio Parisse was a real threat with ball in hand and soon won three penalties of their own. Fly-half Luciano Orquera clipped over two from three – hitting the post with his middle attempt – to give Italy a 6–3 lead after 21 minutes, and things soon went from bad to worse for Ireland.

Ireland had more than their fair share of injury problems throughout the tournament, and their cause wasn't helped as they lost Keith Earls and Luke Marshall from the game in quick succession. When Jackson missed a penalty, Brian's frustration finally reached boiling point, and what followed was a rare moment of madness. Brian had earned a reputation as a tough competitor, but a fair one. There was no reason to consider him a dirty player. This quiet, shy man had been the victim of unsporting behaviour on more than one occasion in his career, and wasn't the type of person who would seek to deliberately injure another player. It was therefore a massive shock to everyone when Brian stamped on Italian flanker Simone Favaro at the ruck, and was sent to the sin bin. The only possible explanation (but not excuse) for this was frustration, not just at the way this match was heading, but Irish international rugby in general.

With Brian off the pitch, Italy tried to hammer their advantage home but could only manage a third penalty, banged over from distance by long-range kicker Gonzalo Garcia. Astonishingly, Ireland then lost a third man to injury as Luke Fitzgerald was forced off, with 21-year-old Iain Henderson coming on at blindside flanker and Peter O'Mahony moving to the wing. They were given a glimmer of hope as Jackson kicked his second penalty with the last action of the half to make it 9–6.

Italy turned up the heat in the second half as winger Giovanbattista Venditti capped his fine tournament with a powerful drive from short range. Orquera landed the conversion from wide on the right, but there was soon another twist as captain Parisse was yellow-carded for a trip on Ian Madigan. During the number 8's absence, Jackson landed three penalties, including one that came following a 20-phase attack that was eventually halted two yards from the line. This cut Italy's lead to one point and set up a tense finale.

Garcia missed a long-range penalty that would have given the hosts a little more breathing space, but when Donnacha Ryan was sin-binned for a late tackle, Orquera made it 19–15. It soon got even worse for Ireland when scrum-half Connor Murray was yellow-carded for a trip, and Orquera's last-minute penalty wrapped up a historic win for the Azure.

With just one win and a draw from five matches, this had been a disastrous Six Nations campaign for Ireland, who ended the tournament fifth in the table. Wales's 30–3 victory over England saw them retain the title ahead of the men in white on points difference. Ireland seemed a million miles away from the team that won the Grand Slam four years earlier, and serious questions had to be asked about the future direction of the side. The reality was that since the Grand Slam triumph in 2009, Ireland had won just 16 of the 40 Tests they had played, while this had been Ireland's worst ever run of defeats in the Six Nations. Ireland were now ranked ninth in the IRB World Rankings, their lowest position since the rankings began.

Within days of the tournament's end, the IRFU's National Team Review Group met to plan the way forward. It came as no surprise when two weeks later it was confirmed that Declan Kidney's contract was not being renewed. The process of finding a replacement was underway, and while this was going on, a huge question mark hung over Brian's future involvement with Ireland. While Brian had been away on Ireland duty, Joe Schmidt had turned Leinster's season around. They and Ulster were the dominant forces in the PRO12, they were playing like European champions again, and with Brian back in the ranks, there was every reason to believe they could claim the title. He made his presence felt in the match away at arch rivals Munster in early April when his 71st minute try was instrumental in helping them to a 16–22 victory. The previous week, without Brian, they beat Wasps 28–48 to reach the last four of the Challenge Cup. Although their wobbly start to the campaign cost them the chance of retaining European club rugby's biggest prize, this was still shaping up to be a very special season.

In the semi-final, they produced a superb performance to beat Biarritz 44–16 at the RDS. Two tries from Jamie Heaslip, with one from Jonny Sexton in between put them 24–9 in front at half-time, and nine minutes after play resumed, Brian's turnover set up the opportunity for Jonny and Isa Nacewa to produce a delightful one-two for the Fijian to score. 14 minutes later, Brian scored a try of his own after another searing attack. This was a fantastic display, and although this was European club rugby's secondary competition, it was clear from this performance that Leinster desperately wanted to lift the trophy. However, they would need to produce another performance of this magnitude if they were to beat Stade Francais in the final, where they would enjoy home advantage.

The following week, the IRFU announced that Joe Schmidt had been appointed Ireland coach on a three-year deal. This was an ambitious but common-sense decision by the IRFU, and one Brian wholeheartedly supported for obvious reasons. Over the course of the last three years, Joe had proven himself to be the greatest coach in European club rugby, and while coaching a national side provided a different sort of challenge, he had enough experience and charisma to reinvigorate the Ireland side. Of course, moulding a group of individuals together from different clubs for a brief period every few months isn't the same as working with them day in, day out, but there was every reason to believe Joe was the right man for the job.

Days after his appointment, Brian gave Joe a massive vote of confidence when he hinted that he might be willing to play on for another year. During an interview with the BBC, he said, 'There is the added carrot now that Joe is head coach. I have made no secret of my admiration for him. He has been fantastic for Leinster and Leinster's loss is Ireland's gain. I do not think they could have picked anyone who could encourage me more to hang on for another year. We talk the whole time, I have a good relationship with Joe. He has spoken to me about my future from a Leinster perspective. He appreciates I am my own man and will make my own decision. That does not mean he cannot try to sway my opinion one way or another. But that is just one aspect of making a decision as big as whether you play on for another year.'

However, Brian was quick to point out that this wasn't just about his own needs and ambitions. He added, 'I need to sit down and talk to my wife and go through different things and see if the body is up to it. I have been lucky to have had a 14 or 15-year career, and I have to understand my wife has a career as well and maybe be flexible to her needs too.'

Within days of Joe's appointment, attentions turned to

the squad announcement for the upcoming Lions tour of Australia, where they would play three Tests, along with the customary matches against provincial sides. There were rumours that Brian would be given another shot at the captaincy, but these were unsubstantiated and Brian hadn't heard anything official to that effect.

Some months earlier, many had been surprised by Lions coach Warren Gatland's selections for his backroom staff. Shaun Edwards had been one of his key lieutenants for the past decade, at both Wasps and more recently at Wales. Edwards, an all-time great at rugby league, had become one of the 15-man code's most respected coaches. Beneath that harsh exterior was a deep thinker, a devout Roman Catholic who was well-read and a good person to turn to for wisdom or encouragement. Shaun had been part of Sir Ian McGeechan's coaching staff at the last Lions tour four years earlier, and many assumed he was a shoe-in for this tour. It therefore came as quite a shock when Warren chose to recruit England coaches Graham Rowntree and Andy Farrell, and Wales assistant Rob Howley. Warren also revealed he had talks with Joe Schmidt, but these had come to nothing.

The time had now arrived for the squad to be announced. Sam Warburton, who had captained Wales to the Six Nations title in the last two years, would lead the Lions in Australia. 12 years after Brian cut the Wallabies to shreds in the opening Test, he was back in the squad. It came as no surprise that the squad was dominated by Welsh players, but it was perhaps most notable for who it did not include. England legend Jonny Wilkinson had been invited on the tour but had turned down a place, while uninvited big names included Chris Robshaw, Andrew Sheridan, Rory Best and Simon Zebo. Brian's fellow centres would be Manu Tuilagi, Jamie Roberts and Jonathan Davies, all of whom were considerably younger. He knew he could not take his place in the Test side for granted.

A few days later, it was announced that former Australian international Matt O'Connor would succeed Joe as Leinster coach as of July 1st on a three-year deal. O'Connor, aged 42, had coached Australia A before becoming the coach of Leicester in 2009. During his time at Welford Road, he guided Leicester to two Premiership titles, and a few weeks after this announcement, he added a third when the beat Northampton Saints 37–17 at Twickenham. Leinster Chief Executive Mick Dawson had met with O'Connor, and had been impressed with his vision for the club, and believed this was a man who could build on Joe's remarkable achievements.

Back to the present, and a Jamie Heaslip try helped Leinster to a narrow 17–15 victory over Glasgow Warriors to reach the PRO12 final. However, this tense victory was overshadowed as Brian hobbled off after just 13 minutes. The following day, Joe confirmed that Brian had suffered a back spasm, and there was speculation that he wouldn't be fit for the Challenge Cup showdown against Stade Francais the following Friday night, the PRO12 final against Ulster the following week, and quite possibly the Lions tour. Furthermore, Gordon D'Arcy also hobbled off with a calf injury during the nail-biting win.

Brian faced an anxious wait to see whether he would be fit to face the French giants. On the Monday, he failed to report for the Lions' initial gathering in London, and three days later Leinster confirmed he had not recovered sufficiently to take part in the Challenge Cup match. Some of the disappointment from that news was relieved that same day when it was announced that he had signed a one-year extension to his contract with the IRFU. However, he made it clear that he would retire from all rugby when this expired. Speaking to the *Irish Times*, he said, 'I really am not ready for a year of speculation, it is going to be just the one. I can't handle that in every interview that I do. I know with my wife, I did agree to do just one more. I did say as well when I was talking about a World Cup, that means three pre-seasons. I don't have another three pre-seasons in me.'

Brian added that satisfaction over the recent coaching appointments had been a significant factor in his decision. He said, 'There were lots of different factors in who was going to come in as national coach and then who was going to come in at provincial level. From a family situation then in terms of what my wife's set-up was, we've a new baby girl. And also how my body was. All of those factors come into things. So it was about weighing up all those options and wondering was I ready to give it up, knowing that I wouldn't be playing anymore and you're a long time retired. I just felt that I still had plenty to give to be able to allow myself one more year.'

In the same interview, Brian admitted his surprise at Ronan O'Gara's announcement that he was taking up a coaching role at Racing Metro. Ronan's role would be as assistant coach, while he would also be responsible for the youth team. Jonny Sexton had recently agreed to join the French outfit for the 2013/14 season, and Brian admitted that while Jonny and Ronan had had an 'interesting' relationship in the past as they competed for Ireland's number 10 jersey, he was confident they could work together constructively at their new club.

Leinster would also have to make do without Gordon D'Arcy for the match against Stade Francais, while captain Leo Cullen would start from the bench as Jamie Heaslip led the team. This would be a massive test of their squad depth and character. In front of a packed crowd of more than 20,000 at the RDS, Leinster produced a remarkable display of clinical finishing as Ian Madigan touched down after just two minutes, while further tries from Sean Cronin, Rob Kearney and Cian Healey helped them to a 34–13 victory.

This was yet another massive victory for Leinster, and

although it lacked the prestige of the Heineken Cup, the Amlin Challenge Cup was still a major trophy and they had to get past some of European rugby's biggest names to win it. However, both Joe and Brian were keen to get back down to earth and not get too carried away until after the RaboDirect PRO12 final against a very strong Ulster side, which was just eight days away. For all their success in recent years, Leinster had never won a European trophy or the PRO12 (in any of its identities) in the same season, and this challenge wasn't going to get any easier as they prepared to face Ulster, who had beaten them in both their regular season PRO12 encounters. More than once, they had let their guard down in the week between a European final and the PRO12 final, and they were keen not to let this happen again.

The status and prestige of the PRO12 had risen considerably in recent years, from something of an afterthought to the Heineken Cup to a respected competition in its own right. Leinster, Munster and Ulster were all very strong sides, and while the Welsh and Scottish sides had underachieved, the Ospreys, the Scarlets, and the Glasgow Warriors were all tough teams to beat. The Leinster brand had grown massively in recent times, in line with the team's success. In 2005, Leinster had around 1,850 season ticket holders, and this doubled to roughly 3,700 in just a year. By 2012/13, this had rocketed to around 12,500, with average overall attendances in excess of 18,000.

The astonishing and rapid growth of Leinster as a professional rugby club was in no small part due to Brian's efforts and status in the game. Everything at Leinster was handled in a way that befits the professional era, whether it be in the boardroom, the training ground, or the academy. Chief Executive Mick Dawson, who'd been in the role since 2001, had provided superb leadership and business acumen in developing the club. Yes, there had been a small number of overseas stars, but the bulk of the squad consisted of Irish players, many of whom had been brought through the academy. It was also worth remembering that much of this growth had taken place at a time when Ireland was going through an extremely difficult time economically, with both the club and supporters having to make tough decisions as to how to spend their limited income.

The day before the PRO12 final, it was confirmed that Brian would return to the ranks, but they would still have to make do without Gordon and Sean O'Brien, who sustained a bruised knee in the Challenge Cup final. Shortly before kick-off, Rob Kearney reported a slightly tight hamstring, so Isa Nacewa took his place at full-back and Andrew Conway came into the starting line-up on the wing.

In front of a capacity crowd at the RDS, Leinster were quickest out of the blocks when skipper Leo Cullen collected a line-out throw from Richard Strauss and, after the pack drove for the line, Shane Jennings spiralled away from the Ulster defence and touched down to give his side an early lead. Jonny Sexton got the conversion and added another three points with a straightforward penalty five minutes later.

Ulster, who topped the regular season table having lost just four matches, began to pile on pressure and had two chances to score through flanker Robbie Diack. Ruan Pienaar opened Ulster's account with a penalty on 24 minutes, but Jonny, playing his final game for Leinster before his big-money move to Racing Metro, missed a chance to restore his side's ten-point advantage on the half-hour mark.

Jonny made amends by slotting away a penalty four minutes later, but Pienaar responded with one of his own soon after to reduce the gap to seven. Indiscipline was a problem for Ulster, and just before half time they gave away another penalty, which Jonny used to restoring his side's ten-point advantage at the interval.

The flow of penalties continued in the second half, with Ulster's Robbie Diack sent to the sin bin for being off his feet in the ruck, from which Jonny extended Leinster's lead to 19–6, putting clear blue water between them and their opponents. Two minutes later, Leinster were also temporarily reduced to ten men when Isa Nacewa, playing in his final game before returning to New Zealand for personal reasons, was punished for a high tackle on Paddy Jackson, who was heading for the try line.

Pienaar kicked the resulting penalty, and when he added two more in quick succession, the momentum was with Ulster as they cut their deficit to four points. The game was becoming an increasingly bruising encounter and the tide turned in Leinster's favour again as Jamie Heaslip touched down again as it entered the final quarter. Jonny's conversion attempt fell narrowly wide of the posts, but Leinster could breathe a little more easily with a nine-point advantage. Pienaar hit back with a superb long-range penalty from just inside the Leinster half, but it wasn't to be enough as the Leinster defence superbly held off a late onslaught to complete a 24–18 victory and claim the title.

Leinster had done it – a memorable double was theirs and it was a fitting end to the Joe Schmidt era. This had been a quiet game for Brian by his standards, but he had certainly played his part in their success. After an indifferent start to the season, Leinster had shown the strength of character to recover, and ended the campaign with two major trophies.

Every season was the end of an era in some ways as familiar faces inevitably departed, but it was especially poignant this time around. Under Joe's three-year tenure, Leinster built on the foundations of his predecessor and had become by far Ireland's most successful province. They had now won four European trophies compared to Munster's two, while the arch rivals were level with three PRO12 titles (or equivalent) each. This had been an extraordinary period, a time in which good players had become great players. Many of the team, probably including Brian, would continue to see plenty of Joe as he took charge at Ireland, but at Leinster, his shoes would be massive ones for his successor to fill.

There was plenty of partying done by the Leinster players and supporters in and around Dublin that Saturday night, but for Brian, there was barely time to take stock, as in just two days' time, he would fly out to Australia for one final crack at glory with the Lions.

Chapter 25

LIVING IT RAW
WITH THE LIONS

Within hours of Leinster's PRO12 triumph, Brian had to say goodbye to Amy and baby Sadie as it was time to join up with the Lions. Brian would travel to join the squad in London before flying out from Heathrow the day after that. He was quite used to going days, sometimes weeks without seeing Amy as his rugby and her work commitments kept them apart, but this was going to be far harder, as he had so far never been away from Sadie for a long period of time. However, he took some comfort from the fact that both wife and daughter were due to fly out to Australia in time for the first Test.

Brian wasn't overly keen on the idea of WAGs being around the tour. One major criticism of the 2005 Lions tour had been that the players had too many of their creature comforts around them and that team bonding suffered as a result. Although the days of several players sharing a room may have been over, in Brian's view, players should be expected to sit down to breakfast together. As he saw it, they could have breakfast with their wives for most of the rest of the year, but for this period, they should focus on the squad, and on getting to know players they didn't normally see much of. That said, fatherhood had softened Brian somewhat, and he was already looking forward to spending some downtime with Amy and Sadie in between matches during the latter part of the tour.

Before the Lions landed in Australia, they were to stop off in Hong Kong for a match against the Barbarians to mark the 125th anniversary of the first Lions tour. The match took place a week after the PRO12 final, and inevitably Brian was still recovering from that game and the long flight. Warren Gatland was pragmatic when picking the side. He didn't want to burn out those who had been involved in the PRO12 final, or the Aviva Premiership final, which had taken place on the same day. While the fixture deserved respect, it was also unwise to use players who had niggling injuries or weren't quite match-fit. In Sam Warburton's absence, Paul O'Connell captained the side, reprising the role he held four years earlier. The Barbarians fielded a strong side containing several stars from both the Northern and

Southern Hemispheres, including Joe Rokocoko and Martin Castrogiovanni. In the sweltering heat, with humidity levels as high as 94 per cent, the Lions treated the crowd of more than 28,000 to a convincing eight-try victory, with a final score of 8–59.

Although there were far bigger challenges ahead, this was a massive boost to the squad as they headed on to Australia. The early part of the tour saw them face all five of Australia's Super Rugby sides, along with a match against a Combined New South Wales-Queensland Country side, specially created for this match. The scheduling of this tour was interesting. With the exception of their final match against the Melbourne Reds, all of these encounters would take place before the Test series. With the matches against the club sides only a few days apart, there was still squad rotation, and either/or players would be given a chance to stake their claim for a place in the Test side, but this had the feel of a united squad, where nobody was that far away from a place in the starting XV.

Their first match against Western Force in Perth came just four days after the Barbarians game, so there was little time to settle in and get much intense training done. With Sam Warburton rested, Brian was named captain, and he was very much aware that this tour could well be the final time he would get to captain a professional rugby side in his career.

Western Force were under-strength, and this should be

a match the Lions would win comfortably, but even so, it was important to get their time in Australia off to the best possible start, and Brian was keen that he and the rest of the side should take the game seriously. What followed was a magnificent display, as the Lions ran riot, with nine tries, including one in each half from Brian, as they romped to a 17–69 victory. Brian's first half try was vital in getting the Lions going, as they led only 0–10 at half-time, but it was a different story after the interval as the Lions put in a blistering performance. The only sour note involved Brian's Leinster teammate Cian Healey, who was accused of biting Force scrum-half Brett Sheehan in the 18th minute, and shortly before half-time was taken off on a stretcher after twisting his ankle. He was later cleared of biting Sheenan but the ankle injury was more serious than initially thought and his tour was over.

This wasn't quite a win on the same scale as their 10–116 victory over Force in 2001, in which Brian scored a single try, but it was a huge win nevertheless. Warren was slightly concerned that they had conceded two tries, and it took them a while to acclimatise and get going in the first half, but these were all things that could be worked on in training.

The day before the next match against the Queensland Reds, the squad was hit by the news that veteran prop Gethin Jenkins was out of the tour. Gethin had arrived on tour with a calf strain from which he was expected to recover, but he aggravated it in training and was forced to withdraw. Alex Corbisiero and Ryan Grant were called into the squad as cover.

On the same day, Brian was the star attraction as a few of the players took part in a signing session at a shopping street in Brisbane. Hundreds of ex-pats, mostly Irish and Welsh, were packed in, 20-deep. They greeted Brian with a rock-star welcome as he took to the microphone to thank them for their support, after which he and the others sat down to sign balls, shirts and other memorabilia.

With just three days between matches, this was inevitably a much-changed side. Brian was rested from the squad completely, while Manu Tuilagi was the sole survivor from the starting XV. This turned out to be a far closer, brutal encounter, with Reds players requiring 50 stitches between them. Until three minutes before the end, there was only a try between them, before Owen Farrell secured the Lions' 100 per cent record with a well-taken penalty, giving them a 12–22 victory.

After the match, Warren revealed that two Lions fitness advisers, Paul Stridgeon and Adam Beard, had pursued and caught a man who was filming a Lions training session in Perth the previous week without permission. The footage was destroyed by the Lions officials. He claimed there was quite a bit of depth to this, with the Australians doing videos on individual players. Warren also claimed that the Australian team had employed cameramen to film additional footage of Lions matches, over and above what was recorded for TV broadcasts. He announced that to remedy this, they would implement a completely new set of calls at some stage. As far as Brian was concerned, there was nothing especially new about this. All four Lions tours he had been on had involved allegations of spying, with various levels of supporting evidence.

Shortly afterwards, the Australia camp responded with an official statement, denying that anyone connected to the Wallabies had been filming or watching the Lions at training. It turned out that the person caught filming the training session had been an ordinary member of the public, who had destroyed the footage voluntarily when asked to do so. Not for the first time in his coaching career, Warren had made crass and inaccurate comments that had rub the opposition up the wrong way.

Around this time, it was revealed that winger Tommy Bowe was a serious doubt for the rest of the tour after breaking his hand against Queensland. It was initially reported that his tour was over, but this was somewhat premature.

Despite their 100 per cent record, the Lions were facing criticism from some quarters for their style of rugby. Former Wallabies Eddie Jones accused them of playing 'Robocop rugby', saying, 'The Lions are a Warren Gatland factory-produced team, who play a confrontational gain-line game based on winning the collisions. Undefeated? No way on this tour.' It was fair to say that Warren's approach had been very similar to the one he used with Wales, which some considered a bit one-dimensional, when taking on Southern Hemisphere sides.

Games were coming thick and fast, and their next encounter against the Combined New South Wales-Queensland Country came just three days after their hard-fought victory over the Reds. Brian returned to the side as captain, where he was partnered with fellow 2009 Lion Jamie Roberts in the midfield, while Stuart Hogg switched from full-back to fly-half. Alex Corbisiero was given a chance to prove himself, while George North and Alex Cuthbert, the likely wing pairing in the opening Test, were given a run-out.

In front of a crowd of more than 20,000 spectators at Hunter Stadium, Brian played a pivotal role as he scored one of the Lions' ten tries as they cruised to a 0–64 victory. This was a promising performance from Brian, as he set up tries for Alex Cuthbert and Jonathan Davies, while he was unfortunate not to score a second of his own late on. After the match, Brian seemed delighted with the magnitude of the victory. Nobody knew quite what to expect from the makeshift opposition, but Brian was delighted to keep them to zero, as they put a lot of emphasis on defence. He emphasised the importance of trying new things and keeping the Wallabies guessing, and firmly believed that they were starting to gel as a squad and understand one another's games, which was quite an achievement considering that in many cases they didn't really know each other before the start of the tour.

Four days later, and exactly one week before the first Test, the Lions faced the New South Wales Waratahs in front of more than 40,000 fans at the Sydney Football Stadium. Inevitably, Brian was rested as Warren began to fine-tune his Test selections. Warren wasn't best pleased that the injury crisis meant he couldn't name a shadow XV, and it seemed as though 11 of those who started this game would play in the first Test. Leigh Halfpenny was the star of the show as two tries, along with a 100 per cent record with the boot, gave him a 30-point haul and the Lions came through 17–47 winners. The one sour note was Jamie Roberts, who limped off with a hamstring injury, and would be ruled out of the first and possibly second Tests of the series. There was still a question mark over Manu Tuilagi's availability for the first Test due to a shoulder problem, but this game showed that Jonathan Davies was in good enough form if he wasn't available.

Hours after the match, there was an extraordinary twist when it was announced that Welsh legend Shane Williams had been called into the squad. The main purpose of his call-up was to play in the coming midweek game against the ACT Brumbies. Shane was already due to travel to Australia to cover the Tests as a pundit for British radio station Talk Sport, but his call-up came entirely out of the blue. He was now 36 years old and had retired from international rugby two years earlier, and was, by this time, living in Japan where he was playing second division rugby for Mitsubishi Dynaboars. Warren resorted to this move due to the extent of the injury crisis among the backline and the need to rest other players, especially those who were to play in Saturday's Test. It was partly a pragmatic move, because the journey from Japan to Australia would be far easier at such short notice than flying someone in from Britain or Ireland. Shane would join the squad for 48 hours, arriving on Monday before departing after the match on Wednesday. Meanwhile, England backs Christian Wade and Brad Barritt were called up as injury cover and were due to arrive in Australia on the Monday.

Until this point, there hadn't been a clear distinction between a 'Test' and 'midweek' squad, however, this was inevitably going to change as the days ticked down to the first Test. Those who lined up to face the Brumbies wouldn't be in contention for a place in the starting lineup for Saturday, but it was still a strong side, led by Rory Best, that also contained world-class players like Rob Kearney, Sean O'Brien, Toby Faletau, and, of course, Shane Williams.

The Lions got off to a good start as Williams, who

became the oldest person ever to play for the Lions, almost touched down after two minutes, but it was all downhill from there, and few players enhanced their prospects of being called into the Test side as they suffered a 14–12 defeat, their first loss against a provincial side since 1997. The Brumbies had come out all guns blazing, and attacked the Lions in the set-piece, as well as being superior at the line-out and breakdown. Losing the 100 per cent tour record was a psychological blow just four days before the first Test, but the side that faced Australia would be a completely different one and the best thing they could do is put this blip behind them. As the days ticked down, Brian became increasingly aware of the importance of these three Tests. Not many players were fortunate enough to be invited onto four Lions tours in their careers. Indeed, Brian was one of just three, and it was a matter of bitter disappointment to him that he had not been more successful in terms of result. It's true that Willie John McBride had taken part in five, but in those days there were sometimes three-year intervals between tours rather than four. This really was Brian's last chance to be a Lions tour winner, and he was determined to make the most of it. So far, he had won just once in six Tests in Australia, and there was a sense of unfinished business on this, his final visit to the country as a player.

Brian didn't want to go down in history as someone who had made lots of appearances in Lions Tests but had failed to win a series. He had now reached the stage where he had heard lots about camaraderie and gelling together, and everyone becoming great friends on Lions tours, but in reality, if they all got on terribly but still managed to win the series, he would now settle for that. He was never going to win a World Cup with Ireland – that ship had sailed – so a series win with the Lions was now the biggest thing left for him. He had been hugely impressed with Sam Warburton's captaincy on tour to date. Sam was a man who didn't speak for the sake of it, but when he did speak, he had the attention of the squad, as he was saying something of relevance. Brian saw this as a contrast with Ireland, where they were more talkative, so he knew he had to tone it down a bit and strike a balance. As a man of experience, Brian was adding his tuppence-worth when he thought he could add something, which was greatly appreciated by the rest of the squad, but he was happy to let Sam take the lead.

Brian was greatly comforted by Amy and four-month-old Sadie's arrival in Australia during the week. The days of him being an obsessive recluse in the days leading up to a big match were over, and while his commitment to the squad and team-building was never in doubt, it was nevertheless a huge psychological boost to be reunited with the two most important people in his life at this time. However, the no WAGs policy remained and Brian continued to room with Jonathan Davies, who had quickly become a trusted friend, and someone who shared his approach to the game.

There was no doubt that Brian's training regime was now very different to the one he put himself through during the previous Lions tour of Australia in 2001. Back then, he was training for 90 minutes twice a day. There was no way he could tolerate that level of intensity at this stage in his career. Sports science had improved in the years since, and the right thing to do was to allow a period of recovery after each match, while focusing on the quality rather than quantity of training.

There were few surprises as the starting line-up was named. Leigh Halfpenny thoroughly deserved the number 15 shirt. With Manu Tuilagi still injured for the time being, Brian would be partnered at centre with Jonathan Davies, who was having a fine tour. Alex Cuthbert and George North were on the wings, while Jonny Sexton came in at fly-half. Paul O'Connell, still bearing the scars of captaincy four years earlier, claimed the number 4 shirt.

Sam Warburton led his side out to a raucous atmosphere of more than 52,000 fans at the floodlit Suncorp Stadium in Brisbane. This was it – the moment Brian and the rest of the boys had waited months for had arrived.

The match had barely started when Australian debutant Christian Leali'ifano was stretchered off after getting his head in the wrong position when attempting to tackle Jonathan Davies after just 52 seconds of play. It soon became clear that the Lions were struggling to get used to New Zealand referee Chris Pollock's interpretation of the breakdown. Whereas Northern Hemisphere referees regarded it as a tactical part of the game, those from the Southern Hemisphere were less keen on delays and wanted to keep the game flowing. The Lions, including Brian, found it hard to adapt and gave away two penalties early on, but James O'Connor missed both attempts with the boot.

The Lions spent several minutes hammering away at the Wallabies defence before the hosts won a penalty in their own 22. Will Genia took a quick tap and surged to the halfway line, where he waited for Leigh Halfpenny to commit before sending a delicate chip into the path of Israel Folau, who picked up and sprinted over for the game's opening try, and this time O'Connor couldn't miss from in front of the posts.

The momentum was all with the hosts, but the tide turned on 23 minutes when James Horwill was penalised for coming in at the side and Leigh Halfpenny's penalty made it 7–3. Two minutes later, George North collected a Berrick Barnes clearance ten metres inside his own half, eluded Pat McCabe's initial attempted tackle and O'Connor's ankle tap and charged towards the left corner to touch down. Halfpenny added a superb conversion, and minutes later North was over in the left corner again when he barged past

Genia and Folau, but the television match official ruled that his left elbow was fractionally in touch. However, the referee had already blown for offside and Halfpenny stretched the Lions' lead.

Australia hit back immediately as Folau, released into space, showed his athletic prowess as he outfoxed Jonny Sexton and Halfpenny to score his second try, but O'Connor's third miss of the night meant the Lions remained in front. Shortly before half-time, Halfpenny missed a penalty for just the second time in 27 attempts on tour, and the score remained at 12–13 at the interval. Eight minutes after the resumption, Alex Cuthbert superbly judged Sexton's pass and powered his way over, with Halfpenny's conversion extending their lead to 12–20. O'Connor's penalty reduced the deficit, but the Lions might have added to their tally after a thrilling breakout, only for the referee to adjudge Brian's delicate offload marginally forward.

Wallabies replacement Kurtley Beale, who was returning to action after receiving treatment for alcohol abuse, landed a long-range penalty to cut the Lions' lead to two. Halfpenny responded in kind, before Beale again made it a two-point game with 12 minutes left after his own thrilling counter-attack had forced the Lions to infringe in their own 22.

The Lions were still struggling with the referee's interpretation, and things got worse when they lost a scrum on their own put-in five metres from the Australia line, but this time Beale could not make them pay and they held on for a 21–23 victory.

There had been many positives they could take from this performance, and a win was a win, but as Sky Sports commentator Stuart Barnes pointed out, if Australia had a kicker of any calibre, they would have won by 14 points. In many ways, the Lions had been damned lucky, and there was a huge amount of work to be done in training during the week.

While Brian was focusing on the next Test, Amy visited an animal sanctuary, where she posed with a koala. She was quite fortunate to have this opportunity, as the furry creatures often sleep for between 18 and 22 hours per day. Also during the week, the second-string, captained by Dan Lydiate, put in an impressive second-half performance as they beat the Melbourne Reds 0–34 in the last match against the provincial sides. The returning Manu Tuilagi, Sean O'Brien, Ian Evans, Richard Hibbard, Toby Faletau and Lydiate himself all staked a claim on a place in the Test side with some superb displays. Competition was always healthy and if things didn't go according to plan in the next Test, or if there were injuries, it was comforting to know that these guys were more than ready to step up to the mark.

Two days before the second Test in Melbourne, the squad for the game was announced, and there were to be five changes. With Paul O'Connell and Alex Corbisiero out injured, Warren drafted Geoff Parling into the second row and Mako Vunipola at loose-head. He also opted to make a further three changes with Dan Lydiate getting the nod at blindside at the expense of Tom Croft following his superb display at midweek. Tommy Bowe had recovered from his hand injury in half the expected time and would replace Alex Cuthbert on the right wing, while Ben Youngs was in for Mike Phillips at scrum-half. With Jamie Roberts still injured, Brian and Jonathan Davies remained the midfield pairing. Roberts's absence meant they lacked the gainline-breaking thrust in midfield that had been part of their gameplan before the start of the series. Tuilagi made his comeback from injury against the Rebels, but was used at 13, not 12, and there was no prospect of him overtaking Brian in the pecking order for this game.

With Brian busy preparing for the game, Amy took some time out with friends to visit the famous Ramsay Street set where the popular soap opera *Neighbours* was filmed. On Twitter, Amy joked that if she didn't leave the set as the 7,000th actress to play Lucy Robinson, she would be disappointed. The part had actually only been played by three actresses in 28 years, and besides, Amy was at least five years too young for the role!

Brian wasn't underestimating the importance of this game. Win here at the Etihad Stadium, Melbourne, and the series would be theirs. Lose, and they faced a difficult series decider in Sydney the following week. The Lions appeared to have learned a lot about the Southern

Hemisphere interpretation of the breakdown in the intervening week, as South African referee Craig Joubert awarded them four penalties in the opening eight minutes, which resulted in Australia being given a warning. Halfpenny landed his first kick, but after a composed start, errors started to creep in, with the scrum a particular cause for concern.

This soon resulted in Leali'ifano, now fully recovered from his first-minute knockout in the opening Test, having two shots at goal in quick succession, both of which he duly landed to give his side a 6–3 lead. Within minutes, it was Australia who were making errors at the scrum, and Halfpenny landed two penalties of his own to make it 6–9. Leali'ifano levelled again when Lydiate strayed offside trying to stem a dangerous Wallabies counter-attack, but as half-time approached, the Lions had the upper hand, and when Mowen was penalised at the breakdown, Halfpenny edged his side back in front. Australia threw everything at the Lions in a tense and scoreless third quarter, but their defence, led by Lydiate, initially held firm, although as time went by there were further problems at the scrum. Brian was not having the best of games, and he made a terrible error when his pass went straight to Israel Folau, which allowed Australia to counter dangerously. Soon afterwards, Brian was penalised for hands in a ruck.

Bringing Conor Murray on for Ben Youngs was an inspired move by Warren, but the score didn't change until the 63rd minute when Australia were penalised at the scrum, allowing Halfpenny to land his fifth penalty. However, Australia were not done yet, as dangerous Folau, stepping off his wing, was twice denied, but the pressure finally told with five minutes left, and James O'Connor sent Adam Ashley-Cooper crashing over. Leali'ifano landed the crucial conversion, but the Lions still had a line-out to save themselves with two minutes left. Replacement hooker Richard Hibbard was unable to find his target, and then with the 80 minutes up, the Lions ran a penalty from their own half and got to the halfway line, where Australia conceded a penalty. Halfpenny's kick fell agonisingly short, and the Lions had lost the game 16–15.

This was an especially painful way to lose a match, and now everything would depend on the following week's third and final Test. In the post-match press conference, Warren blamed a small number of critical turnovers, but in all honesty, Brian had to accept his share of the blame for errors he had made.

If losing the match in such a cruel manner wasn't bad enough, captain Sam Warburton had sustained a tear on his left hamstring and was a major doubt for the final Test. The morale of the squad was low on that Saturday night, and any attempts to start afresh the following day were dashed by the news that Sam's injury was bad enough to keep him out of the match in Sydney. This led many in the media to assume that Brian would be given the captain's armband for the final and deciding Test. For the time being, the squad had to banish the events of the weekend to the backs of their minds and focus on the all-important challenge that lay ahead of them the following Saturday.

Early that week, there were plenty of column inches written about how this was destined to be the ultimate fairytale ending to Brian's Lions career, as he prepared to lead the team to glory after more than a decade of pain and disappointment in the famous dark red jersey. Journalists naturally assumed that he would be paired with the returning Jamie Roberts at centre.

Yet at the Wednesday morning press conference where Warren was due to announce the squad, it soon became clear that something quite different to the assumed plan was taking place. Warren walked into the room flanked by Tour Manager Andy Irvine and Alun Wyn Jones, rather than Brian. Immediately, the mood amongst the press pack changed as they sensed something quite unexpected was about to be announced. They were not wrong. First to speak was Irvine, who, after the initial pleasantries, confirmed that Jones would captain the side for the match. He proceeded to read the team sheet, where he stated that Jonathan Davies would be given the number 13 jersey, while Jamie Roberts would assume number 12. Irvine continued reading out the remainder of the starting XV, before moving on to the replacements. There was still no mention of Brian's name. There was an eerie silence among the journalists as they absorbed the shock news that Brian had been dropped not only from the side, but from the entire squad for this crucial game.

At no point in the last 14 years had Brian been available for selection for any game and not been chosen. This was an extraordinary moment. When questioned, Warren stated that Brian had naturally been disappointed at the decision, but had appreciated being informed before the announcement had been made. He went on to add that Brian's presence around the squad in the next 72 hours would be very important in terms of his experience and leadership. This was by far the biggest disappointment of Brian's playing career, and by far the biggest decision in Warren's years as a coach.

An enormous reaction from the rugby community quickly followed the news. Australian legend David Campese said that the Lions had just handed the series to Australia. All Black Dan Carter, the world's best fly-half, said that Brian should have been the captain. Ex-England player and motormouth Brian Moore described the decision to even omit Brian from the bench as a 'strange call'. Mark Cueto admitted that Brian hadn't had his best game the previous week, but that surely this game was 'made for him'.

Few ex-players were willing to justify Warren's decision, but some fans took to Twitter to defend him. A number said there was no room for sentiment, players had to be picked on form, and that Brian had made silly mistakes in the first two Tests. Some of the comments were quite harsh. While Brian had made several glaring errors, but there wasn't much quality ball given to the backline in the two Tests. Others added that the decision to pick Jonathan Davies over Brian was made based on who would best work with Jamie Roberts. Meanwhile, Brian tweeted that he was 'totally gutted' at being left out, but that all his efforts would go into preparing the boys to see it through.

Brian's most vocal supporter was his predecessor as Ireland captain, Keith Wood. Speaking to BBC Radio Five Live, he said, 'I've been uncomfortable throughout this tour whenever Warren Gatland has spoken about the captaincy. He tries to depower it, he consistently says it isn't about leadership and that isn't the most important thing. Having been on two Lions tours myself under Martin Johnson, I would have said the leadership of the captain was the most important thing. Brian O'Driscoll has been quiet in the two Tests but at every stage, he has been the clarion call once Paul O'Connell got injured. I just think Gatland has made a terrible mistake.'

Meanwhile, Mike Phillips returned at scrum-half following a knee complaint, Alex Corbisiero was back at prop, Richard Hibbard started his first Test as hooker, while in the back row Sean O'Brien replaced the injured Warburton with Toby Faletau taking Jamie Heaslip's place at number 8. The emphasis was very much on power, which was, in a sense, understandable as they failed to make a single line break in the last Test.

On the night of the match, Brian put on his suit and took his place in the stand at the ANZ stadium in Sydney, where he sat alongside Jamie Heaslip. More than 82,000 fans, easily the biggest crowd of the tour, welcomed the teams onto the pitch for the finale to a thrilling series. In the opening minute, Mike Phillips took a quick tap from a penalty, Alun Wyn Jones was held up short, but Alex Corbisiero powered though to score the game's opening try with the clock on one minute and 17 seconds. Leigh Halfpenny added the conversion, and it was a sign of things to come, as he added four from four penalties before the half-hour mark to put the Lions 3–17 in front. Shortly before half-time, James O'Connor stepped past Jonny Sexton and Sean O'Brien to score, and Leali'ifano added the extras to cut the gap to nine points at the interval, but despite this setback, there was a real sense that the momentum was with the visitors.

Leali'ifano landed two more penalties within six minutes of the restart to cut the gap to three points, but after Halfpenny made it 16–22 on 51 minutes, the Lions turned up the heat. Jonny Sexton and Tommy Bowe combined to send Jonathan Davies through a tackle and Halfpenny was on his shoulder, getting his pass away for Sexton to sprint over. Halfpenny's conversion took the score to 16–29, and with clear blue water between the two sides, it got better and better.

Halfpenny, one of a record-equalling ten Welshmen in the starting lineup, stepped inside Will Genia and away from Joe Tomane to send George North surging to the left corner for a third try, and Halfpenny's missed conversion barely seemed to matter. Three minutes later, with a chorus of 'Bread of Heaven' ringing around the stadium, Conor Murray's splendid pass put Jamie Roberts over for a fourth touchdown, with Halfpenny adding the extras. With 10 minutes left, the Lions were 16–41 ahead. The match was secure, the series was won, so they emptied the bench, which resulted in a cameo from Richie Gray, the only Scot to feature in the series. Neither side adjusted the scoreline in the final minutes, and referee Romain Poite blew his whistle to an eruption of cheers from the travelling support.

This had been a magnificent display from the Lions – victory was complete, and, like it or not, Warren's gamble had paid off. They had won the series, the first time a Lions squad had done so in Australia since 1989, and the Tom Richards Trophy was theirs. Brian picked up baby Sadie from Amy and took her onto the field as he savoured the moment. He had previously never been keen on sportsmen, in particular footballers, taking their children onto the pitch to celebrate landmark moments, but now, as a father himself, he understood the appeal and couldn't help himself.

Sadie was dressed in what looked like a miniature Lions jersey with a white overcoat, and her parents sensibly put pink ear defenders over her head to protect her hearing. During the post-match interview, Brian admitted this was a bittersweet moment for him, and that he was still 'living it raw'. He said, 'I haven't really gone and analysed it all and thought about how painful this has been. I'll probably think about it a little bit more over the next few weeks when I have a bit of time on my hands. I have been on four tours and thankfully I have managed to win one. Finally. Not having involvement on the final day does taint it a little bit for me, but it is still a series win. I played 80 minutes in the first two Tests and I did have a big say in what happened as well.'

Brian behaved with his characteristic dignity and it was a mark of his character that he was able to put this into a broader perspective. He added, 'It wasn't exactly as I would have liked it scripted but you don't write your own scripts. Otherwise you'd be scoring hat-tricks every week. The main thing is we won the tour. One man's disappointment counts for nothing when there is a squad full of guys who are very, very happy to have won themselves a Lions series. This squad will always be remembered in Lions folklore as one of the tours that matches 1997, and 1989, and 1974 – 13 is now a number that will be remembered.'

Back in the dressing room, there was a raucous atmosphere. Everyone was on a high. Warren and Andy

Irvine spoke of what it meant, of a job well done. They didn't need too many words, as the achievement spoke for itself. James Bond star Daniel Craig popped down to congratulate them. Brian had met him once before and had been impressed with his knowledge of rugby. He was only too happy to allow him to share in this moment of great joy.

Brian had certainly played his part in this success. It's true there were those who said, harshly, that Brian had been poor in the two Tests he played in, but nobody who understood modern rugby could deny that the leadership and experience he brought wasn't of great value to everyone in the squad, especially the younger players. It's also fair to say that after 12 years of disappointments with the Lions, all of which he had handled in a professional manner, he thoroughly deserved to be part of a successful tour.

The following Monday, writing in the *Daily Telegraph*, Brian admitted that he thought he could have played a useful role in the game, and that he didn't necessarily agree with Warren's decision. He said, 'I would back myself but there is little between myself and Foxy [Jonathan Davies]. Foxy had a solid game on Saturday. His left boot really came into play a couple of times. It was a game I might have looked all right in myself but you cannot say.'

He reiterated that the moments after the game had been a time of mixed emotions, saying, 'No matter what, that is just how it is. It was a massive mix of emotions: delight at being part of this historic moment alongside guys you have battled with, but tempered by not playing. It was hard and I would be lying if I said otherwise.'

Brian did stress, however, that he was delighted to be a series winner. He said, 'You are desperately envious of those who are out there but there is not a sliver of ambiguity about wanting to see the boys win. That is non-negotiable: 100 per cent you want the team to go well. But thanks be to God, I am a series winner with the British and Irish Lions, albeit it did not finish as I would have liked it to. But you cannot write your own script. Other people write it for you.'

The 2009 Lions captain Paul O'Connell, whose arm injury kept him out of the final two Tests this time around, also came out in support of Brian, and believed he should have played in that crucial final Test. Speaking to Irish radio station Today FM, he said, 'I was shocked and disappointed. I thought Brian was playing well. After playing so long with him you end up being a bit of a fan. I wouldn't say it took the gloss off it a little bit for me, but it probably did. It's a shame he wasn't out there. It just felt wrong that he was on the bus with the non-playing squad, not in the 23. I was injured and there were other guys resigned to the fact that they weren't on the team.'

Nevertheless, the majority verdict appeared to be that Warren had made the right decision in dropping Brian, but a sizeable minority believed that the victory would have been just as great, if not greater, had he been wearing the number 13 shirt. That debate could go on forever, and we will never have a definitive answer.

While Brian handled the situation and aftermath in a dignified manner, the same could not be said of Warren, who decided to treat journalists to one of his characteristic outbursts of bitterness when he said, 'I've been absolutely shocked by the reaction. I'd almost say it's been vitriolic. It's my job to take tough decisions and I always stick to my guns. It's true that people are entitled to their opinions, but I haven't enjoyed the last 72 hours and I'm not taking a lot of pleasure in feeling vindicated.' There was little justification for such spiteful comments from Warren. Like all sports, rugby is a game full of opinions, and coaches had to take the rough with the smooth. He had made a decision that he knew would be divisive, and, whether it was the right call or not, people were going to have their say about it. Yet surely this should all pale into insignificance against the great joy of being a Lions tour-winning coach. Warren's attempts to take the shine off the achievements of the team and turn the media's attention onto his own personal vendetta said a lot about his character.

At the start of his final season as a professional player, what does the future hold for Brian O'Driscoll? What is clear is that he is preparing for life after rugby. Back in 2001, at the age of 22, Brian established a company called ODM and Promotions Limited, as part of a bid to capitalise on being the most marketable Irish player of the modern era. His father, Frank, is a director of the firm. In the year end to August 2012, accumulated profits at the company topped €3.19 million, while the amount owed to the firm by debtors increased from €534,128 to €704,697 during the year. During the same period, Brian more than doubled the value of investments the company owns, going from €945,504 to €2 million. Even when his playing days are over, his marketability looks set to continue. The sums of money involved might not be as great as David Beckham's, but the principle is the same, as brands queue to have Brian endorse their products.

Meanwhile, new Leinster boss Matt O'Connor has said that he won't 'play Brian to death' in the 2013/14 season, which suggests he will be used sparingly, mainly for big European games and in the most competitive PRO12 matches. Matt has also made it clear that he wants to put a succession plan in place, not just for Brian, but because Leo Cullen, Shane Jennings, Isaac Boss, Eoin Reddan and Gordon D'Arcy are all now in the autumn of their careers. However, he is keen to maintain and build on the overall ethos of the club, which has evidently been very successful.

At Ireland level, Brian was excited at the prospect of having Joe Schmidt as national coach, and hoped he would replicate his success at Leinster with his innovative, charismatic approach to the job. In late November 2013, Brian is likely to have one final crack at beating the All Blacks when they come to the Aviva Stadium. Provided he can remain injury free and in good form into early 2014, he will have one more shot at Six Nations glory, with his final home match coming against Italy in the penultimate weekend of the championship.

As his playing career draws to a close, the debate about his legacy is, in many ways, only just beginning. He will go down as a pivotal part of the most successful side in the history of European club rugby to date. Of that there is no doubt. At Ireland level, he will be remembered as a great captain and a record try-scorer. However it could be argued that he should have more silverware to show for his talent, with just one Six Nations Championship to his name. While he, personally was often impressive at World Cups and against the Southern Hemisphere giants, the reality was that Ireland were often disastrous on the very biggest stages. With the Lions, Brian has suffered some extraordinary bad luck and was the victim of grossly unsporting behaviour in 2005. He thoroughly deserved his success in 2013, but the debate as to whether Warren Gatland made the right decision by leaving him out of that final Test will never be settled once and for all.

Will Brian go down as the greatest outside centre in the history of the game? Many would say yes, though Frank Bunce, Jeremy Guscott, Will Greenwood and

Conrad Smith all have their cheerleaders on that front. This is another debate that will go on for ever.

The Brian O'Driscoll of 2013 is far more than just a rugby player. He is a husband, father, family man and businessman. In recent years, being married to Amy and becoming a father has brought a sense of contentment and stability to his personal life. He and Amy both know that no matter what the future has in store, they will face it together. One of the most remarkable things about Brian is that for all his success and celebrity status, he has remained a humble, family-orientated man who is never happier than when he is at home with Amy and Sadie, or surrounded by close friends and family enjoying a barbecue in his garden.

Despite being the most recognisable and successful sportsman in his country, he remains entirely level-headed, approachable and loyal to his roots. It is these qualities, along with his outstanding ability as a rugby player, that have made him one of the greatest ambassadors Ireland has ever had.